TO SPEAK IS TO SEE

TO SPEAK
IS TO SEE

GUIDE TO THE DUAL-
LITERATE GENERATION

MAX ELI KELBLY

NEW DEGREE PRESS

TO SPEAK IS TO SEE

Guide to the Dual-Literate Generation

ISBN   978-1-63676-897-7 *Paperback*

978-1-63676-895-3 *Kindle Ebook*

978-1-63676-896-0 *Ebook*

To those who defy the wears of age with curiosity sustained in years advanced, and to those who are young who ask not but stand in wonder of the mystery of it all.

Contents

——

It has ever been my delight to learn
or to teach or to write.

—SAINT BEDE, THE VENERABLE

Introduction

___

VOLUNTARILY ILLITERATE

I never truly remember what it was like not being able to read English before I was taught in kindergarten. Whether or not I simply saw letters as bizarre drawings or symbols I really didn't think about it. To me, signs on the road were more symbolic and were pretty pictures. However, I do recall the learning process.

When we learned our basic vocabulary in elementary, I vividly remember sitting on a tall stool at the kitchen countertop with my parents going through vocabulary flashcards bound by a metal ring. It was time to learn to read what I was speaking and more importantly, listening while also gaining new words. I specifically recall practicing the word "or" over and over again because it sounded like the nearby town "ORrville," the place that had the best movie theater in the world. Oddly enough, the association between that movie theater and the words "or" and "orr" still remains stuck in my memory today.

Other simple words included "I," "can," "am," "a," "see," "of," and "the." I became so frustrated as English made absolutely no sense in pronunciation: "What do you mean 'of' isn't spelled 'u-v'?" The first thing I noticed about English spelling is it seemed to break all the rules of pronunciation we learned when memorizing our "ABCs." I was outraged as any ill-tempered five-year-old was at the discovery of the lack of phonetics in English "phonetics." "I can't believe this! She lied about our ABCs! Our teacher lied!" I shouted at the barstool, shaking my enraged head at the flash cards, fists clenched.

"I give up! I'm never going to learn to read!" I exclaimed to my mother, to which she reassured me with something along the lines of, "You have to learn to read. You can't just *not* read. It's important," followed by, "You can't read? What are ya, stupid?" in her typical rugged-but-hilarious humor. She had no doubt I would learn and in fact, whether I would have admitted it or not, the frustration was derived from the beginning of an understanding of how complex language—in this case English—is. I was already learning.

THE POWER OF THE WRITTEN WORD

In recent years I often look back at this story to illustrate to myself and others what it's like to learn a foreign language, especially learning how to read one. Being an American who has been through the American education system like so many others, I wholeheartedly understand how difficult it can seem to acquire a language. In the United States, most people who know another language were brought up with it or learned by necessity, but outside of that small sphere, many *learn* a language without *acquiring* it. I've been through the system, but I've also stepped out of it.

It is difficult to imagine a life where I could not read Latin script/the English alphabet, but how is this so different from not being able to read Russian, Chinese, Amharic, Kanji, Hebrew, or any other script foreign to me?

In high school, I began exploring an interest in language, especially orthography, or how people spell things in different languages. I began with the basics by learning the Greek alphabet due to its similarity to the Latin script (especially since Latin script/English is based on the Greek). This helped me to read stylistic variations such as the Coptic alphabet of Egypt, and eventually the Cyrillic alphabet—a sister of Latin script, as it is also derived from Greek, but designed for the unique sounds found in Slavic languages, particularly Russian and Bulgarian.

I can now read Cyrillic, giving me an introduction to pronunciation across Eurasia. I remember seeing Russian signs on TV shows and movies when I was younger and having no understanding of pronunciation, let alone meaning. This state of not knowing is really the same as when I was little and didn't know how to read English. At one point in your life you would not have known how to read this text on this page. Take a second and think about how it may have looked to you back then.

This idea of using symbols and characters to express the spoken word became more and more interesting. I am a history nerd, and the development of writing is an important marker for any civilization. The advent of human writing is often remarked as the beginning of history. The fact that humans can take ideas and spoken words, which disappear the second after they are uttered, fleeing into the past, and carve them into stone to live on forever is absolutely amazing.

Did the Pharaohs know that 5,000 years after they began recording their history that some civilization would rediscover what these ancient people were saying? Do you realize what you have written, recorded, or posted online might be read, listened to, or watched by people thousands of years from now?

My story of wanting to learn foreign languages is likely not too dissimilar from yours. Your goals in learning a language are unique to you. This book is designed to act as a thought exercise to find your goals, then learn *how to learn* a language and then for you to choose from the different tactics I provide, which are best suited to your learning style, interests, and goals. My own language-learning experience has taught me there is not a one-size-fits-all method to this arduous process, and the motivations for one person to begin a self-taught journey diverge from one soul to the next.

WHY MEN LEARN ANYTHING

Two years ago, I took a fancy to learning conversational Farsi, one of the languages of Iran, Tajikistan, and Afghanistan. More accurately, I took a fancy to a girl who knew some Farsi. The idea was to impress a girl, as many men reading this must confess is certainly one motivator to learn a foreign language. More critically, it was to impress her father who spoke Iranian Farsi.

As an English speaker, there are several ways to learn Farsi. You can read the transliterated script using Latin characters or you can use the Farsi script, which is a modified Arabic abjad. Yes, an *abjad*. It cannot even be called an alphabet because alphabets contain both consonants and vowels, but Arabic and Farsi as well as other scripts such as Hebrew for the most part ONLY contain consonants in writing. Consonant-only writing systems are called abjads.

To throw another wrench in the works, even though they are spelled only with consonants, the languages still have plenty of vowels that are pronounced, you just don't write them. Some vowels could be spelled using characters that represent a consonant sound.

For example, imagine if English used an abjad, only using consonants to spell. As English is now, the letter "L" might be pronounced in a word as an "el" or "lah." But if English only had consonants, "L" could, for whatever reason, *represent* the sounds of "ah," "eh," "uh," or "aeh" depending on placement, diacritic marks, or implication.

Vowels may also be implied, so to stick with the analogy of a consonant-only English, the word "laptop computer" would be spelled "lp tp kmptr." Now say it as it is written. It is pronounced the same but spelled differently. The vowel sounds are implied. Most of the sound could immediately be understood, and then throw some grammatical rules in there and you have your specially packaged, vowel-implied portable PC. We actually do use this sometimes in English: Think about abbreviations like "plz" for "please."

Funnily enough, some languages use the Latin script, such as Czech and Slovak that have words and phrases that are entirely consonants. Consider the Czech "strč prst skrz krk." This translates to "stick a finger through the throat." How consonants are used in written language is just one of thousands of interesting and seldom talked about things in language. Language is ludicrous indeed. Outlandish gimmicks, foibles, and quirks like the Czech neck decking are what draw me to the study of foreign language and linguistics, as well as the love-hate tension I have with the English language—a product of its peculiar origin.

FRENCH CLASS

In my journey to learn a secondary language to fluency, I wanted to share my experiences and research with those who also have struggled with learning a secondary language, especially when their first language is English (the English speaking world is easier to break into than break out of).

Through my years being a teenager and into college I would be captivated by one language or another. I first took French in high school because I wanted to be *different, unique,* and *cultured* compared to most others who took Spanish. Taking French, I learned the basic question words and a bunch of random sets of words. It was not obvious why we were learning them then and is still not obvious now. I could have told you all the colors of the rainbow, the animals of the zoo, what life was like in a Medieval French castle, how to count from one to a thousand, how to sing "Frère Jacques," and how to conjugate some verbs.

Yet, neither I nor most of the class could tell you how to order food, give or ask for a phone number, ask for and take directions, or relay a problem with your hotel room. So pretty much any question or phrase you would need when traveling to a French-speaking country, we did not learn. Sorry, Madame. I would love to write this off as a cheeky anecdote, but similar experiences are unfortunately the predicament many Americans find themselves in when placed in a foreign language class, either by choice or requirement. The blame should not be so easily placed on the instructors though.

In the United States, language education, retention, and multilingualism are an absolute mess. In many regions of the US, 95 percent of the population only speak English, and nationwide, only 20 percent of students are taught a foreign language. Compared to some regions in Europe where 100 percent of students are taught a foreign language other than their own. If you look at all of Europe, the median percentage of students who learn a foreign language is a striking 92 percent, and the absolute lowest in all of Europe is 80 percent with fifteen of twenty-nine European countries polled having 90 percent or more of their students learning a second language according to the article, "The State of Languages in the US: A Statistical Portrait." Having been to several vastly different regions of Europe, my experience is that most young people there speak *at least* two languages.

To put that in perspective, even the worst educational language programs in Europe produce three times the amount of second language learners than in the USA. As found in the October 2019 study by Karen Zeigler and Steven A. Camarota from the Center for Immigration Studies, any increase of people speaking multiple languages in the United States can mostly be attributed to immigration and growth of immigrant communities, as 67.3 million US residents spoke a language that wasn't English in their home. We also know from the two studies mentioned that 75.5 percent of English-speaking adults fluent in another language acquired that non-English language in their childhood home, i.e., parents, siblings, grandparents, media they were exposed to, etc. Only 16.3 percent of that same population of English-speakers who know a non-English language learned it in school.

The reason I believe Americans are mostly not bilingual and second language education has been rapidly declining in public education is, not solely a failure of educators or students per se, but rather because American society is in an unprecedented geographical and historical anomaly.

LANGUAGE APPS, GENERALLY = THE LANGUAGE CRAPS

Bill Gates, the powerful tech magnate famously said:

> *I feel pretty stupid that I don't know any foreign languages. I took Latin and Greek in high school and got As, and I guess it helps my vocabulary but I wish I knew French or Arabic or Chinese. I keep hoping to get time to study one of these—probably French because it is the easiest. I did Duolingo for a while but didn't keep*

it up. Mark Zuckerberg amazingly learned Mandarin and did a Q and A with Chinese students—incredible.

Not to compare myself to Bill Gates… but like many Americans, especially high schoolers and college students, I have downloaded language learning apps like the one with a threatening green owl (Duo, the Duolingo owl, "It's simple: Spanish or vanish") with the intention to become fluent in French… then Italian… now I mean Mandarin Chinese… sorry, actually German and Czech at the same time… or how about Esperanto? Russian? Ever heard of Klingon?

Every time I would pick up my phone and open up the app to begin a new language, I was committed. I would tell myself, "I'm going to learn this to fluency. I'll keep up my streak by practicing every day! It'll be so cool when I learn this. I'll be able to talk to native speakers about… well… anything!"

Inevitably, after about four days or maybe a week of dedicated practice I would fall off the wagon, lose my immense commitment and ambition, practice every other day, then once a week, and eventually, stop all together, still receiving those "We miss you! Take five minutes to practice Spanish" messages. I would feel discouraged from a lack of progress to only pick up the phone a few months later with the same intentions and increased level of interest—only this time it was with a different language and, far too often, multiple languages at once, returning to the torturous cycle.

Eventually, I got fed up with this cycle of knowing a little bit about a lot of languages, and not knowing one language a lot, and I pushed for change in the way I was going about acquiring a second language. I wanted to make sure the large amount of time I was investing in language education was being used wisely—even if it meant spending some money. I knew that I could always earn money back, but time is a finite resource and so is attention.

I did a ton of research on the psychology and science of learning languages at any age, picked one specific language that I could commit to long term (French), found resources that would best suit my language choice and learning preferences, set out daily, weekly, and monthly traction plans and goals, and finally took action by practicing in ways that were fun AND effective.

Now I have detailed highlights and lowlights of my journey throughout the book.

THE JOURNEY AHEAD

I see a lot of polyglots who give tactics and techniques for learning a foreign language, but rarely do I see these tactics and techniques (some of which seem to contradict each other) listed in a succinct, understandable, and practical manner. Much of what is commonly portrayed is that learning a language in the easiest way possible takes years of gradual, dedicated work. Or, more recently, it is sensationalized and disingenuous such as YouTube videos with titles like "I learned Italian in one week." (I love you, Nathaniel Drew, and still watch all your content, but titles like that are not completely honest.) These perceptions are two extremes with a great deal of truth in both, in the middle, and nowhere on that simple spectrum.

Learning a second language to functional fluency is *absolutely* possible. It can be done in less than two years, and often in less than one. Once you get your foot in the door with the absolute basics of the language (exposure to the 1,000 most used words, basic understanding of grammar, basic phrases, basic questions, and the writing system), you have extraordinary amounts of room to pivot and learn in ways most enjoyable to you.

The key is to have fun with it. Otherwise, your brain will take it as a punishment, and you'll drudge through until you quit on yourself.

Learning, or more accurately *acquiring*, any language is useful. Using your brain to speak and listen through a different cultural lens with different words sharpens the mind like a steel to knife. Learning a little bit or a lot of a dead language like Latin or Greek (and its culture) often helps to understand all sorts of words, phrases, and cultural references in the modern world.

Acquiring an "unpopular" language, or a language really only spoken in its native land, is also totally useful because it makes you uniquely qualified to work in or with people from that country, despite you not being from there.

Imagine an American able to speak Indonesian. That makes that person a cultural bridge between 330 million Americans and 100 million Indonesians, leaving that person in high demand for their unique ability. It is important to be able to span the gap between massive cultures that typically have little interaction with each other. That is a lot of untapped knowledge and opportunity for both sides.

Languages open doors, and that is a major theme of this book, but knowing that and seeing that are two different things. Reality is often unexpected and surprising. These surprises really hit me when I started getting ads in French on YouTube and Instagram.

There I was, sitting in my car listening to a typical English-speaking YouTube video to then have an ad play in French. It's bizarre because I didn't start learning French to get French ads, but that is reality. People in France get French ads. Languages bring with them all the amazing aspects of a culture or society, but also their baggage.

Nevertheless, that should never deter you. When you begin to see the door to another culture gradually crack open more and more as you learn more, the feeling you will have is one filled with joy that makes it harder to give up than it is to keep going until the door is open enough for you to walk through. I believe that, with the aid of technology, we are entering into a language revolution to create the first globally connected dual-literate generation.

With the advancement of technology, there is an emerging generation beginning to harness their full "dual-literate" capabilities in acquiring a second language. It is my mission to help anyone accomplish their language learning goals while I realize mine.

Learning French to fluency and Farsi to a conversational level are my goals, but I know your goals may be different.

This book is for learners of any level because not only does it provide practical, easy-to-digest advice, but it also describes the state of language learning, its history, as well as relay really fun and bizarre firsthand stories about learning a language, as well as things you never knew. Join me on this journey as I chart my language learning experiences.

HOW TO READ THIS BOOK

Since this book is meant to be used in the way you best see fit, I HIGHLY recommend you go to the sections and specific chapters you need. I constructed the book so that there is a continuous narrative flow to it, while each section and chapter can stand on its own; combining the best aspects of a how-to and self-development book, all bound by a compelling narrative.

In Part I, we will spend time exploring language learning across the world to help uncover why so much of the world is so good at speaking multiple languages, while the United States and a few other English-speaking countries like Australia, the UK, and Canada lag so far behind high achievers like the whole of Europe.

In "Anglophonospere," I weave the tale about the time I wandered alone through Amsterdam to convey how prevalent English and English language education is across the globe. Next in "Ugly American" and "Speaking 'Merican," I go into detail of how *not* knowing a second language when in a foreign country can prove disastrous. More on the optimistic side, in "Hope Yet," my friends will tell you how there truly is a growing dual-literate generation.

Part I establishes background, and Part II is where we get into the odd world of languages across the globe through unexpected stories and mind-blowing facts. Here we will talk about the many oddities in the English language, commonly known and lesser understood. Later on, I will build on English and expand to the peculiarities of other languages as told by friends, professionals, polyglots, and linguists alike. This section serves to simultaneously blow your mind, expand your perspectives, become enthralled in riveting stories, flip your perception on what you thought you knew, and humble you (as it did to me) to the vastness of language across the globe.

Finally, if you are primarily interested in the methods to learn a language effectively, I recommend you skip to Part III. The chapters in Part III detail specific methods you can use to learn in a way that best suits you based on scientific research from a variety of fields. In this part, I reviewed dozens of studies, blogs from language educators, polls, and interviews with experienced linguists and polyglots. I let the evidence guide my prescriptions for learning a language. These methods are proven, and I have used them in my own language studies with great effect. I have also found that those I interviewed who have found success in learning multiple languages, by coincidence or intention, used these research-backed strategies.

Allons-y! Let's go!

PART I

CHAPTER 1

To Speak Is to See

———

"He who knows no foreign languages
knows nothing of his own."

—JOHANN WOLFGANG VON GOETHE

If you type into Google "quotes about language learning," you will find no shortage of thinkers, writers, and every type of famous person emphasizing the importance of learning a second language or a foreign language. It is remarkable to see who has chimed in on this age-old discussion or idea of learning a second language other than your native tongue. Here are some more examples:

"One language sets you in a corridor in life. Two languages
open every door along the way."

—FRANK SMITH, PSYCHOLINGUIST

"Change your language and you change your thoughts."

—KARL ALBRECHT, GERMAN ENTREPRENEUR

AND FOUNDER OF ALDI

"You can never understand one language until you understand at least two."

—GEOFFREY WILLIANS, ENGLISH AUTHOR AND JOURNALIST

"The limits of my language mean the limits of my world."

—LUDWIG WITTGENSTEIN, AUSTRIAN-BRITISH PHILOSOPHER

"Learning another language is not only learning different words for the same things, but learning another way to think about things."

—FLORA LEWIS, AMERICAN JOURNALIST

AND WORLD TRAVELER

"To learn a language is to have one more window from which to look at the world."

—CHINESE PROVERB

"To have another language is to possess another soul."

—CHARLEMAGNE, FORMER KING OF THE FRANKS, KING

OF THE LOMBARDS, AND EMPEROR OF THE ROMANS

"One who speaks only one language is one person, but one who speaks two languages is two people."

—TURKISH PROVERB

"A new language is a new life."

—IRANIAN PROVERB

"Those who know many languages live as many lives as the languages they know."

—CZECH PROVERB

Or put more bluntly by another Czech proverb...

"Learn a new language and get a new soul."

Or, perhaps you are feeling a bit more *romantic*... in the graceful Russian sense of the word...

"Love has its own language, but marriage falls back on the local dialect."
—RUSSIAN PROVERB

THE LIGHT AND THE FOG

If you look further, you'll begin to see that most of these quotes, no matter who said them or from what culture they emerged, focus on the idea that *IF* you don't know a second language you're missing out in a lot in life. If you do learn a foreign language, *THEN* you are gaining a whole new perspective on life. Other themes intertwined with this are something along the lines of, "If you learn a second language, it illuminates the first, and when you only know one language you really don't *know* that language." In writing this book the quote I took and ran with most was the following:

"A different language is a different vision of life."
—FEDERICO FELLINI, ITALIAN FILM DIRECTOR

I like this quote because it highlights a weird thing we humans do when speaking English, and actually any language: We equate the idea of *understanding* with *vision* or *sight*. When your friend clears up an explanation you might respond: "Oh!

I see." In French we say "*Je vois,*" which is literally "I see," a phrase used to show understanding as in English.

When we *see* something it's that "lightbulb moment" where everything clicks into context, establishing understanding. I frankly find it bizarre that we use the language of vision to describe levels of understanding. Researchers Alex Clarke and Loraine K. Tyler delve deeper into this phenomenon in a 2015 article in the journal *Trends in Cognitive Science.* The article is called "Understanding What We See: How We Derive Meaning From Vision."

To further illustrate the idea, we use words like *enlightened, illuminated, highlighted clear, clarification,* or *blind, obscure,* and *opaque* to describe these levels of understanding, and perhaps it is tied to visualization in the mind... *the mind's eye,* as Clarke and Tyler point out. I am convinced it goes deeper. Being able to see something is, in part, understanding that thing; being aware, understanding of a problem is the same thing as looking at, being vigilant, or paying attention to that problem. Even the word *obvious* ties back to an ancient root word "*wegh-*" [1] that meant "plain to see," all made clear on Douglas Harper's Online English Etymology Dictionary, *Etymonline.*

We all know the feeling of not fathoming something that could only be described with visual terms: fogginess, grayness, unclear, murky. There is a mental *feeling* of not being able to *see* properly. However, when we do finally reach understanding, all the puzzle pieces snap together, and at least for me, I get a bright, satisfying feeling inside, literally as if a bright light was shining—a crossing of senses in what can only be described as synesthesia ("Synesthesia," 2020). How else are we to see something if it is not cast into the light? How is it we shine through the thick, gray gloom of a foreign language? How do we go from our overcast befuddlement to a clear blue sky of transparency, fluidity, and comprehension?

TO SPEAK IS TO SEE

In my language learning, I have had many moments of irritation and confusion. Yet when I would stick with my daily and weekly routines, take breaks, naps, and come back, I would slowly begin to gain clarity in difficult concepts, grammars, or pronunciations. In my interviews and research, and general life experience, I have observed many people actively hating learning the grammar of a language. Of all my close friends, many of whom love learning languages, I only have known one who *truly* loved spending hours with language grammar. A rare breed, that one. Grammar is conceptual, often really different in foreign languages. At first, it doesn't mesh well with how our brains currently organize sentences and word orders.

When I was first learning Spanish and French, the word order made no sense to me. It was rough, coarse, irritating, and got in the way of how *I* wanted to speak Spanish and French, but particularly Spanish. I remember thinking, "Screw the order of how they speak! I'm stylistic and I'm going to construct the sentences how *I* want to. They don't own *my* words!" My obstinance was a square peg attempting to fit in a round hole.

The funny thing about language is that it does not belong to us even if we are native speakers. It was given to us by our predecessors and our culture. Something valuable like a wristwatch, jewelry, painting, or piece of furniture from a recently deceased relative. At most, we can add or take away bits and pieces. Hardly ever do we dispense with it altogether. In a way, language is the parent of our culture as our parents are the genetic precursor to us.

Regardless, when I kept with it, despite being stubborn to their grammar systems, the more I practiced the language regularly, the more I exposed myself to the way Spanish and French are spoken, the more I subconsciously began to understand the grammar. With French, it came upon me by surprise with those bright shining fluorescent puzzle pieces gliding down from heaven in luminous rays of light, falling into my mind perfectly in place. French grammar suddenly clicked, and I knew what order to put words in, different ways I can construct sentences, and even gained a sense of what *didn't* sound correct because I had routinized the basics of the grammar. I internalized it. Through habitual practice I turned my conscious effort at the forefront of my attention to something like muscle memory.

That is the essence of this book. That gradual knocking away at a difficult task, little by little, allows the work to accumulate to those brink points where it is so rewarding to have chipped at a big task little by little, where speaking or understanding another tongue becomes second nature. Perhaps that vision will come to you in a dream. You will never forget the first time you dream in a foreign language. When you speak and speak and speak, and fail and fail and fail, you aren't a *failure*. To draw from a classic metaphor, in the battle you might be failing, but as long as you win the war by playing the long game, you are golden!

Each battle in which you fail to be PERFECT in the language, you are actually progressing because you are gaining understanding of what *is* correct and what *isn't*. Yes, you insulted someone's grandmother by calling her a horse because you didn't pronounce a word right in Chinese, but guess what? You are establishing boundaries. By failing you are setting up a framework of understanding, of sight. When you speak and speak and speak and then fail and fail and fail, you are really building a path and training your brain to *see* what it means to be able to *speak* a language. The more you speak, the more you'll see. When you *speak* you will, in time, *see*. And when you can *see*, there is no limit unto what you can *speak*. In short, *to speak is to see*.

WHEN? NOW!

As I stated in the introduction, I want this book to serve your specific needs and desires with learning a second language. I love learning languages, studying linguistics, uncovering etymology (word origins), and using native and foreign language as a tool of communication to better connect with people in my community, cultures I am a part of, and with people around the world. With this keen interest in language, despite not being a trained linguist or teacher, it is my mission, ambition, and purpose to make language learning accessible to those who have and continue to struggle with acquiring a second language.

This book serves as a "how-to guide" for learning another language, but this rests on the larger frame, the skeleton, or overarching narrative of the book that we live in the PERFECT time to learn *ANY* language to fluency. "You mean right now?" you might say. Yes, now! Why? Because the best time to learn a new language is always *now*, regardless of how turbulent life and society may seem. There is no better time to learn a language than NOW, and *now, when*ever you are, is the only time there is. Everything else is a memory, hope, or prediction.

Although we only ever live in the present moment, as we grow with the passing of time, a lot more responsibility gets placed on us as individuals to get done what might have been done in groups or by others before.

Time management is a competence everyone confronts. Why? To be alive and to be keen to the fact that you are alive is to understand you must eventually die. To accept your mortality is to accept that the more time you spend on Earth the less time you have left. Thus, time becomes increasingly valuable as she resolutely marches forward.

If our time is not managed for us by our job, our responsibilities, our family, or any other structure and relationship in our life, it is up to us to carve out our time in a way it is used effectively. The 168 hours in a week need to be acknowledged and contended with. Without such rigid structures of how a workday goes or when classes, sports, and activities are, it is up to us to establish routine. We have agency in our lives and by understanding our finitude, we have the opportunity to schedule time to pursue what is meaningful by learning a language.

Here's the *ugly* truth that I know many are coming to terms with in all areas of life: You have time, and if you don't have time, it's not really that you don't, but rather that you won't schedule for it.

To not make time for the things you love consistently indicates that you do not value your time enough to rearrange it. Again, that is another concept not wholly bound to any pandemic or epoch. No one is too busy; it is about making the time for the things you value. If you don't have time to learn a language you don't value a version of you who knows that language. When you picked this book up, you presumably knew I would say this. If you really don't think you have time to learn a new language, just remember you took the time to pick this book up. If you "don't have time," make it.

Not only do I plan to provide tools, tips, techniques, and tactics to learn another language, but I also provide personal stories from myself and others, as well as detailed research about topics including why English is such a bizarre mixture of languages, the decline of language education in America, why people in other parts of the world know so many languages, and all the science behind language learning and acquisition.

FOOTNOTE:

[1] The asterisk is used to indicate the word is a "Proto-Indo-European" reconstruction. The asterisk is always used to show the word is a theoretical construction and not directly attested.

CHAPTER 2

Anglophonosphere

———

ANGLOPHONOSPHERE:

noun

1. Geographical areas where English is commonly spoken by the inhabitants, considered collectively.

"India and Canada are part of the Anglophonosphere due to British colonization."

2. The collective of all English speakers globally.

"Dominika's Czech classmates began to learn English, gradually bringing them into the Anglophonosphere."

3. The physical, cultural, or metaphorical location where Anglophones feel at home.

"He speaks the language, so he must be from the Anglophonosphere."

ORIGIN

Anglo- (Medieval Latin) "of or pertaining to English" + *-phone/phōnē* (Ancient Greek) "voice, sound, or speaker of" + *sphere* (Latinized spelling of Middle English *spere*) "cosmos; space, conceived as a hollow globe about the world" = *Anglo-phono-sphere*; literal sense: "space pertaining to speakers of English"; *Anglophonosphere*. A word I constructed not possible without *Etymonline* (Harper, 2020).

THE ODD POSITION OF ENGLISH

English is notoriously a troublesome language to learn, as popularly attested to and accepted by many native speakers and foreign learners alike.

English, being a rare language that belongs to several different language families at once (evolving from and mixed with Romano-Celtic, Anglo-Saxon, Old Norse, Norman French, and influences from Latin, Greek, modern French, and German, oh, thousands of minor influences from dozens of other languages), has seemingly contradictory pronunciations and grammar rules when you take the spoken word and reference it with its written counterpart.

English's diverse mix of influences and dialects presents challenges for any student of the language, yet also gives it a unique international status that makes acquisition more accessible than most other languages. English is a rare hybrid of languages while also sharing common roots with hundreds of languages and dialects, but that's a discussion for the later chapter "How to Count In Ten Languages at Once."

The increasing omnipresence of English is the bridge between why it can be such a difficult language for primary and secondary learners, as well as why English is so easily accessible across the globe.

NO SLEEP IN THE NETHERLANDS

In December 2018 I was returning from the lush, tropical Uganda, Africa, headed home to Ohio. For the layover, I waded through the snow and sleet-fettered winter Amsterdam, the grand capital of the once mighty Dutch Empire. From the colorfully humble, ever-growing, semi-agrarian metropolises of East Africa to the stark Gothic edifices held in a four-hundred-year standstill in staunch battle with the perilous waters of the Dutch coast on the North Sea.

On the eleven-hour flight from Entebbe to the Netherlands I barely slept, being in that awkward half-awake state nodding in and out of consciousness, gazing out the window to a flat, black landscape and navy blue sky. That sky was illuminated by the equatorial sideways crescent moon rising far above the Earth. In my dazed stupor such an image of the moon would be indistinguishable from the grin of the Cheshire cat, but I won't go down that rabbit hole. I later found out that the flat, vast, sleek yet open shadowed ground was the Sahara.

I was on a research and immersion trip with my university scholar cohort. We traveled to Uganda and voyaged across the country, trekking through substantial urban centers, through unpaved jungle roads that ridiculed our bus's suspension, and through the tawny thicket of the savanna. Our objective: to research the unique Ugandan educational systems and how locals rose to the call to solve schooling challenges.

Since our in-country investigation was over, I had made prior arrangements to splinter from the group at this point to spend the next week traveling both alone and spending time with family friends in the Czech Republic. It was two hours prior to sunrise when our group arrived at Schiphol (the main Dutch airport right outside of Amsterdam). Any rose-tipped fingers of dawn to hint at a rising sun were muted through a drizzly lens.

There were over twenty-four hours between my flights and six hours before my check-in time at the hostel, and I had booked my stay unknowingly in Amsterdam's famous Red Light district. I had to kill a lot of time; more than anything, I wanted a quiet bed to sleep in. In this instance, I had to kill time with what seemed like a rusty butter knife, and a groggy, sleepless coordination—about as effective as a toddler doing taxes. Really, I could have slept on the luxuriously knobby cobblestone ground outside if it weren't partly frozen, fettered by dank, melted sleet. Sleep deprivation hit me like a truck. My eyes fluttered increasingly with every passing minute. The words of Dr. Gradisek, our research trip leader and cohort advisor were on repeat in my head: "Remember: Be flexible." A laconic phrase that still sticks with me.

In the Dutch airport, I wandered around, lugging a massive forty-pound lovechild of a backpack and a briefcase, checking out duty-free stores and kiosks, biding my time, keeping my feet moving so I wouldn't slip into unconsciousness, despite how much I wanted to fall into the sandman's embrace. My eager march turned to a sapped shuffle.

With my sleep-deprived brain, my judgment was impaired equally to the drunk businessmen and husbands of all backgrounds at the airport bar getting a reprieve from their wives and legions of screaming children. A universal phenomenon. I thought I might join, but a skinny lad whose mind was full of more grog than what would lie at the bottom of a pint had no need for more bewilderment. One's eyes can only cross so much before they pop out of the head.

In the not-so-drunken lassitude, I converted a lot of my American dollars to euros, not realizing until later that they ripped me off on the exchange rate. Like a lighter taken to an uncashed check, the service fee vaporized a chunk of my money never to be seen again. Yet, I still had a pocket freshly filled with euros. With that, I was ready to stimulate the Dutch economy. Money goes a long way, but was English enough to navigate this foreign country?

FINDING A RIDE

While getting to know the massive airport by roaming around for hours like a lost cow in an unfamiliar pasture, I decided to get a train ticket to the Amsterdam city center to find a dewy field to graze. Perhaps a place to ruminate on my trip thus far, to chew my cud. Keep in mind I had no understanding of public transportation, either in America or abroad, nor any grasp of the Dutch language. Dutch was simply the language they speak in the Netherlands… you know, the country I was staying in for the next twenty-four hours.

I'm from rural Ohio after all. We don't have city buses or subways. We have cows and tractors. Even rideshares like Uber are a scarce, and therefore expensive, commodity.

In the town where I grew up, a handful of people blatantly spoke another language, but Dutch? No way. To compound that problem at this time in my life I had minimal people skills. Asking for help in the US in my native tongue, let alone a foreign country where I didn't know the language, was anxiety provoking. "Remember: Be flexible," I thought.

Here I was, living the paradox of having the extreme confidence to throw myself into a foreign country I'd never been to, yet zero confidence to ask a stranger or attendant for help.

However, it was time to buck up and find a solution, as in the words of Alfred A Montapert: "Expect problems and eat them for breakfast."

It took time to figure out where exactly I should go to get a cheap one-way train ticket and who to ask for that ticket. Not wanting to look like the "ugly American," I knew it was time to do what all sleep-deprived college students do and implore my study skills to study the night before the test.

I whipped out my phone, logged onto the Schiphol Wi-Fi where I was nearly out of the signal zone, pulled up Google translate, and memorized the absolute basics in Dutch. (No, this is not one of the tips to learn a language effectively.)

After doing this for a good half hour, completely unaware of how to correctly pronounce the words and phrases I had just memorized, I walked over to the ticket table. An attendant in his fancy navy blue vest, white dress shirt, sleek glasses, and yellow name tag was sitting at the marble desk looking down at his computer monitor. My presence alone made no difference to his focus on that screen. There I was, the skinny 125-pound, twenty-year-old, rural Ohioan with a backpack bigger than his torso slung on his back, hunched over, greasy two-day travel hair all wrapped up in a size-too-small beanie.

To project some semblance of confidence, I took Dr. Jordan Peterson's advice and "stood up straight with my shoulders back" (as much as I could with the weight of a boulder on my back) and asked myself, "Okay, now how do I clear my throat without sounding like I just cleared my throat?"

I took a swallow and began to speak in this horrifying parody of Dutch.

"Hallo. Alstublieft, een ticket to een Amster—"

Without moving a single muscle or changing his posture at all, the attendant's eyes darted up to me and gave me the expressionless look of "Okay dude. What the hell are you even trying to say to me right now?"

I froze as a good five seconds dragged by, as it felt like an eternity with a buzzcut-wearing, beefy Dutch dude staring into my soul.

Then, he said in impeccably fluent English, "Yeah, I speak English. What kind of train ticket do you want? And to Amsterdam, right? We have one-way and return trip tickets."

In my shock, I stammered, "Uhhhhh. One way. Uhh, one way please."

"No problem. That is eight euro."

I dug through my pocket, extracted my wallet, and fumbled through its contents. I double checked my money to make sure it was the right amount and flipped him the eight euro. He gave me my ticket, instantly went back to his computer screen, and I was on my merry way.

I turned and said, "Uhh, bedankt!" ("thanks" in Dutch).

The man turned his head from his computer screen again, his eyes peering above his glasses, deadpan, paused a second, and said, "You're welcome."

ENGLISH OR DUTCH

Despite the embarrassment, it was probably for the better that he spoke fluent English.

Unbeknownst to me, 90 to 93 percent of the Dutch in the Netherlands speak fluent English.

English is learned by *necessity* and because of its ease. English is so widely spoken individually and used in Dutch institutions that English is no longer considered to be a foreign language in the country. Over 50 percent of classes offered in university are taught in English as reported by DutchNews.nl in January 2018: "English Is No Longer a Foreign Language in NL, But It Has a Unique Character Here" (*DutchNews* 2018).

The Netherlands is a small country. Its partial dependence on foreign trade, consumption of foreign entertainment industries, and historical closeness with the UK has exposed the natives to English at length. Both Dutch and English are extremely similar languages branching from the same ancestral language, Western Germanic, over one thousand years ago.

Plus, the UK and the Netherlands are right across the sea from each other. Once upon a time, the Dutch and British were huge trade rivals on the high seas, hence the "Dutch East India company" and the "British East India Company." Additionally, for a time Britain and what would become the Netherlands were ruled by a single king, William III, more commonly known as William of Orange. This is all a historical reminder that it is easier to break into the Anglophonosphere than it is to break out of it.

ENGLISH'S SISTER LANGUAGE

More interestingly, a tiny group of people live in small coastal communities in the Netherlands and Germany speak a language even closer to English than Dutch.

No other language is closer to English than the dialects of Frisian, yet chances are you have never even heard of it.

The Frisians number no more than half a million, and their communities are fairly separated and spread out along the North Sea coast of Europe, some relegated to tiny islands offshore. And yet, they retain a strong sense of community responsibility and culture.

These people were known to be distinct from the Dutch in the way in which they combated the floods from the sea: by living on man-made dirt mounds called *terpens* instead of building dikes. Since prehistoric times, the Frisians, or the Frisk as they call themselves, have had their culture survive by fighting off the ever intrusive, watery chaos of the sea and preservation of the Frisian language, all creating unifying factors to rally behind (Encyclopaedia Britannica, 2020).

English and Frisian dialects are part of the same language sub-family: the Anglic languages, also known as the Anglo-Frisian languages, or even cooler yet, Ingvaeonic.

From around 500 AD to 1,200 AD when English (what is now called Old English) was first spoken by the Anglo-Saxons, and Old Frisk was spoken by the Frisians, the two languages were so close they were mutually intelligible. In fact, some of the Frisians along with some of the Angles, Saxons, and Jutes were the peoples to leave continental Northern Europe after the collapse of the Roman Empire to colonize what is now Britain and lay the linguistic groundwork for Old English/Anglo-Saxon and actually became the Anglo-Saxon people as now might be obvious.

However, what mutual intelligibility means is that an Anglo-Saxon and a Frisian could understand each other's languages just as closely as how in America today a Bostonian can understand a Texan's accent and dialect, and vice versa. Closer than a blood orange and a Florida orange. To add, the Viking language of Old Norse was also mutually intelligible with Old English and has since emerged and divorced into Danish, Norwegian, Swedish, and Icelandic—all of which are mutually intelligible among each other to an extent.

Old English and Old Frisian were so close that they technically weren't different languages at all, but dialects of "Anglic." Nowadays, Frisian and English still share a lot of words, but are *not* mutually intelligible. However, even after 1,000 years of separation, some cherry-picked phrases are still mutually intelligible.

If you ran into a person in Friesland, Netherlands, they might speak West Frisian. If they hear you speak English, they might say this rhyme to you: "Bûter, brea en griene tsiis is goed Ingelsk en goed Frysk!" If you had subtitles while they were talking, you might think "Why are there floating words in front of my face?" but more likely, you'd notice that this person REALLY can't spell. Can you guess what they were saying in West Frisian? (Mitch, 2020).

What they are trying to tell you is, "Butter, bread, and green cheese is good English and good Friese."

Obviously, they wanted to share with you how your culture and theirs appreciate the merits of buttered bread and horrifically moldy cheese. Europeans and their cheese, am I right? Doesn't quite have the same rhythm in English, though.

Regardless, here are two languages—one you know and one you have likely never heard of—that are outrageously similar. We will explore the nuances and advantages of mutual intelligibility later on in the book. But now, let's look beyond the North Sea to the world as a whole.

A GLOBAL LANGUAGE

When Britain colonized one-fourth of the world's land mass, the British brought with them their mutual language: English. English quickly became the *lingua franca* of most of North America, being used in the thirteen colonies, Canada, and Belize, that little country tucked away in Central America.

India, the "crown jewel of the empire" would use English to unite the sub-continent of 1.2 billion people in the world's largest modern democracy. As reported by Rukmini S. in May 2019 on LiveMint.com and the 2011 Census of India, India makes up a massive portion of people learning English globally. The Indian Census discovered English is the second language of 83 million Indians, and the third language, (yes you heard me right, the third language), of forty-six million people (Rukmini, 2019). As of June 2021, the CIA World Factbook reports that English enjoys status as the subsidiary language critical for national, political, and commercial communication. English is a necessary unifying factor as the country otherwise remains linguistically divided: 43.6 percent speak Hindi, 8 percent Bengali, Marathi 6.9 percent, Telugu 6.7 percent, Tamil 5.7 percent, Gujarati 4.6 percent, Urdu 4.2 percent, among many others living up to Mark Twain's adage: "The country of hundred nations and a hundred tongues…"

This may be shocking for many monolingual Americans, but outside of the United States, it is common for people to know more than one language or dialect. I often find that those I meet who know more than one language more often than not know more than two. Why the United States is confined to one or two major languages and why most Americans only speak one language is the focus of the next chapter.

India's neighbor and rival Pakistan uses English to a similar extent.

It is said in a not-so-inaccurate generalization that half of Africa speaks English and the other half French. Zimbabwe, Uganda, Zambia, Botswana, Namibia, Kenya, Sierra Leone, Liberia, South Africa, and Nigeria all use English on a national scale.

Australia, a continent and country, almost exclusively speaks English! (Let's not forget neighboring New Zealand does too.)

With such prevalence and ties to the Anglophone world (an anglophone is someone who speaks English), many countries in Europe have strongly integrated English into their educational curriculum, and Anglophone culture has made its way into these cultures.

One is hard-pressed to find someone who doesn't speak English when traveling through the cities of Germany, Switzerland, Sweden, Norway, Denmark, Finland, Belgium, the Netherlands, Estonia, Austria, Slovenia, Greece, Croatia, and Liechtenstein. In my own travel experience, most people in the often-forgotten country of Albania speak it as well!

Other countries predominantly use English in tandem with their native languages, such as in Israel/Palestine, the United Arab Emirates, and Hong Kong. English is taught in many other countries across the world as well, and much of the world has a great demand for native speakers who have the desire to teach it (Vega 2018).

It needs to be mentioned that a major reason why English spread especially in the last few decades and continues to spread like wildfire is because many of those computer scientists who developed the early forms of the internet and modern computers spoke, you guessed it, English. Thus, because English was prevalent among those early developers, English has been the bedrock for coding languages and general computer functions. Social media and smartphones, a cultural extension of this, has become a vector by which English is spread.

The wide world seems to exist in this strange balance between native languages and the dominance of English throughout the globe. An accomplished world traveler who also happened to be my high school literature teacher, Mrs. Brianne Pernod, had this to say about being an anglophone abroad:

> *I'll never forget looking at street signs in Russia or Norway and realizing I didn't even know what the letters were, let alone the sound they made. I'm grateful that while I only speak one language, it happens to be a universal language of business. I love that I can travel the world with a relative comfort that I won't be abhorrently stranded. I still try to learn a few phrases—and the tipping procedures—but mostly I feel pretty good about taking off for anywhere and being able to get around. In Romania we [Mr. and Mrs. Pernod] had the Uber app; they had it in India too, but I wasn't brave enough to try Ubermoto there! Basically, I guess I'm saying that while language may be a barrier, it doesn't prohibit experiencing other countries and cultures, and for that I'm continually grateful.*

SPEAKING VERNACULAR

So, English is widely spoken throughout the world, and in some instances, fluently, as I discovered during my brief time spent in the Netherlands.

Nevertheless, it is important to keep in mind that even though much of the world may speak English, that does not mean the people there want to, and that still leaves the rest of the world who might not know how to. Dave Barry, an American author, comedy writer, and columnist for the *Miami Herald* said it best:

"Americans who travel abroad for the first time are often shocked to discover that, despite all the progress that has been made in the past thirty years, many foreign people still speak in foreign languages."

A large portion of the world knows or is learning English at this moment in history and having a language—like English— that bridges people together across borders is extremely useful. Yet, when traveling, working, living, or interacting with different parts of the world, something is to be said for the person willing to meet "foreigners" halfway, especially when we are the foreigners in their countries.

Master the English language, join in on the Anglophono-sphere, but pick a foreign language you want to learn and chase it. English has bridged the world, but those who speak multiple languages on top of English end up bridging the world several times over.

TAKEAWAYS

1. The Anglophonosphere is the English-speaking world.
2. The English language has always been a collection of many languages including Latin, Romano-Celtic, Anglo-Saxon, Old Norse, French, and bits of Greek among dozens of smaller words and phrases from other origins.
3. English is so prevalent in countries like the Netherlands that English is no longer considered a foreign language.
4. English's sister language is known as West Frisian (or Frisk) spoken in parts of North-Western Europe, and for nearly 700 years English and Frisian were mutually intelligible coming from a common language spoken around the time of the fall of Rome (~500 AD).
5. Colonization by the British Empire brought English to much of the world, as the empire at its height controlled one-fourth of all land on Earth.
6. English is used as a national language throughout different regions of Africa and is taught to fluency in many countries in Europe, Asia, and Africa.
7. Much of the world knows English, but when traveling it is a best practice to learn—at minimum—the basics of the native language; meet native speakers halfway.

CHAPTER 3

Speaking 'Merican

———

LANGUAGES EVERYWHERE

Right now, stop what you're doing! I want you to guess how many languages are spoken in the world today! Okay. How many did you guess? Better yet, how many languages can you name? Ten? Twenty? Forty-two? One hundred and ninety? Okay.

As attested by the *Ethnologue: Languages of the World* database, in 2021, 7,139 languages are actively spoken around the world! Can you believe that? I hardly can. For reference, there are only 195 countries in the world today.[1] If you do the math, that is roughly thirty-six unique languages per each country. Many countries have one dominant language such as the Czech Republic speaking Czech. Or in China there are Mandarin and its gobs of dialects in addition to tons of different languages spoken by a tiny minority of citizens. Some other countries have groupings of dominant languages based on region and religion, such as Nigeria. The country with the most spoken languages in the world is... well, can you guess?

A tiny country on the Pacific Ocean below Asia and above Australia and New Zealand called Papua New Guinea. As maintained by Niall McCarthy at Statista—my favorite statistical website out there—as of 2019, in Papua New Guinea 840 languages are actively spoken. Indonesia, its neighbor came in second with 710, and Nigeria was third with 524.

With all that said, have you ever wondered why English, and not Spanish or French, is the dominant language in the United States? Why is Spanish a close second? How can English be the culturally dominant language if the United States has no official language? (Did you know the US has no official language?)

AMERICAN PECULIARITY

The reason I believe Americans are mostly not bilingual and second language education has been rapidly declining in public education is because American society is an unparalleled departure from typical geographical and historical patterns.

Let me break that down. For most of history all around the world (and for most of the world currently), the native language one would speak would be confined to a small area of land or among a specific organization or social class.

THE HISTORICAL NORM, THE FRENCH EXAMPLE

A historical example is how after the fall of the Roman Empire, new kingdoms and nations were forming all across Western Europe, and in the former Roman province known as "Gaul," an unheard-of kingdom was forming between all sorts of peoples that spoke different languages in a small geographical sphere.

In the region of Brittany, you had the Celtic Breton speakers and the Gallo speakers. On the North and Eastern frontiers of Gaul you had Franks (the namesake of the kingdom) who spoke an ancient Germanic language as well as all sorts of other Germanic languages and dialects, and all throughout the whole of Gaul you had Romanized Celts who spoke a dialect of Latin.

Keep in mind, handfuls of languages and dozens of dialects were all spoken in this emerging kingdom known as Frankia.

A kingdom that would produce famous kings and emperors such as Charles "the Hammer" Martel and Karl the Great, or as you may know him: Charlemagne.

Eventually the various dialects that descended from the Gaulish dialect of Latin would produce a family of dialects known as the *langues d'oil* (meaning *languages of "oil,"* oil being the way they said "yes"; oil evolved into "oui") that grew far enough in difference from Latin to be considered a new language. This language with its family of dialects would come to dominate the Northern half of Gaul, eventually becoming the early French language.

The early French dialect of an old Roman and Celtic settlement known as Parisius, or *City of the Parisii tribe*, would later come to dominate all of Frankia. Frankia would become West Francia, West Francia would become France, and Parisius would become Paris according to the entry "Kingdom of West Francia" in the *Ancient History Encyclopedia*. Even today, France has several different languages in its borders along with dialects of French different enough to be considered foreign languages!

THE HISTORICAL NORM, THE CHINESE EXAMPLE

To further illustrate, for most of history and in the modern age, you could go a few dozen miles or more rarely a few hundred and find that a completely different language was spoken or a dialect so different from your own that you simply could not understand without a guide.

Gavin van Hinsbergh in his 2019 article "Modern Chinese: Mandarin and Chinese Dialects in China Highlights" gives a breakdown of the country's linguistic profile from which I derive and infer the following example. China, a country that largely speaks Mandarin in its most populous areas, has such a large dialect continuum that if you, a native Mandarin speaker from Beijing, go from Beijing into Qingdao city in the neighboring province, there is a good chance you cannot understand their Mandarin dialect as well as, say, an American anglophone can understand someone speaking a Scottish accent.

THE HISTORICAL NORM, THE INDIAN EXAMPLE

If you look southwest of China to the subcontinent, the world's largest democracy, and the country with a population of 1.4 billion (nearly 20 percent of all humans on Earth) you'll find India, the "land of a hundred tongues."

As the *CIA World Factbook* indicated and Mark Twain vivified in last chapter, India is host to hundreds, if not thousands, of cultures, languages, and ethnicities, despite being a third of the physical size of the United States, a country in which the vast majority of people only speak English or Spanish, and seldom both. Even though India does not have as many languages as Papua New Guinea or Indonesia, I want you to imagine how many dialects there would be in a country with dozens and possibly hundreds of languages.

THE HISTORICAL ANOMALY, THE AMERICAN EXAMPLE

Back to the United States, where an English-speaking American finds himself in a peculiar situation. This person can go hundreds of miles in any direction within the United States and be in a completely different landscape, climate, or culture, yet have no worry that the people there will speak a dialect of English that could not be understood.[2]

Of course, there are parts of the country such as Cajun Louisiana, Spanish speaking communities in the Southwest, German Texas, French speaking towns in rural New England, and Native American reserves, but these are the exceptions, not the rule.

Extrapolate this out globally as I did last chapter, and Americans can go to major tourist destinations around the globe such as Western Europe, East Asia, the Caribbean, and Oceania (not the one that uses Newspeak) and have little doubt that those they interact with wouldn't know enough English to carry out the traveler's needs.

The fact that most of the globalized world uses English as a *lingua franca* makes life easier on the global and local stage for Americans and other primary or strong English speakers such as Australians, New Zealanders, Irish, Swedish, Dutch, Germans, and the various British.

ORIGINS OF THE UNITED STATES AND THE ANOMALY

After reading that, you are probably thinking, "Okay, America is absolutely weird. So why does such a large country like America only have one common language?" Well, to partially answer your question, English is just that: a unifier. Well, again, I should specify that is one of the arguments and one of the aspects that make English *the* dominant language, but it is not the origin.

From the last chapter and what you likely already know if you are American or a lover of history, America arose from the British Empire several hundred years ago. If you are not familiar with this history, I'll keep it brief.

As pilgrims escaping religious persecution in England and Europe arrived, they increasingly created larger and larger colonies. As the British crown began realizing the wealth of resources and land in the New World, expeditions like the Virginia Company were set up to find precious resources like gold in the Americas.

In time, more colonies popped up along the coast of what is now the Eastern Seaboard of the United States. The coastal areas of the West Atlantic were the easiest to access by the British (and other European empires) in the Northwest Atlantic.

From when the pilgrims landed in Plymouth in 1620 to the American Revolution in the 1770s, the continent of North

America became more populated by Europeans with large cities like York City (the New one), Boston, and Charles Town (Charleston) already firmly established.

The British competed with other powers, especially their ancient nemesis, France, for control of all of North America. As much of the history of the Americas goes, the land that would become the US and Canada, specifically the Ohio Valley and Great Lakes region had a commodity bought by the bushel in Europe.

Can you guess what it was? Yes, your first guess was right! Beaver pelts! That is what you guessed, wasn't it?

Unfortunately for the Brits, France controlled much of the Ohio Valley and Great Lakes region, but Britain wanted it. So, Britain got all of it from Florida up the Eastern Seaboard through Canada (except for the Louisiana land, which was nearly all of the land west of the Mississippi, which went to Spain). Britain gets what Britain wants (except when it comes to good food despite the efforts of Gordon Ramsey).

Long story short, that was the French and Indian War as we call it in America, as both sides used alliances with Native Americans. Us 'Mericans also call it the seven-year war, but in Europe they call it the nine-year war.

Clearly language is not the only difference between the two of us, Americans and Europeans; our understanding of math, and time for that matter, seems to be fundamentally irreconcilable. You say po-tay-to, I say po-tot-o; you say five plus four equals nine, I say I'll settle for seven, take it or leave it.

That seems to go beyond metric conversions and commas as decimals and decimals as commas.

Shortly after the seven-to-nine-year French and Indian (but also British) War, Britain imposed heavy taxes on the British colonists to pay for the massive debts incurred by the conflict. The colonists had enjoyed many freedoms the English back in England did not get to enjoy, such as home rule, where locals essentially make up how the government and society are to work, therefore were closer to what those people wanted.

When the taxes and greater top-down rule came down, the British had their soldiers quartered in people's homes rent-free, and trade with anyone other than Papa Britain was prohibited. The colonists became infuriated.

Of course, this is an oversimplification, but the case still stands.

Colonists of thirteen separate colonies threw off the British and their tyranny to be free, equal in the eyes of the law, independent, and soon to join these thirteen separate colonies turned countries into thirteen United States. But the United States, despite throwing off the British rule, inherited so much of English culture.

FRENCH AMERICA VERSUS ANGLO-AMERICA

As historians, both amateur and professional, have pointed out that the fate of the entire North American continent would be decided in the seven-year war. If the French won, America, if it exists in this alternate reality, would not speak

English as it does now, but French. The vestiges of French colonization remain in Canada, primarily in the province of Quebec, as well as in small communities in the Canadian maritime provinces along the Eastern Seaboard.

Plenty of place names are French in Canadian provinces and northern states such as Michigan with names like "Grand Maraias" (great swamp) and Sault Ste Marie. Other vestiges lie in the United States, famously with Cajun culture in Louisiana. The Cajuns being French colonists who lived on a Canadian island known as Acadia. During and after the war, the British massacred and forced the Acadians (*Acadiens* in French) out of the region where they would settle South in Louisiana, eventually dropping the "A," calling themselves *Cadiens*, which in French sounds extremely close to *Cajuns*; thus, the name "Cajun" was born.

Other cultural themes from the English were inherited by Americans such as a system of common law, a certain freedom of speech, and representation in parliament, or as we properly call it in America: Congress.

This hints to an important fact in understanding American culture in all manners of life. America is famously individualistic, meaning there is a societal emphasis on being independent, sovereign, and self-reliant, which fits into and creates the American conceptualization of extreme freedom and liberty. This is often distilled into a maxim: *One is free to do what one wants so long as it does not harm others.* Although that last part is often contentious or forgotten for a more libertine attitude.

Self-reliance is a principle I would not live without. However, there is a balance between self-reliance and responsibility for one's life and actions and having the humility and curiosity to ask for help and search for answers outside of what we know. That's the spirit of learning a language!

This curiosity often does not extend to learning other languages. Yes, many of us Americans are curious to learn that second language, and if you are an American reading this, you've already indicated yours. BUT, this curiosity is not so undying that we rise up out of our recliners, brush away the Cheetos dust from our shirt, and march on our schools, city halls, and state legislatures demanding superior language education from kindergarten up through university.

DESTINED TO PART

I can't talk about language and culture in America without bringing up a certain Frenchman, who documented the social, political, religious, and linguistic aspects of America in his famous 1835 book *Democracy in America*. Alexis de Tocqueville is this Frenchman's name.

Tocqueville commented that America—the American project, democracy in America—is the child of Europe, as America is made up of many immigrant groups from all over the continent of Europe (at the time: English, Scottish, Irish, Dutch, Swedish, French, Polish, Swiss, German, among many others). However, he makes sure to mention that America is not only a child of Europe, but the Americans also are a child of Britain, particularly in its language, laws, and customs.

America was at the time and still is wholly unique in a way that no other countries have been quite before, and many in the last 200 years have attempted to emulate it with wholly different results. Even though the United States of America had politically separated from Great Britain on July 4, 1776, American culture and language were nevertheless rooted in that original British culture. As it is written in the United States Declaration of Independence:

> We have appealed to their native justice and magnanimity, and we have conjured them by the ties of our common kindred to disavow these usurpations, which, would inevitably interrupt our connections and correspondence. They too have been deaf to the voice of justice and of consanguinity. We must, therefore, acquiesce in the necessity, which denounces our Separation, and hold them, as we hold the rest of mankind, Enemies in War, in Peace Friends.

Essentially affirming that although the British and Americans are glued together by a common history, language, culture, and even by blood at that point in time, the two must bid each other adieu. Having once been a colony of Britain forever changed the culture and language of those who lived in the thirteen colonies that would become America, and from the American Revolution onward, America was on a completely different path.

Today, the cultures of Britain and the United States are, of course, similar, as they both are in the Anglophonosphere, but truly, they are distinct peoples. One of the few things keeping us Americans and British similar other than our shared language and common law is our competing obesity rates, but I suppose that is a preferable problem than starvation.

DESTINED TO MANIFEST

As colonists and American settlers spread West beyond the Appalachian Mountains, English, too, was spread. In the nineteenth century (that's the 1800s for those of you who skipped history class), there was a prevalent doctrine in the United States called "Manifest Destiny," which held that American expansion out West, even to the Pacific Ocean, was justified and inevitable.

Justified? Perhaps, in some sense retrospectively, but probably not for the sense the expansionists had in mind. However, it was inevitable as land was sold to the US by countries like France and became the target of several wars (Mexican-American war that gave the US California, Nevada, Arizona, Utah, Texas, Colorado, New Mexico, Wyoming, Kansas, and Oklahoma). With the British still in Canada and the Americans reaching the Pacific Ocean, English dominated North America and still does today. The country of Mexico and cultural enclaves within the US, Mexico, and Canada are the only exceptions.

With the Americans dominating North America, being able to pivot both in the Pacific and Atlantic Oceans, American military and economic dominance over the world would be inevitable as Eurasia, and a disunited massive continent was blocked in by both sides by a singular country with a more or less coherent culture patched together from hundreds of subcultures tied by English. Many powers in Europe and

Asia throughout history have tried to control the continent of Eurasia (the Mongols, various Islamic Caliphates, the Soviet Union, the British Empire), but the US was the first country both powerful enough and in the right geographical position and with the right allies to exert major influence. The US is on either side of Eurasia and in the post-WWII era, its allies were Western Europe capping off the western end and Japan, Taiwan, and South Korea capping off the eastern end of Eurasia.

I write all this about geography and American expansion because it helps explain in part why America and its culture are dominant throughout the world today. Yes, I am missing major parts such as American military dominance established over several wars, but this isn't a history textbook (and don't use or cite it as one). I still believe those direct causes were made possible through the foothold the United States was able to establish from "sea to shining sea."

ENGLISH IN AMERICA

There is a practicality of using English, rather, continually using English: prevalence around the world due to aforementioned British mass colonization and American dominance (militarily, economically, and culturally), making English an official language that could act as a unifying factor. Whether this is ethical is not my assertion, but the stoic in me says to accept the current situation and work with what we have rather than wishing reality to be other than it is. David Ibekwe and Fraser Moore have a fantastic 2017 article and video called "Why Universal Languages like Esperanto Won't Catch On" published in *Business Insider* about why changing the world language by force or committee is and has been a fruitless battle.

Some argue that continuing to not have an official language would help embrace America's truly multilingual nature. English has always been dominant, but cities are filled with communities that speak dozens if not hundreds of different languages. If you have the opportunity to visit New York City, you will see hundreds of cultures and languages converge in one single, compact space. If not, check out any big city in the US. In Ohio alone, we have considerable communities of Poles, Germans, Nepalese, Lebanese, Serbs, Vietnamese, Iraqis, Amish, among many others.

Many federal and state government documents are composed in English first, and then Spanish, and even many other languages, but primarily English with due consideration to Spanish.

American companies put their labeling and advertisements primarily in English which perpetuates the use of English in everyday reading and consumer shopping.

Proximity to Canada, a country with a tenth the population of the US but mostly English speaking, makes English the *lingua franca* between the two countries. In Canada, labels, signs, advertisements, and other reading material that would have two translations are almost always in English first than French, with the exception of Quebec. Quebec is the French-speaking province of Canada, where the roles are reversed or English might not be offered at all. Having been to Quebec, many speak English, but not everyone wants to. You'd better be prepared because that absence of English on signs is the norm (again, an exception). Although it is a federal requirement to learn (more accurately: teach) French in schools in Canada, most Anglophone Canadians know just as much French as most Anglophone Americans know Spanish, i.e., nada, *rien.*

The process of obtaining American citizenship includes an English literacy test. This test requires a certain level of English speaking and reading ability. The American federal government expects new immigrants to know or learn some English, despite English not being the official language.

Lastly, studies show that immigrant children also show a strong desire to learn English and learn it well so they do not stand out more than they might already do. Having all been kids once upon a time, we had a desire to be unique, but we also did not want to stand out in such a way as to be pushed out from the "main group." Americans are human too; we seek belonging. Balancing humility with a desire to be unique and to be seen as unique to others, while also not being so unique you don't fit in, is a human balancing act we all play out. How can we conform while also being one of a kind? That seems to be a lifelong process.

IMMIGRANT FAMILY
Another factor is that immigrant groups in the United States (and in many other countries) tend to lose their "foreign" language within a few generations.

An example of this can be seen with my friend Emily Ghazoul, United Nations Holy See intern extraordinaire and fellow

Walsh University graduate. She comes from a culturally rich immigrant family background:

> *"My dad's side of the family is from Syria, so growing up I've always heard Arabic, BUT my siblings and I are the only ones in our family who don't speak fluent Arabic because our mom is the only American married into my dad's family. English was my first language, but hearing Arabic all my life I know how to pronounce words, how to move my mouth and everything, and I understand a lot more [Arabic] than I can speak."*

Children brought in at an early age or raised in a new country will often adapt to that new culture, being an intermediary between family culture and host culture.

Also, there is economic utility in learning the language of the country you are in, as you can then navigate the larger society and thus the job market, entrepreneurial opportunities, ease of negotiating a close on a new home, or any economic activity or choice that would greatly impact someone's life. It's not such a cold or callous decision over what choice *makes me the most money* and *how I can get the most things*. Rather, it is about using our resources and *resourcefulness* to maximize our lot in life, immigrant or otherwise. Language simply factors in. A tool in the toolbox.

On the other hand, if you dropped me off in China and told me to go start a business, negotiate rent for an apartment, and use a taxi to get from point A to point B, I would first wonder where you got the money for me to do such a thing because I sure ain't paying for that, and second, I would have no idea what to say or how to ask for help or read absolutely anything as I know approximately 0.0000001% of Mandarin. But if my life depended on it, I might be inclined to learn. In a situation like that everything becomes interesting, and learning becomes a necessity. That necessity comes from an implicit expectation, but where do these expectations come from and what are there consequences in larger society?

POLITICS OF LANGUAGE

In the United States, it is simply a fact that there is a societal and individual expectation for English to be spoken and used in almost every facet of life. America is bizarre in that—historically and currently—massive groups within the country speak a variety of languages but still conform to learning English in some capacity—if not themselves as individuals, then by proxy through their children or family as interpreters. A similar argument can be made about pockets of the US where there are majority Hispanic populations where Spanish is expected.

When conversing with Ivorian economist Germinal Van [3], author of *The African 'Nobel Prize'* as well as *The Economic Development of West Africa in the Twenty-First Century* and *Political Decisions and Economic Outcomes*, we discussed how language and culture play a unique role in the United States unlike any other democracy. I had pointed out that many democracies across the world divide into political parties and coalitions, not on the basis of a set of political ideas but along ethnic, religious, linguistic, cultural, or even racial lines.

For example, in a stable and model country like Germany, the majority political party is defined on religious terms, Christian Democratic Union, and the most radicalized parties come from East Germany, which is steeped in cultural differences from the rest of Germany. Even ideologically-based and uniform governments like the Soviet Union were held together not by communism, but by rallying around Russian nationalism and Soviet identity.

To further illustrate, Germinal explained to me that in Africa, democracy is widespread but is often held back and falls prey to opportunist dictators because allegiance is not given to institutions like rule of law, and parties are *not* formed around policy but rather tribal supremacy of one identity over another.

We came to agree that even though America certainly has a history of issues with racial and cultural relations, the American political system manages to avoid membership to a specific racial, linguistic, ethnic, and religious identity as being necessary to be part of either party or to find a place in government. Both Democrat and Republican parties, as dysfunctional and corrupt as they may be, are made up of religiously, ethnically, racially, vocationally, and linguistically diverse groups of people. America has mostly managed to avoid strong identitarian politics and identity politics (two sides of the same coin that place group identity over individual dignity and merit) within the institutions themselves relative to other countries. The largest war in American history was the American Civil War, which was a conflict to stamp out identitarian stratification.

The American language, English, really doesn't belong to any one group of Americans because in American culture it has been separated from something simply owned by people in England; it has become all our language. A paradox. A peculiarity. This is the *sweet* part of the bittersweetness of *speaking American*. With that said, are Americans and other anglophones doomed to only English? Is there a special quality in acquiring multiple languages that native anglophones lack?

I'M NOT SPECIAL AND NEITHER ARE YOU

It is often thought among people who only speak one language that acquiring a second language is impossible, and that knowing multiple languages is a special skill. However, there are many precedents across the world where societies utter several languages all their lives. South Africa, Germany, the Netherlands, Singapore to name a few.

Now consider this: Chances are learning English or your first language was probably pretty easy. Of course, there were probably humps to overcome with the grammar in English class, but overall, you speak the language natively and understand others who can speak the language without trouble. So, is it really such an accurate statement that you can't learn a second language because it's too difficult or a special skill for special people?

This should teach us two things:

1. You certainly can acquire a second language easily or similar in difficulty to how you learned your native tongue, and

2. we would want to replicate the methods that taught you that first language in order to learn a second one.

There was a point before high school where I could *ONLY* speak English. Then I took French class for two years and picked up the basics, along with a bunch of random vocabulary. Fast forward to sophomore year of college, after not practicing French for four years since my last French class, and I traveled to France.

In France, I was able to understand bits and pieces of conversation and read 90 percent of street signs, advertisements, and menu items. Even then, I could barely string together a sentence. Less than a year passed, and all flights are grounded. International travel was made impossible. I was living in my apartment, kicked off campus because it was May 2020 and the coronavirus pandemic was in full swing. I had barely practiced any French since traveling to Lourdes and Paris, but I decided that hopping from tongue to tongue like a French kiss on a deluge of language apps without a plan would never result in fluency of any kind.

I decided it was time to choose ONE language, and I chose French. Now, as I write these words, it's summer 2021 and, because I made an evidence-based plan and stuck to it, I can speak French at the intermediate level.

I say that because in regard to learning a language, I am not special. I don't possess a magical or innate skill set you don't as it pertains to memorization or speech. In fact, I may be at a disadvantage in some cases. Memorization in studying has always been difficult for me, whether it be retaining the information or simply executing on the will to sit down, remove distractions, and study. Historically, I would also stutter and get anxious in social situations, even with family and close friends I was fully comfortable around. Nevertheless, practicing foreign language with strangers and people I didn't know too well has helped me build confidence in another language, moreover, a confidence of personality overall.

LANGUAGE CLASSROOMS IN THE ANGLOPHONOSPHERE

Lastly, the lack of actual language learning within language classes should indicate that there is an obvious issue with how Americans and other native English speakers are taught a second language. Or, perhaps, how it is approached. I am not in the business of blaming teachers for this issue, as I have outlined other reasons why learning a second language is not a cultural priority for Americans.

However, unless you are going to a language-centered school the classroom as it currently is configured and approached is rather useless for acquiring a second language. Why? This is a multifaceted issue with many explanations. I'll blitz through a few examples inspired by the 2019 blog post "Why Learning a Foreign Language in School Doesn't Work (and How to Make it Work)" composed by the YouTuber, blogger, and Italian polyglot Luca Lampariello.

Languages are treated as a subject and NOT as an acquirable skill. Languages are taught similar to how we teach other subjects: memorize facts and rules. The classroom is often competitive, favoring those few students who have a specialized eager interest in mastering language as a skill, whereas most students see it how it is taught: as a subject. To learn language as a skill is an improvement from it being taught as a stale subject, but acquiring a new tongue with the understanding that language is simply something humans do like eating, playing, working, and creating, language is thus humanized; not a book to memorize or a special skill for the few.

The given language is rarely used to actually communicate and even more rarely to communicate something relevant to the student, such as lifestyle of the youth, trends, home-life, and popular music in the target culture. Textbooks and lesson plans often use outdated phrases no longer applicable to the current generation of learners (or native speakers). For example, in French classes you will still be taught that "comme ci, comme ça" is the way to say, "I'm doing alright; I'm doing so-so." Whereas in France, no one says this anymore; you would simply say, "Bof!"

The education of language is teacher-focused whereas it needs to be focused on a student's genuine desire to acquire a language. What I mean by this is teachers are viewed as the ultimate conveyor of knowledge, and it all must pass through them. Instead, students need to reorient their mindset and have a genuine desire to acquire fluency and not put so much pressure on the teacher to perform. You get out what you put in. Students spend a minimal amount of time with the language outside of class beyond minimally effective worksheets, and most importantly, students don't understand why they are being taught a language.

When we lack a purpose or interest in any facet of our life, we lose engagement because its utility is not obvious, especially if it is boring. Having a positive association and purpose (your motivation or your *why*) is crucial for the simple fact that it will keep you interested.

TAKEAWAYS

1. For most Americans there is little to no incentive to learn a second language. America's largest border is shared with a primarily anglophone country. English is the dominant global trade/business language, successive world powers primarily used English (British and Americans), and American culture has been exported so widely it is hard to find a place in the world where English isn't used on some level.

2. The American Anomaly: America is a peculiar country in that it is massive geographically yet retains the same language across most of the country, whereas most places for most of history would have a different language every few miles (think modern Europe, China, and India).

3. The British Empire and France competed for control of North America, after which the British victory cemented English as the dominant language of most of North America, although French culture and language is still prominent in pockets of the continent, mostly in Eastern Canada.

4. Self-reliance is crucial but must be balanced with responsibility to others. You can learn a language on your own but be willing to ask for help and use it as it is meant: to communicate with others.

5. The USA was originally a child of Britain in its traditions of customs, language, laws, and culture, which still holds

to some degree today. America is also a child of Europe (and more broadly the world) as the country is a patchwork of cultures, languages, and ethnicities.

6. The primarily English-speaking United States controlling much of North America blocked Eurasia from both sides, making American cultural and English language dominance beyond the fall of the British Empire inevitable.

7. Seemingly every community in the US, big or small, has groups of people who speak a wide variety of non-English languages… even in the middle of nowhere Ohio.

8. Immigrant families tend to lose their ancestral language within a few generations of arriving in a new country.

9. Most countries and political systems, even Western democracies, divide into political factions centered around ethnicity, language, religious, and/or racial groups, whereas in the United States, political factions are determined along ideological lines.

10. Learning and acquiring a secondary language can be as easy as how you learned your native language.

11. If you are to acquire an additional language as seamlessly as you acquire your primary language, you are best served to imitate how you acquired your primary language.

12. Make a plan to acquire a language and stick to it consistently.

FOOTNOTES:

[1] The number of countries in the world is somewhat subjective; in order to become a country/state, one has to have a permanent population, definable borders, functioning government, and recognition from at least one other country. With that, whether a country like Palestine, Israel, South Ossetia, Transnistria, and Republic of China (Taiwan) is considered a country depends on which country you asked,

as all those have limited recognition. By legal definition, a country that declares independence but is only recognized by itself and no other state is technically not a country. The recognition by France (a major world power at the time) of the United States was crucial in the founding and survival of America.

[2] Similarly, the British Isles, Australia, and New Zealand have no pressing geographical reason to learn a language other than English due to the fluency of English on the islands, the surrounding countries being mostly fluent in English, and any other languages spoken on the islands such as Irish Gaelic, Scots, Maori, or Welsh being spoken by less and less people each year.

[3] Germinal G. Van, born and raised in Abidjan Cote D'Ivoire in West Africa, is a trained economist and contributor with the Mises Institute and the Foundation for Economic Education (FEE) and in the time between my interview with him in June 2020, he has written and independently published four books on Amazon adding to his grand total of nineteen published books.

CHAPTER 4

Ugly American

—

IN-FLIGHT SHOW

It is not often you get stuck in a floating tube with people who don't speak English 30,000 feet in the sky, far above the clouds of a raging blizzard ravaging half a continent. Yet there I was, on one of the world's oldest airlines, Czech Airlines, circling over the Václav Havel international airport amid a whiteout that blanketed all of Central Europe. We were minutes away from landing in yet another country I did not accurately prepare for.

On the plane, I had a window seat, and all I could see was a fleece covering that gently enveloped all of the land stretching past the horizon and the crystalline baby blue dome of the wild blue yonder. Not even the mountains of nearby Southeastern Germany could poke through that puffy haze. It was a moment of serene calm that emanated from the natural beauty of the sky and a tad bit of anxiety from the uncertainty of when we were going to land at the airport or whether we would be sent back to Schiphol Airport in Amsterdam.

Depending on whom I would look at, the level of concern displayed on people's faces varied from the extreme of the couple in the row across me, whose expressions said, "Will our engines freeze midair causing us to fall several thousand feet face down into the ground and shatter into a million tiny cold pieces like an icicle off the roof of a building?" to the young Czech woman beside me who said in perfect and jovial English, "This is a pretty rough storm. I hope we don't get sent back!" to the unfazed squad of male Slav icons who sported Adidas tracksuits head to toe, flat caps while joking with each other, and eating homemade food wrapped in tin foil they smuggled on the plane. Don't ask me how they got that through the metal detector.

This was also the same group squatting in the ticket queue before boarding, eating sunflower seeds all in true gopnik fashion. Here, I was presented with an unmistakable stereotype of a Slav, and they were presented with an unmistakable, and glaring, example of an ugly American.

Not being able to understand the pilot or the flight attendants in their native tongue, and having the fortune to be sitting next to someone who spoke fluent English, highlighted to me: Why would I come to a country with no experience with the main language spoken there and with little interest in doing so? I wanted to visit my family friends—duh, of course! Nevertheless, I found myself falling into the position so many Americans and other anglophones fall into that I avoided like the plague before the actual plague was in vogue—that of the Ugly American. I was literally being an American traveler who goes to a foreign country with sparse interest in learning the language and subconsciously or consciously expects the natives to meet the traveler halfway by speaking English and adopting to American customs. The exact definition is as follows:

Ugly American, noun

Definition of *Ugly American*

: an American in a foreign country whose behavior is offensive to the people of that country [1]

Coming to that realization, I first felt awkward and out of place; I was entering a culture with which I had no experience. And second, because I knew I would not be getting nearly as much out of the experience as I would hope for because I did not put in much effort going to the country. I taught myself the bare minimum of Czech, and the little I acquired was learned via basic Polish, the cousin of Czech, due to a lack of convenience for Czech learning apps at the time.

Do not let inconvenience sideline you. If you are traveling, always plan out at least a month ahead of time to add a few minutes every day to practice a language. Do at least thirty minutes or an hour of research to find resources online, order books, and find flash card decks. Think of this research and practice of the language before leaving as important as buying an airplane ticket, packing the essentials, finding lodging, and how to get food. A ticket takes you to a country, but a language opens all of its horizons. Prioritize practice by making it quintessential. Stumbling around without any of the country's language can be as embarrassing and derailing as unzipping your suitcase to find you didn't pack any pants.

Keep in mind when learning a language (or anything), you get what you put in and how consistently you put forth effort.

Lastly, I thought, *How can I make this experience the best I can for myself, my hosts, and all those I meet and interact with?* This question became the prime focus of my curiosity and mission statement for that trip. In my search for a better experience for myself and others in Czechia, I found the cure to Ugly Americanism, which, in turn, is a major stepping-stone for learning any language.

CENTER OF THE WORLD

Finally, after over an hour of flying through a massive snow-storm with all the bumps and turbulence one could ever wish for, our Czech Airlines flight touched down in Václav Havel international airport. It was surreal when the clouds dispersed to reveal a soft layer of snow blanketing airplane hangars and old, tiny houses. As we were landing, dozens of giant snowplow trucks (no larger to the eye than the most minuscule toy truck) plowed snow away from the terminals and other landing strips as the precipitation continued to coat any flat surface. It looked as if little beetles were scudding through a fluffy white pastry, scraping away the frosting in neat little rows.

Upon landing, the experience became surreal, as I was truly apart from any of my friends, family, or contacts in a country at the heart of many historical events. Events I had delved into during my time in high school and college. Communism has become a sort of myth to young Americans like me because our generation has not grown up in a time where such an ideology posed an existential threat to our way of life. Entering a formerly communist country is tantamount to visiting a graveyard people live in who are slowly converting it into a modern city with the specters of the past visible in every brick, every walkway, every bookstore, every edifice, and nearly every face. I saw something from a past era I never knew sewn into the fabric of that country as both a haunting specter and propelling spirit.

To be in the Czech Republic, specifically Prague, was astounding. This city and this country were the head of the Czechoslovakian state that emerged from the ashes of the Austro-Hungarian Empire after World War I. It led the anti-Bolshevik coalition against Lenin and other Communists in Russia and Europe. The country enjoyed relative peace in the interwar period, then was annexed and invaded by the emergent Nazi Germany. Finally, liberated by the Americans and (ironically) the Soviets, it suffered under Communist rule until 1991 when the poet Václav Havel led his country to freedom, then split into Slovakia and the Czech Republic.

Wow. This country, the Czech and Slovak peoples, and all other folks within their borders were truly at the center of *the* major events of the twentieth century: the Great War, Bolshevik Revolution, World War II, the Cold War, and the collapse of the Soviet Union.

ALL UN-BOARD
Due to the weather conditions, there were more delays. We could not simply go from the airplane to the terminal

because it was apparently too dangerous for the airplane to dock with the terminal. Like most international flights flown, the pilot gave paragraphs upon paragraphs of details and notice in their native language over the radio, and then a five-word sentence summary in English of what was going on. It was really reassuring to know a several-minute status report about the various aspects that would indicate how much or how little our lives were at risk by stepping on that plane could be condensed to five words for us English natives.

Our plane was on the tarmac when a portable staircase came to let us out. Then we were signaled by the neon green vest-donned worker to walk a few hundred feet across the tarmac to a small glass-enclosed shelter on the exterior of the airport. There we waited, most people confused, shoulders shrugged until a tram picked us up... well, except for the other half of the passengers who couldn't fit on ours. I hope they're doing alright; it's been three years since I've seen them.

From there, we went up to the baggage pickup area, went through a security post, got our bags after wading through more delays, and finally were released to the public like wild animals after being raised in captivity. I'll never forget waiting by the pickup area along the street looking for my friend Domi and not seeing her anywhere. My then-skinny bones with minimal insulation quivered in the gentle snow filled breeze with not a familiar soul in sight, only the mutterings of Bohemian strangers fell on my ears.

I was to then be nearly tackled from the opposite direction I was looking, being bear-hugged by that curly headed girly. I didn't see her at all, nor did I see her face when she had her arms around me, so it could've been a baby bear for all I knew. I was in former Russian territory after all. But, in all seriousness, it was great to see my friend whom I hadn't seen for half a year. It was sweet to hear the words, "Max! I missed you so much!" not only because of the meaning, but also because it was English.

It was obvious when I got on the flight that Amsterdam was the last I would be hearing of English from most people. Outside of the Václav airport, there really was not an immediate need to use English. Why would there be? Everyone spoke Czech or Slovak and the country is surrounded by countries that speak Slavic languages or German. The history of the Czech people is unique because they are a Slavic-speaking people greatly influenced by German and Austrian culture in architecture, education, music, law, and to an extent, religion and politics.

Domi led me to the car her mother, her *maminka*, had parked by the curb. Maminka's face lit up with a bright smile and glittering eyes, "Ahoj!" I said. "Hi, Maaax, how are you?" she replied. "I'm good, how're you?" She paused for a second, looked at Domi, then back at me, and said, "Good!"

We got in and we were off. Václav Havel Airport was a hop and a skip outside of Prague proper, so we had ways to go to get to Prague. Domi and her parents lived in a village thirty minutes outside of Plzeň, which is a city one hour south of Prague, so the ladies wanted to show me the city of Prague before we would be spending the majority of the week between their village called Horní Bělá and that of Plzeň.

A-HAH! PRAHA!

Similar to the Amsterdam fiasco, despite having months to research where I was going and the language spoken there, I didn't. I did use the threatening green owl app to an extent, but my effort only went so far (Czech or get wrecked). The time I got in the car to when we reached Prague was a good hour.

Prague, I would find, is a primate city. No, not a city of orangutans, gorillas, and bonobos. A city so large in population and economic importance that no other city in the province or entire country could compete. Like a mini Paris or Moscow or Mexico City.

Prague has a dense, historically preserved European style city center with cultural landmarks, shopping districts, gargantuan cathedrals, fortresses, and huge open squares. Whereas outside of the core there were massive sprawling urban residential areas. A desire to be super close to the city center, dozens upon dozens of Soviet-esque block tower apartments were no less than thirty stories tall. To get to the core, we had to take the highway inward past open fields then through the miles of the residential jungle to then get to the outskirts of the city center that the outside or tourist world knows and loves. Instead of going through the urban jungle via car, we took the metro. Again, something I was not at all used to, hailing from rural America.

Maminka parked the car in the shadow of one of the skyscraper towers. Domi and Maminka led the way. I had no idea where we were going, except the clues revealed by Domi's intermittent narration of Maminka: "My mom is buying us three metro passes from this newspaper salesman."

In Amsterdam, you buy metro passes from a sharply dressed public worker at a sleek, clean desk. In Prague, at least where Maminka went to get the passes, the tickets are sold by a disheveled newspaper salesman smoking in a little kiosk separated by Plexiglas covered in random stickers, newspaper articles, and logos and adverts for absolutely everything—all of which are underground in a grungy, sketchy, to be exact, tunnel to the subway.

The US is famous for the never-ending stream of adverts on television, the internet, mail, billboards, and really everywhere else. I was humbled by the Czech Republic, thinking this is a uniquely American issue. When we drove in, dozens of billboards were spaced every few feet along the exits, which sounds ridiculous, but is even more ridiculous to see. This is the one time I was glad I couldn't read or speak Czech, I could tune out the adverts, but then again, with the number of them, I'm sure the locals were too. However, Domi argued they were distractions that lead to car accidents. In that, there is another important language lesson: Keep focused on the path of the language you are studying and don't veer into another *lane-guage* or be pulled away from an individual practice session by distraction.

Maminka picked up the passes, gave them to us, and off we went walking down the tunnel that turned into a staircase. The corridor was round and sleek brick, which eerily reminded me of pictures I've seen of the Soviet-era Moscow metro tunnels. Grabbing a train ride, we were soon to be in the city center to discover the depth and breadth of modern European culture.

CZECHTUCKY FRIED KITCHEN

I remember years ago in a Skype call with Domi, she told me flat out, "What the hell, Max! I do NOT understand English. Why would you have these words 'chicken' and 'kitchen'? Which is which? They sound the same right? Why would you have two words so similar? Do you cook a kitchen in a chicken, or do you go to the chicken to find the kitchen?"

My English bias was showing because I frankly never realized how close the two words were. I was preoccupied with my own frustration in remembering the difference between cause and *effect*, and psychological *affect* or being completely blind to the fact that eminent, immanent, and imminent were three completely different words. What words in your study language sound similar or are spelled the same?

Nonetheless, the issue was brought back up when the three of us, Domi, Maminka, and I, were looking for a quick place to refuel on food. I certainly did not know Prague well enough, nor did Domi who spent most of her life in Plzeň and her tiny village, so we trusted Maminka to pick out a niche local spot, perhaps rich with history. After all, Maminka and Raclav, Domi's dad and Maminka's husband, met while studying in Prague and participated in the Velvet Revolution where tens of thousands of students protested the authoritarian communist regime by gathering in that very place, Wenceslas Square, and jingled keys in the air as a peaceful act of civil disobedience.

After hearing this harrowing and inspiring story translated to me via Domi, Maminka guided us to a culinary bulwark of Czech culture on that very square where Communism was annihilated and the tree of liberty planted. KFC. Kentucky Fried Chicken. Right next to the "Irish Pub." One of three pubs on that side of the street alone.

This time around I wasn't imparting my Ugly Americanism, the concept itself had beat me there. Even if a country is seemingly hermetically sealed from the English language, one cannot avoid the beatific omnipresence of the American fast food empire. All seeing, all knowing, and by all means, all consuming. Their omnipotence was clearly at play, as I actively avoided fast food in the United States only for it to be placed before me 4,300 miles from home in a country that prides itself in not being fat like my fellow countrymen (and women; I wouldn't want to be exclusionary).

CULTURE
The seldom-overlooked aspect of learning any language is the significance of the culture and the impact culture has had on language.

Language is not simply what people speak, write, and listen to. It is a grand storybook of sorts that encapsulates an entire people's history, culture, origin, and direction. Bridging what we know into this concept can be difficult as many people do not have expansive knowledge about the cultures and history that informed prevalent world languages like Chinese, Spanish, Portuguese, or the many dialects of Arabic, for example.

By coincidence, learning French in the minds of many non-French, and definitely many Americans, is about learning the language of berets, mimes, accordions, the Eiffel Tower, baguettes, croissants, ascots, cabaret, Napoleon, Marie Antoinette, storming of the Bastille, fine dining, wine, and waving white flags (how the might of Napoleon and surrender are associated with the same culture, I do not understand). I am hard-pressed to think of any language that has such a strong connection between culture and language in the eyes of the average person.

The fancy, and sometimes pompous, association with French culture is expressed in the Parisian accent and pronunciation and inflection of words.

Where Spanish might give us detached phrases and words like "adios amigos," "no problemo," or "hasta la vista (baybee)," French gives us phrases closer to actual French culture and everyday use. In English, using bizarre or flat-out incorrect and fictitious usage of French phrases is commonplace. For example, "c'est la vie," "bourgeois (bougie/boujee)," "coup d'état," "au contraire," "connoisseur," or "encore" are all French phrases that retain the same or similar meaning when used in English. Much of this has to do with the interwoven histories of French and English. If the previously discussed West Frisian is English's sister, French is English's evil stepsister, married in and hard to get along with.

When we learn a language, it is not simply a word-to-word exact translation from one language to English or vice versa. In fact, this is nearly never the case, even with related languages. In the beginning of learning a language we often start with direct translations or phrases with slightly different senses that could still be understood in the English sense.

But, when we go further into learning a language, we begin to encounter challenges where sentences, phrases, sayings, idioms, and even individual words do not directly translate into English, and where there are translations that do not make sense.

Take the French phrase, "C'est le petit Jésus en culotte de velours."

Literal English translation: "It's like baby Jesus in velvet underpants."

Yes, you read that correctly. The actual meaning is not obvious, nor should it be, but is understood within the French culture as meaning, "This wine is delicious!" My thoughts exactly.

Here is something profound. Every language has a unique logic that arises from a culture's understanding of the world and their perception of the world. A phrase like the one above that talks about Jesus probably is not going to arise in a Buddhist and atheist country like China, which also does not drink wine as much as it does beer.

Think back to the chapter "Anglophonosphere," and consider this concept that culture creates language and language thus reflects culture and history. English is an amalgamation of several different languages, some extinct and others still around today. This history of absorbing new chunks of language in order to evolve and survive produces the culture of English speakers. That is, to absorb a ton of words and phrases from other languages, and place them in common speech, while also not learning other languages. The culture of English is to absorb a little bit of a lot of languages as opposed to adopting bilingualism.

This is a bittersweet feature that gives us words from Chinese like *ketchup* and *brainwashing*, or German that gives us *hamburger* and *nix*, or *cartoon, piano, broccoli,* and *cauliflower* from Italian, from Japanese we get *honcho* and *origotto*, from Russian we get *disinformation, shaman,* and *mammoth,* and last but not least, Spanish gives us *vanilla, savvy,* and *tobacco.*[3]

Oh, and before I forget, inexplicably enough, the exceedingly distant cousin and reticent language of Czech gives us a few words: *pistol, polka, Absurdistan, kolache, howitzer, koczwarism,* and *robot.* English words from Czech have a special name: Bohemisms, after Bohemia, the name for the Czech lands in the days of yesteryear.

UGANDA VERSUS CZECHIA

When I was in the Czech Republic, I had barely come from Uganda and found it was a completely different experience culturally and also on a personal level. My time in Uganda was spent with fifteen other extraordinarily curious students, two incredibly intelligent faculty advisors, and a plethora of extremely hospitable Ugandans, including a hilarious bus driver named Peter.

Our research cohort, a part of a global scholarship program, was studying the topics of "education, equity, and opportunity." We, the students, were to take charge in interviewing local educators, religious leaders, tribal elders, government officials, aid workers, and overall local heroes in organized meetings. Thus, a lot of talking, listening, and verbal communication was done and almost entirely in English. Outside of these interviews all of us in the cohort were constantly chatting, making jokes, playing games, and interacting with locals who would make a great effort to use English with us. Constant talk.

In Czechia, the experience was the opposite. Not in a bad way. Where Uganda was a "loud" experience, all sorts of voices, accents, and chatter, Czechia was quiet. Quiet and introspective. In Uganda, I found myself dizzy by the amount of information given to me and my peers, unable to keep up in my journal with notes and reflections, going to one meeting after the next, having one social gathering after the next. The Czech Republic, although hectic in its own way, gave me time to sit with my thoughts.

The twist is that Uganda is a country of dozens of spoken languages and the Czech Republic is a country of one: Czech.[2] I had far more connections in Europe than I did in Africa, but I spoke less, understood less, and remained quiet more. My time spent in Czechia was one of silence and introspection. This was not to its detriment as this vast contrast made me realize a lot about each culture, the conditions surrounding both trips, and myself. In Uganda. I was with a big group with the aim of engaging with the people in the communities who hosted us.

In Czechia I was by myself with one family, and they wanted to show me their country, more so by seeing the sights, as opposed to telling me about them. My lack of practice of Czech, combined with my introversion, and the quieter

Czech culture produced a quiet trip. It didn't have to be this way, but I accepted it.

However, I will impress upon you that even if you are more introverted, you will regret not taking the time to learn your target language and using it. Don't cause yourself to have regrets. Take chances! You have to create your own opportunities. You can't expect anyone to hand them out to you.

Intriguingly enough, with all these differences, these two countries had two things in common. A love for beer and hospitality. If you would ask my Slovak host dad, these two would be the same thing.

MURDERER FOREST SAUNA

All throughout the time in Uganda we passed billboard after billboard, advert after advert about beer, whether it be the South of the county in Entebbe and Kampala or in the North in the city of Gulu. Two brands stuck out in particular: the Nile Special (a local brew) and Pilsner Lager, a highly favored Czech import. Not only was this a Czech import, but it was brewed in the Czech city of Plzeň (Pilsen). Why is this important?

After Dominika, her mom, and I finished our adventure in Prague, *czeching* out all the amazing sites we could fit into in one afternoon we drove off to their home village, a hamlet of 500 people by the name of Horní Bělá, just outside of that very same hometown of the world-famous beer: Plzeň.

One evening in the little village, Dominika's parents felt a little restless, so they planned for all four of us to go on a marvelous journey to the "sauna," a word that does not need translation. I had never been to a sauna, and quite frankly I didn't know what it was, other than pickle slices on your eyes and steam. I was apprehensive, then curious, and quickly interested. Shortly before it was time to go and everything was packed, Domi became pale and noticeably sick and stayed in her room for the night, leaving me to take on the "sauna" with her parents.

I was a little sad at first that my favorite Czech friend wasn't able to come, but I took this as an opportunity to get to know my Czech mom and Slovak dad a little better. And it certainly was. After all, what could be more personal than sweating, showering, drinking, and bathing in the same rooms together? Towels and swimsuits packed, we were off.

The combination of being completely directionally challenged and the winding nature of the Czech roads through the countryside left me with no understanding of how far we had traveled. Being December, seeing out the windows into the evening sky was like staring into the abyss and the abyss staring back.

The first objects I could make out through the shadowy haze were perfectly upright spruce trees, aligned side-by-side like pencils protruding from the ground. We had made it from the vast Czech plains and entered into the haunted woods. I could only see the trees through the dim glow of the headlights and the navy blue hue of the December twilight that peaked so slyly through the clustered groves.

Domi's parents and I shared a combined one hundred words or so of Czechoslovak and English that were somewhat useful in communicating with each other on that excursion. Nonetheless, nonverbal cues went a long way and I followed the two, trusting them.

When we got to what could have been the most remote part of the ominous forest, we pulled into a quaint parking lot to a massive resort facility contained in a single building. Giant glass windows radiated turquoise lattice patterns of waves of the pool reflected onto the outside trees, appearing almost as if we were approaching an alien shuttle that crash landed in the middle of the woods.

SECRET RESORT

After getting through the admission, I was instructed to put on my swimsuit by Domi's dad via pointing at his trunks. This I remembered because Domi gave me basic instructions in English before we left without her. We then proceeded from the locker room, upstairs to a hallway of showers with rooms at the end with translucent glass doors where the saunas were.

What Dominika did not tell me in her detailed instructions is that everyone had to strip down butt naked and wrap themselves in towels before entering the actual sauna room. That room was a little pine box chamber no bigger than a walk-in pantry where you are to sweat it out with ten other sweaty, naked people. Reluctant? Absolutely. Out of my element? Perhaps. But when in Czechia...

It was in the sauna where both of Domi's parents decided it was time to make a considerable effort to make small talk to me in English. Not in the car, but when we are all naked together. I could hardly breathe. The air was so hot and dry. Looking at the thermometer, I refused to believe its reading: 199 degrees Fahrenheit. Despite the suffering inside the naked furnace, I played along, chatted, and religiously kept eye contact with them more than I have ever made eye contact with anyone else in my entire life.

Afterward, we showered in front of the other disrobed patrons awaiting a rinse, re-wrapped ourselves in new towels, and went to the snack stand. Up to this point in my life, I'd had alcohol maybe twice. Sips at best. Domi's dad, Raclav, bought… you know what he bought? You guessed it: Pilsner Lager. He poured a near-liter into my plastic cup and the same in his. If we were in Bavaria, they would have been stein-fulls. Maminka abstained. Beer wasn't her thing. Neither was it mine. "It is good!" Raclav reassured me with a waxing grin. "Good for health in sauna." He gave me an ear-to-ear smile shaped like the crescent moon I saw over Africa.

I drank as much as I could, hiding my innermost desire to vomit profusely across the smooth tiled floor. Not from his hospitality, that is what compelled me to drink it in the first place, rather, the sheer taste of liquid, distilled ear wax not in one swig but a tall glass. How would I know what that tastes like? I was a kid once, do the math.

The image crossed my mind of how gracefully the chunks I could blow would gleam across the shiny floor; luckily that moment never came. I politely declined to finish the last tablespoons for fear of that mental image manifesting before our eyes. He said with the same smile as he leaned closer, "No worries, Mox."

That day I learned that the best place to be naked and sweat is with your friend's parents who don't speak English nor does anyone else.

CZECHTUCKY FRIED FISH

The best way I have found to minimize the appearance of an Ugly American is to speak less, follow more, and let "custom be king," as the historian Herodotus once said. Also to not be afraid to ask questions. Luckily, Czech Christmas with the Faboks a few days later didn't involve us all having a good intercultural chat while sweating naked. I was especially grateful as we were celebrating with Domi's grandparents, no slight on them, but I am sure you understand what I'm getting at. In the Czech Republic, it is customary to celebrate Christmas Eve, December 24, in all manners from feasting, to fellowship, to the exchange of presents. The twenty-fifth is reserved for visiting the graves of deceased family and visiting friends.

At dinner we all had champagne, clinked glasses, and toasted, shouting "na zdraví!"—to health. After we had the traditional Czechoslovak dishes and dishes of the family, we did rituals like splitting apples and counting the seeds to predict our luck for the coming year. The most important part of the meal was the fellowship and gratitude, but the second was the fish. It was Czech and Slovak tradition to have cooked fish as the primary or only meat to remember the plight of their ancestors who under serfdom could only consume meat once a year, which was the carp fished from local estuaries and ponds.

It was time for the exchanging of the gifts. Raclav, Domi, and I were sent out on a walk around the village in the gelid winter night, while Baby Jesus brought the gifts to the household. At least that's the state story. We came back after twenty minutes to a humble little Christmas tree parked in the middle of the living room with presents galore.

The family understood my love for reading and history and got me several books on Czech history as well as a treasure trove of Czech candy, some of which I am still going through nearly two and a half years later. Before coming, I had no idea what to get them, but I found something of value and insight to American culture at a bookstore back in the US.

I had Dominika open the present with her parents and grandparents flanking her on either side. Dominika burst out in laughter when she read the title and saw the cover. Her parents were confused at the initial preview of the cover.

"Max, this is perfect!" Domi said, gaining composure to explain what it was. Without notice, Domi's grandpa burst out in uproarious laughter, shouting something in Czech, laughing, and then saying what I can only remember as, "Trumpsky HAHAHA!"

What I got for them was the best representation of American culture: a quote book of former President Donald Trump's tweets, the best and the worst. They all laughed and loved my bizarre humor gift, and in that moment, I became the Ugly American, not in shame, but in some sort of oddball triumph.

TAKEAWAYS

1. An "Ugly American" is an American in a foreign country whose behavior is offensive to the people of that country.
2. Asking questions is a crucial way to motivate yourself. Why? Asking questions reveals to yourself what your motivations are, why you have these motivations, and how you can act on them. Curiosity is not only asking questions to the world, moreover, posing questions to yourself… a mirror of sorts.
3. Ask yourself in all parts of your language acquisition journey, "How can I make this experience the best I can for myself, my hosts, and all those I meet and interact with who speak my target language?"
4. Consider learning part of a language as essential to travel as booking a flight, packing your bags, and finding a place to stay. Knowing a tiny fraction of the country's language will open more doors than you can even walk through.
5. Language is not simply what people speak, write, and listen to. It is a grand narrative of sorts that encapsulates an entire people's history, culture, origin, and direction through the act of its expression.
6. Even if you are more introverted, you will regret not taking the time to learn your target language and using it. Don't cause yourself to have regrets. Take chances. You must create your own opportunities as no one is guaranteed handouts.
7. Learn to toast and say thank you in your target language.

FOOTNOTES:

[1] English is so widespread that any one invasion of different language speakers couldn't force the change of English entirely like the Norman French did to the English in 1066. We don't live on a 50,000 square mile tract of land anymore.

[2] Slovak is also widely spoken in the Czech Republic; however, Czech and Slovak are so close and mutually intelligible that they can be more accurately considered dialects of each other, in the same way American English is to Australian English.

CHAPTER 5

Hope Yet

A BOLIVIAN, AN AMERICAN, AND A NORWEGIAN WALK INTO A CAR

You really didn't lose the language you were once taught. I often hear the trope, "I studied Spanish in high school for three years, and as soon as I graduated, I lost everything," or "I used to know Chinese; my grandma would teach me Chinese words and phrases, and when I was little it was my second language. When she passed, I lost and forgot most of it."

Situations like this are extremely common for most Americans. Despite America being a majority-monolingual country, most people have encountered a language to some degree throughout their life, be it through school, travel, work, religious affiliation, family, or any other avenue. Some obviously have more contact with other cultures and languages over time or on a regular basis than others. Painting a picture of a *monolingual United States of America* is quite complex because our various experiences vary so widely. In my own experiences through the connections I have made, it would seem commonplace for people to not know where their family is from, but also common for other people I know to be from a family who has recently immigrated to the United States.

When my Bolivian friend Adri and I picked up a Norwegian student from the airport, we were all talking about our families and where they are from. Oskar, from Norway, said he is almost entirely Norwegian, and Adri said, "Bolivian, that's what I am." When they asked where my family was from, I replied, "I'm mostly Swiss French, German, and English on my dad's side, and on my mom's side, I am Irish, French, Italian, and German. Oh! And I'm 3 percent Norwegian."

They told me, "That is the most American response you could have said." The comedian Russell Peters has a similar line "Oh, don't start. If you have to go back five generations just say you're American." Despite having far more connections to different nationalities and ethnic groups via my blood, I was the only one in the car that *really* spoke only one language. Adri spoke Spanish and English, and Oskar spoke Norwegian, English, and could understand some Danish and Swedish. Adri mentioned her aunt moved from Bolivia to the United States, had kids, and now those kids only speak English. Losing the language of your ethnic or national origin is rather common after several generations, as previously touched on.

LOST
How can a family language be completely wiped out from being spoken in the matter of one or two generations? This was the case for much of my dad's side of the family with French and German, and with Italian and Irish on my

mother's side. This is often the case where it really only takes the grandchildren of immigrants or conquered people for the language to be completely lost. Sometimes loss occurs within a generation with parents who refuse to speak their native language with their children, so they are forced to learn English and learn it well, which is a common immigrant experience. Those communities like the Amish, Native Americans, Texas Germans, Hoi Toiders of the South Atlantic, and Hasidic Jews are the rare exceptions that retain their language, accent, and culture for many generations.

For those of us who lost our ancestral languages, how do we get them back into our families? How do we become fluent in Spanish or some other language we broached in high school? Is there hope?

BUT NOT FORGOTTEN

In May 2019, I joined a student pilgrimage going to Europe to see Holy Sites of the Catholic Faith. I knew most of the people in the group by name and not much else, only really knowing two (Josh and AJ) from our university marching band. Our journey would span from the heart of the Roman Catholic Church in Rome, Italy itself, to other major core economic and high cultural European cities such as Paris, Bordeaux, and Barcelona to the humble hinterlands of Europe in the agrarian valleys of the Balkans and Pyrenees resting between great coastal cliffs and inland mountains.

It was toward the conclusion of our trip across the continent that we had driven four hours south of the French city of Bordeaux to the border village of Lourdes, France. There at the foot of the High Pyrenees, before their towering beauty, we took in the fresh air of the not-so-distant Mediterranean. Lourdes, once a tiny village, has grown into a pilgrimage destination for Catholics all around the world.

A series of apparitions in the mid-1800s of Mary, the mother of Jesus Christ, to a young girl named Bernadette Soubirous (Lasserre, 1906) prompted gradual interest by Catholics, as well as skeptics around the world. Now being an official Holy Site, the town attracts millions of pilgrims per year (Barrère, 2014).

When we were there, we saw how a small market town of 13,000 people hidden away in the borderlands of France and Spain was a crossroads for people of every race, ethnicity, and tongue. The multitude spoke French and to simply hear the language of my required high school language class, even when I did not understand all that was said, invoked a part of my memory untapped since 2015. During the massive procession we participated in with thousands of other people, the prayers were rotated between eight or so languages, notably French, English, Hindi, Latin, Spanish, German, and Italian.

It was in that procession that our group really took notice of our university president—who led much of the pilgrimage—embracing his mother tongue. As a child of a French Canadian immigrant raised in a French-speaking community in Boston (a fact not a single soul in our group knew a day prior), President Richard Jusseaume recited the "Our Father" and "Hail Mary" in perfect French.

Marching in the procession alongside individuals from all corners of the globe sharing a common faith, I truly saw how core beliefs of humans can transcend all language barriers; there are ideas and desires that all of mankind can grasp, hold, and work to embody. I saw the oneness of man in those around me, but especially in President Jusseaume. Here was a man I had known for several years to only speak English, holding a deep belief system that went past his English and French to something more fundamental—French, an echo of his childhood ancestry, and English representing his professional and American life.

SEEING IS BELIEVING

Through the living example of President Jusseaume, I learned that language is not just a way to communicate within a culture, but across cultures. Language is an expression of culture, but more importantly, an expression of ideas fundamental to the human experience. To understand what someone is saying is to share in the human experience. At its core, language, although diverse and plentiful in manner of expression, is attempting to bring us closer, not separate us. We all have a common language; it just sounds different when you go to different patches of dirt on this rock we call Earth.

My exposure to the French language and knack for remembering weirdly specific aspects of my past is what set me apart from our group. Here I was in France for the first time, hearing natives speak French. I was four years out of my high school French class, and random words, phrases, and cultural insights kept popping into my head.

Our time at the beginning and end of our days in Lourdes was spent in the basement dining room of our cramped yet cloud-piercing hotel. The names of French cuisine percolated in the back of my mind. We didn't have hot coffee with warm milk or butter or jam on our croissants, but *café chaud et lait avec beurre et confiture pour nos croissants.* I do not recollect ever setting my ears or eyes on a French word in the four years since high school, yet the memory had stuck.

This was an odd discovery and one that gave me the ability to functionally communicate with our hostess and waiters in the town when on our independent adventures. This was especially odd to me because when I was in French class in school, I had no confidence in my ability to understand spoken French, let alone utter it myself. After all, I had passed French I with a low B and barely escaped French II with a B, getting many Ds and Cs on my speaking tests.

But for four years, the language had been fermenting in the cobwebbed portions of my mind like a good wine forgotten in the moldy recesses of a dark cellar. I realized I had been given a functional understanding of the very basics, including an Americanized French accent. In school, I never dared to attempt an accent. How ironic it is that pronouncing a language correctly in an American classroom was looked down upon by peers, but keeping a clunky, sing-songy Midwestern accent was socially acceptable.

THE FRENCH CONNECTION

This retention of past knowledge became increasingly bizarre as I was able to read entire signs in Paris when English wasn't available. My reading knowledge was lightyears ahead of my speaking ability and having already come to the realization that I never really forgot the French I had learned—simply stored it away—why I was able to read so much better was no mystery.

In high school, my French instructor Madame Ferris had given us a plethora of methods to learn from. Every day we would have group recitations of vocabulary, one-on-one question and answer, stories requiring us to repeat our comprehension to the class, memorization of verb conjugation charts, and lastly, weekly small group reading sessions. Every Friday, we would get in small groups and take turns reading through a chapter in a French short storybook. We would often have reading assignments over the weekend as well as tests of comprehension on Mondays. This, whether intended or not, became the biggest proportion of how we learned basic French. I am grateful Madame placed an emphasis on reading as I believe, and as you will see, it is a critical skill and practice to compound your progress in language acquisition.

All this is to say any experience you have had with languages uniquely prepares you to get back into that language. Even more excitingly, that past experience with any language helps train the mind to a certain way of thinking about languages you otherwise might not have. It's that perspective building.

WHY YOU FORGET

Benny Lewis, one of the internet's most prominent polyglots, once wrote, "*Why* you forget is the opposite of *why* you *learn*." (Lewis, 2020)

Would you be surprised if I told you the way polyglots learn languages is not at all the same as how you were taught in primary and secondary school? The reason the approach you have tried has led to failure is because you were taught to forget and not to learn. Ponder that. Do you think your high school Spanish, French, or German teacher expected you to be fluent by the end of the class or the two or three years you had to have with them? Going in and during the classes, did you expect to become fluent from those classes? The answer is probably not. Even when I was in high school, I romanticized the idea of learning a language and really getting into my Spanish and French classes, but the thing is, I wasn't learning in a way in the class or by myself that would lead to fluency.

Going back to Benny Lewis and the polyglots (that would be an amazing band name by the way, and no, it's not taken), there is a way out of the cycle.

Our ancestors often speak different languages lost within the matter of a few generations and when we try to learn, we forget... but partially. We seek the balance between learning a language so fast that you forget it just as fast as you learned it, and taking your good old time to gradually learn the language that it takes years to learn near to nothing. Learn everything quickly or learn a little tiny bit over months, years, and even decades.

There is hope you can straddle this balance while also crafting a plan that works best for you. Benny talks a lot about how he used different methods of language learning with different time frames suited for the specific goal he had. He says the antidote to resolving the issue of people struggling with a language both systemically and individually is a rather obvious one. The obvious and simple secret is:

> "... consistently using the language so it is **always** fresh in your mind. Of course, you can come up with lazy excuses why this is not possible, but the truth is that you can always find ways to use those languages. Find natives to meet in person via social networks, use certain sites to find people to talk to by Skype, be friendlier with tourists, join clubs and actively monitor your social circle and environment for opportunities to use the language. All of these are ways you can speak your language immediately." (Lewis, 2020)

Consistency. That's it.

Well, it's a bit more nuanced than that, and as Benny showed, there are many ways to keep up with consistency.

THE CONSISTENT, PERSISTENT PURSUIT

To my ears and many others, consistency sounds like something you sign up for and do, but it really isn't.

Consistency is not so much a noun as it is a result to be aimed at, a target, a goal. It is a result and description of active participation, whether thirty seconds or thirty minutes a day done *repeatedly*.

In America, we have an odd cultural mix between business and self-help, which pushes for action and execution, the "do

do do," "accomplish great things... become independent...
do this for YOU." And if you aren't doing anything, you are
lazy. It's do or die. In America, we simultaneously attempt
to do so much while also doing so little. A culture of seeking
accomplishment, but not without instant gratification. It is
a desire to want ourselves and others to be efficient and productive without the compassion of asking how they might
become that way.

Even when we are "resting," we feel as if we must eat, listen to music, text, or watch television. We can't sit still even
when we are sitting still for hours on end. We lump activities
together to save on time. Examples: working lunch, fast food,
drive-thru pharmacy, listening to music and podcasts while
working out, in-flight movies, taking pictures of anything
and everything. We refuse to simply *be*.

Consistency is not a noun, and not even a verb, but an *adjec-
tive* to describe the essence of the result of persistence in
doing—in this case, language learning and acquisition. And
it needs to be understood this way.

Consistency is the result of the process of positive persistence
to work on your positive goal, while also understanding the
negative consequences of not meeting your goal.

You aren't going to come home after your first day at your
new job and say, "WOW! Look how consistent I am with
going to work." Bruh, you've only been there once. Similarly,
no one becomes *fluent* in Hungarian when they practice
once a month or speak with a Hungarian speaker once,
period.

Here lies the hope: In order to tackle the systemic problem of declining language education in schools and the declining bilingual literacy in the United States and other parts of the Anglophonosphere, you have to embrace your power to change this trend with simple, persistent consistency. This is what David Meltzer, co-founder of Sports 1 Marketing, speaker, and author calls the "consistent, persistent pursuit." (Meltzer, 2018)

The best part is that the aim does not have to be so monumental as fixing the system, but the positive effect on our societies is felt by you choosing to have fun in your *consistent, persistent* pursuit of becoming fluent. Change doesn't begin and end in protest on the streets or with the signing of a new law, but in your concerted choice to live radically different from what institutions lay out for you. Your mere existence then becomes a protest and model for others.

THE SOCIAL WHY

With all that said, you might be wondering: What about the many people who disagree on whether lack of bilingual fluency is a problem? What about motivating people to make this change for themselves, for me? The struggle between the advocates who want more language education and those that do not think it necessary can be distilled down to the "*Why?*" The debate over *why* we should learn.

The *why*, of course, should be the amazing societal benefits such as being able to understand alternative perspectives, countless economic/business opportunities, increased travel experiences, increased learning in schools, improved relationships with other countries, the ability to make and deepen friendships with members of other cultures, and so on. I hope, I believe, and I know these effects will materialize in time, and you should too because the expanding world keeps getting smaller as it is brought closer and closer via social media, the broader internet, and increasing accessibility of long-distance travel. The world is learning English, meeting us anglophones halfway. Soon, it'll become obvious we need to meet the rest of the world, closing the gap.

FINDING YOUR WHY

Friedrich Nietzsche, the German philosopher who famously lamented the "death of God" in *Thus Spoke Zarathustra* in 1884 also famously declared, "He who has a *why* to live, can bear any *how.*" I'm starting to think I can come up with strangely worded tidbits of wisdom too: "She who knows *what* can find any*where.*" Jokes and incoherent sentences aside, I think Nietzsche was onto something: Those who have a purpose in life (a *why*, a *reason* to live) are more ready for the difficulties of life (the *how*, the details, the happenings).

More strictly applied to goal setting: If you have a purpose for acquiring a language, it'll become more obvious what you need to do and how you are going to go about it.

So here I say to you, in a world where doing the expedient thing is often rewarded, bear some responsibility to delay gratification by learning a language for your own development for *your* own purpose. This purpose needs to connect to you, but if it helps, I recommend you connect it to someone else. For example: acquiring Mongolian so you can better know your father from Mongolia; watching Bollywood movies with your Hindi-speaking wife to connect with her language and, consequently, her.

What is your purpose in learning a language? How does this fit into your life purpose? How will the *process*, the *persistence* in learning a language make your life or the lives of others better?

The ultimate hope is that by finding your purpose in learning your language you may be a better person for yourself and for those around you, and that many other people are taking advantage of the incredible tools of the internet to plug themselves into all sorts of different cultures and to learn languages like never seen before. The hope is in the understanding that *you* are capable of acquiring a language to fluency.

FROM REMEMBERING A LANGUAGE TO SIGNS OF HOPE

All that is fine and dandy, but the dilemma becomes obvious: What if you are one of the many Americans, or really anyone around the world who has never been taught another language even in bite-sized classroom chunks? There is a myth that if you miss a window of childhood to learn a language, learning it will become next to impossible; this is simply not true.

I assure you, my newfound friend, that taking up the responsibility endowed in a new language adventure is a voyage worth taking, even if starting from nothing. This is your call to adventure, and encapsulated in the journey of learning a language is the hero's journey to go out into the world, confront a tremendous challenge, and come out alive, making a stronger, wiser, more intelligent, more compassionate person with new profound perspectives.

FOUR SIGNS OF HOPE IN THE ANGLOPHONOSPHERE

If you are like me and have been concerned about the state of language education in the States and the English-speaking world, here are four altered perspectives and signs of a new wave of language education:

1. The war between STEM and the humanities/liberal arts: Many school curricula are already inundated with a huge emphasis on STEM (science, technology, engineering, and medicine) at all levels from elementary to middle, secondary, and especially university. This is easily seen in the push for universities to transform into *de facto* STEM schools to attract larger attendance, to signal modern relevance, and become an easier, safer object for donors.
   a. Within the last decade, the major school in my area of Ohio, the University of Akron, was the center of a major controversy when it shifted to become a "polytechnic school." My own alma mater, Walsh University, which holds a special place in my heart—my memories, my best friends, and most of my checkbook—axed language programs and placed greater emphasis on science-related programs like nursing at the expense of the humanities.
   b. There is little room for the humanities in the current conception and trajectory of many American universities. For those disheartened in the Western world at

this great shift, the humanities are seen as the besieged bastion of language learning. However, there is other hope as language and linguistics are thriving in a scientific context at other, more forthright and rigorous academic institutions. Computer coding languages are the behind-the-scenes *lingua franca* of the tech literate. Linguistics and philology have expanded into fields such as forensics, search engine optimization, translation, and many other spheres.

2. The American education system, be it public or private, has shown massive flaws and signs of continual decline in language programs, which is why I firmly believe the power to make a shift toward a multilingual society is not through dependence on schools or government mandates or opposition to governments, but rather a turn toward those who have always had power: the people, both individually and collectively. The problem has actually created an opportunity for a surge, a massive push, for a multilingual society. Problems preface solutions.

3. The internet and increased access to technology has made learning *any* language easier than it ever has been. Popular phone apps like *Duolingo, Pimsleur,* or *Memrise* have made learning a language tangible and accessible to most. Browser extensions like Google translate give you the ability to translate articles into a target language, and *Toucan* is an app that attaches to your browser and translates random words into your target language. Additionally, *Etymonline* is a website and browser extension that shows you the etymology of English words and phrases, helping with English literacy and making connections to other languages. There are countless other tools such as *iTalki,* thousands of language podcasts, millions of

songs in foreign languages on YouTube, Spotify, and other streaming platforms. The simple exposure to the media of other cultures in other languages alone opens up the world of possibilities. As of 2019, the online language learning industry is worth approximately $5.13 billion and is expected to grow to $10.5 billion by 2025 (Intrado, 2019). Internet penetration in the United States is also at an all-time high, with 85.8 percent of American adults having access to the internet in 2020, and by 2021 this number is projected to be at 87.2 percent. Although, I believe that percentage will be far higher for the whole population as nearly no child today is raised without some level of internet access (Johnson, 2020).

4. Skype, Zoom, FaceTime, and other video and audio chat platforms have made it possible to easily speak with someone from the complete opposite side of the globe. Writing this book would not be possible without teleconferencing as authorship meetings were held over Zoom, and I used various platforms to connect with friends and experts living all around the United States and the world. Imagine using these tools to talk to someone in your target language. That is one of the ways I improve my French listening and speaking skills, by using Skype via the tutor platform *iTalki* to have weekly meetings with my Swiss French tutor. Prior to the pandemic, teleconferencing was how much of the private sector conducted language education. For instance, English teachers holding classes over Zoom to instruct a growing number of children tuning in from China.

HOPE WITHOUT ACTION IS NAIVETY

This book is meant to make language learning as positive as possible, and I truly believe no downsides are too great that invalidate the process or the result of learning a language. However, the world is so interconnected via the internet and travel, and there is so much wonderful technology and services for free or affordable prices. There is no excuse outside of you that prevents you from learning a language to fluency. Resources, access, and the general environment are not valid excuses. There has never been a better time or climate to acquire a language.

As the jiu-jitsu rolling, podcasting, motivational speaker, and consultant retired navy SEAL Jocko Willink often says to his following on social media, "ALL your excuses are LIES." And if you meet adversity, "GOOD." Take up the challenge.

Think about that.

If you are making an excuse for yourself, are you really being honest with yourself or to others? Is it really that you don't have time to learn a language or is that you won't make time? Is that the impenetrable barrier the world set up against you or is that what you told yourself?

If you are young, people will give you the benefit of the doubt of your excuses and sometimes let them slide, even if they are *just* excuses (lies) you tell yourself.

But there comes a certain time, a certain age, where those excuses you told yourself come to bear bad fruit, where others see the culmination of habitual excuse making for what it is: a failure to act and a failure to discipline to make life better for you and those around you. The lies you tell today compound in the darkness. We think a baby bear is harmless, but when ignored, it will grow into something that is far more than capable of destroying you and those you care about. That is what a lie is. A lie is a monster you create, you let grow, and you must confront. But often it is not one monster, more like a pack of wolves, hyenas, or a den of vipers.

In short, don't be so damn flippant when it comes to making excuses and lies. They change you and attack you, whether you think they do or not.

Heavy, yes. Scary? Also yes. But every decision in life comes with consequences, and as psychologist, author, and professor of psychology at the University of Toronto, Dr. Jordan Peterson says, you don't have an option to *not* choose. You have to make hard decisions no matter what, and not acting on something *is* a decision. Pick your poison: laziness now and painful regret in the future? Or a little discomfort and difficulty now for lasting joy in the future?

Truly, consider all the questions I asked in this chapter. They will not only help you uncover your language goals, but they might also give you a broader orientation to what you truly want to see in your life that includes a new language. More than likely, your life will have to adapt to the language, not the language to your life. Find those dreams, articulate them, aim, and work out your balance. It's time to uncover the bizarre world of languages.

TAKEAWAYS

1. We remember more of what we were taught than we would like to admit. Even if you think you didn't learn anything, you may have very well learned more than you think.

2. There is hope within the world and the United States for creating a bilingual, dual-literate generation.

3. To learn a language you have to come to terms that it isn't that you *don't have time*, it is that *you haven't made time*. You must make time for it.

4. If you want to stick with a language, it is important to know your *why*. *Why* are you studying *x* language? What is the purpose of doing so? Knowing your *why* is understanding your motivation.

5. In colleges and universities, languages and linguistics have migrated from the humanities into the sciences, where they are alive and well under different forms.

6. The failure of the American education system in combination with all the free and inexpensive language learning tools out there have created a massive opportunity for individuals and groups to learn languages on their own terms suited to their needs.

7. The internet gives people access to thousands of language learning apps, podcasts, websites, browser extensions, and learning tools—it is no longer a matter of finding resources, it is a matter of choosing which ones you use.

8. The internet is becoming increasingly multilingual, and becoming "dual-literate" via social media will only be an increasing phenomena.

9. ALL your excuses are LIES… making excuses for yourself, to yourself, is the first step to self-pity, and self-pity is the path to self-destruction.

PART II

CHAPTER 6

Foundation of Linguistics

———

WHAT A LINGUIST ISN'T

Would you be surprised if I told you many linguists speak only a few languages, and most are only fluent in their native language? Would you believe linguistics has little to do with how many languages someone speaks?

"Since you're a linguist you must speak a lot of languages!" If you are a linguist or an amateur language enthusiast like me, you probably hear this a lot and see why it's silly. But for those who don't see why this is silly, allow me to get into the weeds so you don't have to.

WHAT IS LINGUISTICS? WHAT DOES A LINGUIST DO?

Despite popular misconception, a linguist is not someone who can speak several languages. They might, but that is not what *linguist* means. A linguist is someone who studies linguistics. Okay, but what are linguistics then? Seems like semantics, right? Well, no. Semantics is a branch of linguistics. Linguistics is a science.

According to the Oxford dictionary, linguistics is:

"the scientific study of language and its structure, including the study of morphology, syntax, phonetics, and semantics. Specific branches of linguistics include sociolinguistics, dialectology, psycholinguistics, computational linguistics, historical-comparative linguistics, and applied linguistics."

A lot is involved in this scientific study of languages and there are more sub-fields and focuses than listed above. So, what do you call someone who can speak multiple languages?

Simple.

My friend Elioth from Haiti who speaks French, English, Spanish, and Haitian Kreyol is NOT a linguist, he is a polyglot. "Poly" meaning "many" and "glot" or "glotta" meaning "language," but literally, "tongue" (Etymonline, 2021). So if you want to have more than one tongue become a polyglot.

Linguistics is not some pretentious study where all language majors go to die, but it is a robust field that intersects with many other fields and professions such as computer engineering, anatomy, psychiatry, speech pathology, cognitive science, history, archaeology, advertising/marketing, and data science. Careers such as interpreter, editor, translator, forensic linguist, a language teacher (foreign or native), geographer, military interpretation, and many other unexpected professions of diverse interests are all united by a curiosity toward language. It is a wholly practical study of languages applicable to most fields.

FIVE THEMES OF LINGUISTICS

At the heart of linguistics are five major themes, as claimed by Monica Macaulay and Kristen Syrett at the Linguistics Society of America:

1. The unconscious knowledge that humans have about language
2. How children acquire language
3. The structure of language in general and of particular languages
4. How languages vary
5. How language influences the way in which we interact with each other and the way we think about the world

Those are fairly simple and straight to the point, but I find that to be a useful breakdown of the field. Allow me to expand on that and show you how deep linguistics reach into everyday life, and well, everything!

1. THE UNCONSCIOUS

So much of what we do is already done for us, unconsciously. So much goes on in our mind, behind the curtain, that we often underappreciate what's really happening there. The vast array of automation and operations being conducted in our minds without us even having to consciously engage with them is astounding.

There is a misconception that in order to learn a language you *must* be paying attention and actively engaging with your chosen method of learning a language. Yet, this is so far from the truth it isn't even funny. YES! Of course, you need to actively study, but so much of how we learn our first language, and any other language, is done without us even realizing.

We might read an article and see a word we don't recognize, but our brain fills in the gaps through context clues. Or, if we are new to a language, hearing words or phrases being repeated in the background or seeing them written without much second thought happens all the time. A baby isn't actively taking notes in their diary on the language that is going on around them. The unconscious aspect of linguistics even goes beyond learning.

Despite what some philosophers and psychologists may assert, humans are not a blank slate. This idea that humans are born *without* any innate mental content is called *tabula rasa*, or in Latin, "scraped slate," often translated as "blank slate" (New World Encyclopedia, 2021). This propounds that we are born completely impressionable to our social environment, essentially created by our upbringing, where we are, who we associate with, and what we learn… and that even all aspects of the unconscious are impressed upon us. That sounds all well and good, and a lot of that is true; we are products of our environments and what we input, but it neglects that humanity has commonalities within our minds upon initial brain development rooted in our common evolution. Evolution does not simply occur below the neck and cease to do so above.

Perhaps I am biased, I am often a Jungian when it comes to psychology. I believe that *humanity* possesses a nature that comes from within us and that in each of our minds, within our unconscious, we have knowledge of the world in primitive imagery, stories, formulas, and frameworks. Sort of like a background operating system, we all share, or like the processes that bring food to our table: We don't typically see the farmer bring in the harvest, slaughter the animals, process the food, bag it, and ship it to market, or even see it cooked, yet we know it happens and our reality arises from the "background work."

Languages have to be *learned*, but our *understanding* of *language* is innate. See the difference? We have an operating system that goes beyond our consciousness that dictates how language is learned and what qualifies as language as opposed to word salad.

Noam Chomsky, touted as the "father of modern linguistics," is famous for developing his theory on a universal grammar (UG). That is, below the surface of any and every language and its grammar is a grammar built into our own way of thinking, shared by all people, that could have come from genetics itself. *Grammars* are the set of rules *languages* operate under, but *universal grammar* is the set of rules nearly every *language* operates under. This makes sense that a part of our brain would be created from our genetics that dictate roughly how language works.

Further, we unconsciously understand concepts of what people, places, and things are and what make them up. A television does not cease to exist being a television if there was no word for it. Living in an age where millions of things are being invented and discovered every day, we come up with things faster than we can give them names. Often, we struggle to use words to describe concepts, and, in fact, there are words in many languages that describe such a specific concept that it only exists and can be understood in that language.

English, a language that acts like a sponge, absorbs words and concepts in other languages into its own language. Words that cannot be translated and must be imported. For example:

Schadenfreude (German)—
Deriving pleasure or joy from
the misfortune of others.

Wabi-Sabi (Japanese)—A way of
living that finds beauty in the
imperfections of everyday life.

Toska (Russian)—Great spiritual anguish
often without specific cause, also a deep
yearning and pining for both nothing
and something or someone specific,
sometimes deriving from boredom.

For more examples, including untranslatable words that have NOT made their way to English, see the appendix of the book!

2. HOW CHILDREN ACQUIRE LANGUAGE

In order to understand how to learn a language, it would only make sense to look at how languages are first learned. That is, how children learn languages. Here we broach the topic of "the best time to learn a language is when you are young," and while there is truth to this, language can be learned with simple methods in any period of a person's life. Nevertheless, the study of language acquisition in children really gives us a transparent understanding of the basis of language learning.

Adults make for a difficult control group as they already know a language (hopefully), but a child is still learning, and a baby does not know much if anything about speech, let alone what to say. The brain is developing in youth, and observing how a child learns in this critical period of development not only gives insight on language learning, but also the development of the mind overall.

Some children struggle with pronunciation and others may experience lisps, hearing problems, stuttering, or learning disabilities that require speech pathologists to facilitate a tailored learning path. Language is the primary mediator of ideas between people, and to understand the basics of how it works and help those who need it goes a long way.

I cover this concept of learning from babies in the later chapter "Embracing the Inner Child."

3. LANGUAGE STRUCTURE

The fact that we have different languages tells us immediately that language has structure to it. If it didn't, then there would be little differentiation between how people talk and communicate generally. The rules of a language and the logic of how language is spoken all define parameters of what a particular language is. The grammar of one language can be different than the next.

Is it subject-object-verb, or subject-verb-object? What case do I use for this declension? The locative, genitive, or ablative? Did I put this in the correct tense? What is not commonly known is that languages overall hold the same basic principles and structures.

As mentioned, all languages obey certain rules of the UG, which may arise from the structural aspects of the brain (anatomy) and genetic components. This is crucial to understand because it implies language is not just sensory (sounds or words on paper) and subjective to the world, but it is bound by biology itself.

Language structure is studied by using syntax and semantics. Syntax is the study and the arrangement of words and phrases to create a well-formed sentence or idea within a specific language.

For instance, in English, correct syntax would be, "Let's take it on the camping trip at his house," but in French we would say, "*Prenons-le lors du voyage de camping chez lui*," which word for word translates to, "Let's take it that time on the trip of camping house his." The word order seems jumbled and new words are added in to get the same exact idea across. Nothing is wrong with it. Syntax is relative to each language. Some languages are strict in their syntax; for others, the order matters not.

Semantics on the other hand is, yes, a study about splitting hairs. Not literally, but its purpose is to sort through the metaphorical wheat and the chaff to find and define specific meaning of parts of language and define the logic behind the sense or meaning. It is looking for that subtle nuance. It sometimes does come down to "splitting hairs." Semantics takes two or more seemingly same meaning words or phrases and puts an end to that naïve little notion that they are the same.

Semantics is to pick apart the difference between "final stop" and "destination." They can be used to mean the same thing, but they are subtly different.

My friend Mare, a professional writing major, illustrated the concept: "Something can be in the *adjacent* neighborhood to my house, or I could say it is in the neighborhood *near* my house. Yes, they can mean the same thing, but they are different definitions, not the same, but similar, and they actually are different things entirely."

Why bother with semantics? Why not just say what you mean or stop looking so deep into minutia?

Simply put, our daily use of semantics is how we distinguish at all. Semantics is also how we uncover implied meaning. You, again, might be thinking, "Why not just say what you mean?" Because it's not necessary. I will never tell you to be lazy; however, I will suggest you make productive use of your words when communicating. When your roommate, spouse, or parents ask you, "Can you take out the trash?" they are not directly saying, "Can you take out the trash from the kitchen under the sink to the trash can outside of the garage right now?" Yet you understand all of that, and it's implied.

Why bother with all that extra information if it is understood by both the speaker and the receiver (you)?

Yes, that is what is meant when you're asked to take out the trash, but none of that information is necessary because you have the context and because the rest is implied.

We all know someone who constructs these absurdly long and unnecessarily specific answers that seem to miss the original point of the question, or someone who uses fluffy language to look like they are being specific in order to sound smart but are actually vague. I've been guilty of that one before. Apply semantics to your life by using implied language, while also not being so vague you are not understood. Speak concisely.

Au contraire, semantics is also commonly associated with splitting hairs, getting to precise definitions. This is also an important concept to adopt. When we are writing or speaking, it is important to be precise in our language because that is how we articulate our beliefs and communicate ideas. Speak precisely.

Truth lies in the detail, and often we use vague statements to not compromise our beliefs while also not disagreeing with others. That is a lie of omission, which creates distrust and misunderstanding. When we are precise in our speech, we can better articulate for ourselves what we want, what we need, who we are, why we are here, understand where we precisely came from, metaphorically, and where we want to go. Speak precisely yet concisely. Speech is how you think and how you think is how you navigate through the world.

Semantics appeals to me because I love splitting hairs to the chagrin of those around me, moreover because it is the tool of discovering nuance. Semantics is a fulcrum, or balancing point, where we find the compromise of too much and too little specificity while articulating the truth. I am always blown away by thinkers who can convey a complex concept in a single sentence that it takes everyone else pages and pages to even come close. Perhaps this is why quotes are so potent to our ears, our eyes, and our hearts.

Language structure is a large topic of linguistics with no end to variety. A cornucopia of grammar. Yummy.

4. LANGUAGE VARIETY

Comparative linguistics shows us how language can vary when compared to other languages. Languages did not arise in a vacuum chamber with no access to the outside world, rather they developed organically, interweaving with the development of other languages and within changing cultures.

How can there be someone who speaks a language like English, a language like Arabic, and a language like Chinese so vastly different that there can be no accurate similarities?

Languages share the UG, but past that, languages can seem so far and different from each other. How do languages vary? What are the characteristics of similarities and differences between languages? Where do the variations come from?

Although we will almost certainly never know what the first human language sounded like since it was spoken thousands if not millions of years prior to the invention of writing, we do know how language has evolved over time.

Language varies in space and in time.

Go to Japan and the people there will be speaking Japanese. Go to Northern Uganda, and the people there will likely be speaking Acholi. Go to Greenland, and the people will speak Greenlandic (yes that's a language), Danish, and English. Language varies across geographical space.

Today, there are hundreds of dialects of English, variation across space. But if we go back in time, variations emerge the further back we go. The dialect of English George Washington spoke would sound nothing like modern English, nor would it sound like a modern "British accent." After all, modern British accents are less than one hundred years old. The accents of the time would be so far different, they'd leave us scratching our heads.

Further back, different American dialects would be found originating from different immigrant groups from across England, Scotland, Wales, and Ireland, even as specific to the town. Continuing the trend, if we go back to the time of Shakespeare, roughly late 1500s early 1600s, the English spoken then would have so many words we do not understand, and the accent would sound something like a weird German accent. No. I am not kidding. Now try imagining Romeo and Juliet being performed in a wacky Germanic accent.

Go to the 900s and English, Old English/Anglo-Saxon, would be completely unintelligible to us. We might understand every tenth word, but the meaning would likely not have shifted to the meaning it has for us. In 150 years, our great-grandchildren will be speaking a form of English so different from ours we would have a hard time communicating with them. Just think of all the stuff our grandparents' generation don't understand about us.

Have I freaked you out yet? I did? Excellent.

Culture is a major influence on the variety of languages. I think a lot of us have the notion that culture is this monumental structure that is immovable, unchanging, and simply *is*. Indian culture is Indian culture. Black culture is Black culture. French culture is French culture. But that ain't it, chief. Culture and language are something of an endless feedback loop, influencing each other, constituent of each other (Scott, 2010).

To illustrate, think of the Taoist symbol of *yin* and *yang*. Language is shaped by culture, and culture is shaped by history and environment. So to have culture, things had to happen to and among people, and people had to get there somehow. Also, there isn't a single culture on Earth today or in the past that wasn't influenced by other cultures or earlier cultures that came before it. Being influenced by other cultures and adopting aspects of other cultures is not immoral, it's a feature of culture itself.

If a culture has a concept for something it will have a word for it, and likewise if it doesn't.

5. LANGUAGE SHAPING PERSPECTIVES

Whether we like it or not, the language we were taught and learned has a great impact on how we see the world. Language arises from cultures, and cultures are shared ideas, beliefs, behaviors, and customs adopted by groups. Each culture arose from its own environment and the experiences of its people, so no two cultures can be the exact same, and many are different.

How do these experiences and environmental conditions shape the attitudes and beliefs of a people? The language we speak is a way of describing the world in our culture's perspective, and thus by learning another language you are learning more than just words—new senses of words and grand perspectives never before imaginable.

Culture is shaped by shared experiences of a people, a commonality; yet culture manifests itself uniquely in every individual. How we see the world is heavily dependent on the environment in which we spend most of our time in. The world is infinitely complex, and we can spend an unlimited amount of time fixating on any particular detail of something that catches our eye or piques our interest.

For example, just take a moment and look at your hand.

Yes, your hand.

Notice the ridges, the color, the ridges within the ridges, your fingerprints, and every which way they twist, curl, and swerve. Feel the texture and how it changes, where it is soft, where it is coarse. The detail of the space between your fingers. Freckles or beauty marks. Scars. The skin tone and hue. How your hand connects to your wrist. The more you look and the more you feel the more you see. You could even research the anatomy behind human hands and all the physiological and chemical processes on the microscopic scale in all their complexity. The evolutionary adaptation of hands. You can spend hours, days, weeks, and years diving into this specific topic.

Now think about this with any other part of your body, or any animal or feature of a plant. Any topic at all. The most mundane has infinite complexity. Yet, if you are a normally functioning human being, you aren't spending every waking moment of your life counting and examining the unique detail of every grain of sand on the beach. Why? Why not?

What does this have to do with culture?

Culture is a way to acknowledge this vast complexity of life as well as to counteract the danger with vast complexity. We cannot hope to ever learn even a fraction of 1 percent of all knowledge to be had. In fact, most knowledge is not useful at all because it is not relevant to our finite existence. The unending complexity of life and our inability to comprehend most of it individually is one of life's great paradoxes and mysteries.

Culture does not just exist because people come together and say, "Howdy there, I want to do a bunch of random traditions. What d'ya say, fella?" Culture arises from utility, but not simply as a tool. Rather, a whole *tool set* used by its members; and part of that tool kit is restriction. Culture by definition is a *set* of traditions, values, norms, practices, beliefs, and perspectives. By acceding to specific aspects, it discriminates from all other cultural traditions in existence. It focuses, disciplines, and relieves the individual from the burden of unimaginable complexity by creating a system of comprehensible complexity. Every culture and belief system does this, and more often than not, a belief system explains and contains infinite complexity (the universe) in the story or complex framework.

Yes, this is a vast oversimplification, but this isn't a book about theories on culture. In short, by a given culture having specific practices and beliefs it, by definition, discriminates against all other forms of cultural expression not agreed upon by those within that culture. The Navajo don't wear Japanese kimonos in their ceremonies, and the Xhosa aren't fluent in Russian. Culture is creative, but it is also well-defined order. Every human being uses culture to limit themselves in such a way as to not subject the individual or group to an infinite number of distractions, and quite contrarily focusing on like-minded goals. That's not to say cultures haven't or don't bring in elements of other cultures. If I was saying that, I would be contradicting my first point. The United States of America is an example in itself of a culture that wraps in other cultures. The English language as well!

Now that we've discussed the five themes of linguistics, I want to cover a few other bases.

GRAMMAR NAZIS, MY MOTHER, AND SOCRATES

No matter how young and naïve or old and cynical you may be, I am sure you heard the generation before yours say something along the lines of "the kids these days don't know basic grammar and spelling. It's ridiculous!" Perhaps your parents have said this; perhaps you have said this. I can tell you that any time someone says "me and [insert name here]," my mom has a hissy fit: "It's '[insert name here] and I'!" Okay, Mom.

Whether you think your culture is collapsing in on itself and language usage may indicate that (and it may very well be), this is not a unique phenomenon to our time.

Let me explain.

Actually, I'll let world renowned Canadian American cognitive psychologist, linguist, and pop science author Steven Pinker tell it all:

> "The thing is that complaints about the imminent decline of the language can be found in every era. such as 1961, in which a commentator complained, 'Recent graduates, including those with university degrees, seem to have no mastery of the language at all.' Well, we can go back before the advent of radio and television. In 1917, a commentator wrote, 'From every college in the country goes up the cry, "Our freshman can't spell, can't punctuate." Every high school is in disrepair because its pupils are so ignorant of the merest rudiments.' Well maybe you have to go back even further to the glory days of the European Enlightenment, such as 1785, in which a commentator said, 'Our language is degenerating very

fast... I begin to fear it will be impossible to check it.'
And then there are the ancient grammar police, said,
'For crying out loud, you never end a sentence with [the
hieroglyphic of] a little bird!'" (Pinker, 2015)

Socrates, the most famous of the ancient Greek philosophers
wrote on the subject around 300 BC:

> "*The children now love luxury, they have bad manners,*
> *contempt for authority, they show disrespect for elders*
> *and love chatter in place of exercise. Children are now*
> *tyrants, not the servants of their households. They no*
> *longer rise when elders enter the room. They contra-*
> *dict their parents, chatter before company, gobble up*
> *dainties at the table, cross their legs, and tyrannize their*
> *teachers.*" (Goodreads, 2021)

In another instance Socrates also exclaimed:

"If the whole world depended on today's youth, I can't see the
world lasting another one hundred years."

I would venture to say this phenomenon of bad grammar
and disobedience among the next generation really should
not be so absurd to us. After all, we as humans did not
evolve to read words written on a paper. Think about that
for a second.

The invention of writing has cropped up in several civili-
zations around the world independently, and the earliest
instance can be attributed to 3400 BC in ancient Mesopota-
mia (Pinker, 2015).

The Shang Dynasty in China from roughly 1300 BC developed the first fully-fleshed-out writing system. So, the earliest being 5,400 years ago (Clayton, 2019).

By comparison agriculture was invented as recently as 7,000 years ago and as distant as 12,000 years ago. Yes, farming. If you are not a history, science, and archaeology nerd you almost certainly think that is a *really* long time ago, but to me, a history major, that is a drop in the bucket. Nothing. Twelve thousand years of that initial wheat farming to get that bread to where we live now in the twenty-first century—altogether that is only 0.48 percent of human history… a history that spans more than 2.4 million years and goes even further back if you want to include our pre-human ancestors.

"Speech is the representation of the mind, and writing is a representation of speech."

—ARISTOTLE

The fact we could train our brains to write the spoken word, understand what we wrote, and read it back aloud is by God a miracle in my estimation. Just as the discovery of fire propelled our biological evolution (Gowlett, 2016), the discovery and invention of writing propelled our cultural evolution allowing us to organize beyond small nomadic tribes of a few dozen to forging steel and concrete metropolises of tens of millions of people. Writing allowed us to converse beyond the person in front of us, all the way to our future selves and people we may never meet.

The same species that discovered fire, hunted mammoths, and made cave paintings is the same species that colonized the whole world, flew to the moon and back, and created the world's largest information storage system that out competes the memory and processing of the smartest of us combined: the internet. Language and writing specifically is a technology that has outpaced our mortal limitations.

DESCRIPTIVE VERSUS PRESCRIPTIVE LINGUISTICS

When it comes to spoken and written language, there is the ongoing debate, as alluded to above, between the people who advocate for language to be used as it is said and the people who stand for language to be used as it *should* be said. This is descriptivism versus prescriptivism.

Descriptivists believe there is no objective language to be used. That "ain't" is just as valid as "isn't," and "me and you" has the same footing as "you and I." This group is cool with slang, pidgin languages (made up combo languages to help two speakers of different languages understand each other), dialects, and vernacular.

I am sure you, dear reader, have certainly noticed I am more in keeping with descriptivism just by the number of contractions and bits of slang throughout or the number of prepositions I use to end sentences with. If you are an ardent prescriptivist, you probably tore out all your hair and went hoarse before the end of the introduction. But thank you for sticking with it.

I sit somewhere between both camps because I do believe there needs to be a standardized form for languages like

English in order to provide consistency, yet there is an undeniable utility to being subject to an evolving language. Just as culture sets a common framework for a people to deal with overwhelming complexity, standardized language can do the same thing.

Prescriptivism is what I think should be taught and referred to when organization, a discipline of sorts, will help make things run smoother—say, a classroom, computer programs, record-keeping, public signage (roads, buildings), etc.—whereas descriptivism is the undeniable reality outside of formal settings.

I think the debate is rather silly. Language both describes the world and prescribes it. We need to mold language to adjust to differing perspectives, but we also need a backbone to refer to.

For example, before the time English was standardized, the word we say today for "church," was spelled no less than thirty ways, with variations not just from country to country, but neighboring town to neighboring town. Could you imagine if all the towns next to yours all used English but used a completely different way of spelling? Standardization *and* free choice are both needed. A balance of creativity and order, a classic battle in human thought, and a tension wholly necessary.

ETYMOLOGY

"the study of the origin of words and
the way in which their meanings
have changed throughout history."

"the origin of a word and the historical
development of its meaning."

PICKING FAVORITES

I am no linguist, but anyone who knows me will have already guessed that a portion of a book written by me would include etymology. By the definition alone it sounds like a dry subject found in the dark dusty dank corners of an academic's bookshelf. Of all the categories of linguistics, etymology is certainly not one of the flashier fields like psycholinguistics, speech pathology, or sociolinguistics. Fair. It's not incredibly trendy, not even within linguistics. Nevertheless, I argue no other branch of linguistics is as powerful and deep cutting as etymology. This will sound crazy, but etymology is something of a spiritual pursuit for me. It is the means by which I uncover hidden meanings, shrouded before our very eyes.

No, I am not talking about reciting some ancient magic words to summon the aid of the Norse gods to my cause. The study of word origins, *etymology*, comes from a Greek combination of words meaning *to find the true sense* (of a word) and -*ology*, which means "study," from *logos*, "word." Words obviously have meanings, but the origins of those meanings, what the word literally means, and how they have changed over time is not always obvious, especially to the untrained eye. As mentioned before, *Etymonline* is an excellent way to uncover the true sense of a word.

With etymology, we discover that science literally means "to discern," or more literally "to cleave, or split apart." Or perhaps, that a barn is a "bere aern," or in modern English, a "barely house." Similarly, ransack is a house raid, and garlic is a spear (gar) leek. How about one more? A terrible calamity is a disaster, quite literally, an event "ill-starred." With the same root we get asteroid (meaning star-like), asterisk (little star), and constellation (that which shines together/together stars). I could go on, but this book is filled with etymology as is.

To save you the brain ache and to keep this story going, in the next chapter we will explore how it is possible that so many languages are related, how that impacts the modern world, and, of course, why understanding this may prove helpful in learning any language.

TAKEAWAYS
1. Linguists study linguistics, which is the scientific study of languages; polyglots are people who can speak many languages.
2. Languages have to be learned, but our understanding of language is innate, which manifests as a universal grammar that nearly every language conforms to.
3. How children learn language is important to understand in order to learn language at any age.
4. What may make learning a second language difficult, is that different languages order their sentences differently.

5. Languages vary as much as cultures, and the two shape each other in a never-ending cycle.

6. Culture is a tool designed to rightfully restrict us from focusing on the infinite complexity of the world, while also reaffirming it in unique expression.

7. Descriptivists believe there is no proper way to use language, while prescriptivists believe there is a standard way it should be used.

8. Writing is a uniquely human invention discovered much later than the spoken word that has enabled humanity to record and accumulate information more efficiently leading to technological progress.

FOOTNOTES:

[2] The word for "language" in many languages often means "tongue" or it shares an origin with the word tongue. *Language* comes from the Latin *Linguaticum* which comes from *lingua* which literally means "tongue." In fact, both the English words *language* and *tongue* come from an ancient Indo-European root, "*dnghu-," which means tongue, the organ of speech.

[10] *Meso* meaning *between* and *potamia* meaning *land of rivers,* thus *land between the rivers* (the Tigris and Euphrates; modern day Iraq). Compare this with *Mesoamerica,* which means Middle America or Central America and hippo*potamus* (*hippo* meaning *horse* and *potamus*, you guessed it, *river...* river horse).

CHAPTER 7

How to Count in Ten languages at Once

———

YOU SPEAK AN ANCIENT LANGUAGE.

I won't mince words with you. You speak a *dialect* of a language that is 6,500 years-old, spoken in prehistoric times by nomadic horse archer warriors who invented pants and chariots, were some of the first people to tame horses, worshiped an eternal sky father god at the top of a pantheon of gods and to add, these people lived in the fields of modern-day Russia and Ukraine.

What? Sounds a bit... strange, doesn't it? It sounds like the premise to some sort of weird mythological fantasy book, a culture's origin story, or even a hero origin story... all for good reason. I will explain what I'm talking about, but it will make more sense if we work backwards. With that, let's do just that.

YOUR MONTHS ARE NUMBERED

If you have some exposure to Romance languages, have you ever noticed that some of the months of the year in English sound like numbers in Spanish, Italian, French, or Latin?

September sounds or looks a bit like *siete* in Spanish and *septem* in Latin. October unmistakably looks like octo (as in octopus, an eight-legged animal). November like *nueve* or *novem*, or December like *diez* or *decem*. If you take a look at the chart, you'll notice these names come directly from Latin, but you probably also noticed that *Sept*ember is not the seventh month. *Oct*ober is not the eighth month, *Novem*ber is not the ninth, and *Decem*ber is not the tenth. They're the ninth, tenth, eleventh, and twelfth (Etymonline, 2021; *List of Greek and Latin Roots in English*, 2021).

Well, that's because they used to be in correct order until a pesky Roman named Julius Caesar shunted in January and February at the beginning of the ten-month calendar, creating a twelve-month calendar. However, those two months were the last two of the Roman calendar, quite different from today. Two thousand one hundred years later, and the number and name of the months persist. But the precise astronomical calculations used to create the Julian calendar weren't precise enough, so Pope Gregory commissioned the creation of our calendar: the Gregorian calendar.

Yes, the Saint credited for inventing a fantastic style of singing in the Catholic Church, later employed by boys to sing the *Halo* theme in high school bathrooms, was the same guy who made sure your calendar works out all right.

Perhaps some more examples? A preponderance of evidence is better than none.

COMMON THREADS

These commonalities extend past simple numbers and months. I have to assume you know what *bonjour* means in French, but in Italian we get *buongiorno*. Similar pronunciation, same meaning, both cognates (of the same origin).

If we want to write the verb *sing* as in, *I sing*, in French we get *chante*, Italian *canto*, Portuguese *canto*, Romanian *cânt*, Spanish *canto*—all from the Latin *cantō*. We can repeat this exercise with dozens of verbs, and as long as we know the rules for how they change between languages. Verbs, specifically because what people *do* or *act out*, scarcely change but nouns may differ because what people interact with can change frequently across diverging cultures.

The Latin spoken across the Roman Empire began shifting into dialects. With an empire spread so far and wide, the diverse range of dialects and slang became unmanageable from any central organization, and quickly these dialects were called "Vulgar Latin"—not because they were particularly obscenely reproductive, but rather because they were of the common people as opposed to the elite senators, praetors, consuls, and other members of the Roman upper crust. *Vulgar*, the word we use today, comes from the Latin *vulgus*, a term for commoners and was a synonym with *plebeian* or *pleb*. Funnily enough, the modern words *pagan* and *heathen* come from terms to refer to these normal, typically farming, common folk as well.

ROOT LANGUAGES

Those brief examples of the similarities among various Romance languages are to illustrate that modern languages and dialects come from earlier spoken languages, e.g., Spanish, French, Romanian, Italian, Portuguese, Catalan (among many others), which originate from Latin. This logic applies to other branches, e.g., Danish, Swedish, Norwegian, and Icelandic coming from Old Norse or Russian, Polish, Czech/Slovak, and Bulgarian coming from Proto-Slavic dialects. With this logic we can also infer that Latin, Old Norse, and Old Slavic were languages that came from older languages.

In fact, most languages of Europe are something like distant dialects descended from that 6,500-year-old horse culture tongue. And before I am accused of "Eurocentrism" take a look at the chart provided in this chapter. That proto-language, Proto-Indo-European as academics call it, is the language that would branch off into many branches across Eurasia and into Africa.

NUMBERS ONE THROUGH TEN IN INDO-EUROPEAN LANGUAGES:

English	West Frisian	Spanish	Latin	Greek	Sanskrit	Hindi	Farsi	Russian	Irish Gaelic
One	Ien	Uno	Unus	Heis	Ekas	Ek	Yek	Adeen	a haon
Two	Twa	Dos	Duo	Duo	Dva	Do	Do	Dva	a dó
Three	Trije	Tres	Tres	Treis	Tryas	Teen	Seh	Tri	a trí
Four	Fjouwer	Cuatro	Quattuor	Tettares	Catvaras	Char	Char	Chitvri	a ceathair
Five	Fiif	Cinqo	Quinque	Pente	Panca	Panch	Panj	Pyat	a cúig
Six	Seis	Seis	Sex	Heks	Sat	Che	Shesh	Shest'	a sé
Seven	Sân	Siete	Septem	Hepta	Sapta	Saat	Haft	Sem'	a seacht
Eight	Acht	Ocho	Octo	Okto	Asta	Aaht	Hasht	Vosim'	a hocht
Nine	Njoggen	Nueve	Novem	Ennea	Nava	Nau	Noh	Devit'	a naoi
Ten	Tsien	Diez	Decem	Deka	Dasa	Das	Dah	Desit'	a deich

Note: Each of these ten languages has a different orthography (the differing conventions of spelling and pronunciation with words and letters between languages). However, general patterns of spelling and pronunciation can be observed across these languages regardless. For example, the "ch" spelling in Hindi, Farsi, and Russian translations for "four" hold the same pronunciation for the letter "c" in the Irish number for four, whereas the "ch" sound in the Irish number ten is a similar sound to the "c" or "k" in Latin and Greek for ten. Also, note that Greek, Sanskrit, Hindi, Farsi, and Russian use unique writing systems separate from the Latin alphabet but are put into the Latin script for ease of comparison.

BIZARRE SIMILARITIES

When talking about languages with my friend Madalyn Staudt, she flat out told me, "Irish is more similar to Hindi than it is to English," which certainly got my attention. Madalyn was a few years ahead of me in the history program at my university and specialized in Irish and Scottish history. To my visible shock, she went on. "Yes!" she told me, beyond my surprise. "The number systems are almost exactly the same [in Irish and Hindi]. The words *are* the same."

She went on:

> "I actually got that demo. When I was in Ireland our tour guide pulled over an Indian lady, and he said, 'Do you speak Hindi?' and she said, 'Yes.' And he said, 'Would you mind participating in a little experiment with me? I will count to ten, and as you say each number in Irish you will repeat after me in Hindi.' She said,

*'Okay,' and so they did! And with a few minor pronun-
ciation differences, every number was the same!"*

If you haven't noticed, India and Ireland are on opposite sides
of the globe (*The Celtic-Vedic Connection*, 2018; Peadarson,
2019).

Okay, what the hell is going on? If you take a good look at that
chart, you quickly begin to see there are similarities between
the languages you might expect such as Latin, Spanish, and
English, but the patterns don't stop there. English and Frisian
are obviously very close (*Of Languages and Numbers*, 2021),
and all the "ones" for English, Frisian, Spanish, and Latin are
close and Sanskrit, Hindi, and Farsi are close, but different
between these groupings.

But take a look at all the "twos." What do you notice? First
off, they all have what is called an "alveolar" sound of "t" or
"d," which literally means you touch the tip of your tongue to
the bony alveolar ridge on the roof of your mouth. When languages change and evolve, it is common for similar sounds to
split off, or even mispronunciation to occur without change
to the entire language. Go through the list of "twos" and say
them aloud with that in mind. It is apparent that these words
are all related in some weird way. Even the spelling indicates
this—the "t" or "d" sound followed by a vowel, sometimes
with a "u," "w," or "v" wedged in there.

Some of these languages are so close that the spelling and
pronunciation is nearly the same. Look at "dva" in Russian
and Farsi, "char" in Farsi and Hindi, *ocho, octo,* and *okto* in
Spanish, Latin, and Greek. With the exception of Greek and

Hindi, the whole line of "sixes" barely changes between the nine languages. You get the point.

THE INDO-EUROPEAN CONNECTION

So, why are all these languages that seem like they have no connection so similar? Where else do the similarities extend in the languages? Is it a coincidence? Did one of these languages, perhaps one of the notably older ones like Latin and Sanskrit influence all the others? Yes, but it goes far deeper than that.

Up until you got to this point in the book you likely believed that these languages, some of which you may not have heard of, were completely unrelated. But we have gone down the path far enough where holding that belief is no longer an option.

These ten languages, which represent a few different language families, are a few of dozens of languages that all fit into a massive evolutionary tree of languages. This massive family of languages is spoken by more than 50 percent of the entire population of the world, and it is called the Indo-European family. All of the languages above and all the languages not mentioned apart of this tree stem from a single language. That's right, a single language. A single language was spoken as recently as 4,500 years ago and as far back as 6,500 years ago by people who live in what we consider modern-day Russia and Ukraine.

PIE IS FOR DESSERT, Π IS FOR MATH NERDS, BUT PIE IS FOR LANGUAGE NERDS

We have a pretty good understanding of the structure of the language, the rough grammar, and pronunciation. We also know a good portion about their customs, religion, and lifestyles. Scholars call this language "Proto-Indo-European," (PIE for short… yum!) and thus the people, Proto-Indo-Europeans, or simply Indo-Europeans. They are called this because it was spoken so long ago in the part of the world in which writing was not yet invented. Wait, so we know this language exists even though no written records exist? How could we possibly know what it sounds like or know anything about their culture?

When I first heard of this culture and how linguists and scientists were able to discover the treasure trove of information about these people without conventional methods, I really could not believe it. I struggled so hard to believe it because the methods were so off the beaten path and, frankly, clever that I myself never would have come up with them.

The idea of this single ancestral language was first posed by William Jones. Jones was an Anglo-Welsh philologist and judge in colonial Bengal (modern-day Bangladesh and part of colonial India) in the 1800s, where he studied the prominent language of law and religion in the region: Sanskrit. He began to realize striking similarities between Sanskrit and that of European languages such as Greek and Latin. Other scholars had noted this prior upon visiting India and neighboring cultures who used Sanskrit and Iranian languages. His work was expanded upon by scholars to follow and the research efforts grew bigger and bigger, and they continuously grow today.

That was merely the catalyst. Nevertheless, DNA evidence of ancient corpses, as well as broader archaeological evidence show a group of horse riders quickly spread across the Eurasian continent, conquering, interacting, and having children with other prehistoric peoples. The evidence is overwhelming, but with the focus of this book elsewhere, I do not have the time I wish I could go into length on that evidence, but citations are provided.

This language family compromises the languages of Northern India and Pakistan (Hindi and Urdu), Iranic languages (Farsi, Pashto, Kurdish, Tajik), Baltic (Latvian and Lithuanian), Slavic (Russian, Czech, Polish, Serbian, Croat, Ukrainian, Bulgarian, Kashubian), Celtic (Irish, Scottish Gaelic, Manx, Welsh, Breton, and Cornish), Romance (Spanish, Portuguese, French, Italian, Romanian, Romansch, English), Germanic (German, **English**, West Frisian, Norwegian, Icelandic, Danish, Dutch, Swedish, Scots, and Faroese), with Armenian, Albanian, and the extinct Anatolian (Hittite) branches isolated on their own in their part of the PIE tree.

COMPARING PIE DIALECTS, PIE-ALECTS, IF YOU WILL

By using comparative linguistics, where similarities and differences in languages are charted, it can be determined whether or not a language belonged to the family. These comparisons helped show how language can preserve itself over an immense amount of time or show in what ways words and phrases change, and the shifting of their sense of meanings. By looking at what has changed and what has remained the same, as well as comparing that with archaeological evidence showing the movement of people through time, we can make extremely educated guesses on what the PIE language sounded like and what features this culture would have had. We also have an immense amount of archaeological evidence and even DNA evidence to track the migration of these peoples from the steppe to the rest of Eurasia and their mixing and subjugation of local populations.

Since they lived on the steppe of Russia and Ukraine, horseback riding would be paramount to be able to organize into small societies, gather sufficient food, and spread outward. This is backed up linguistically by the fact that many Indo-European languages use very similar words for kinship, people, pronouns, numbers (duh), animals, body parts, bodily functions, food, farming, actions (verbs), mental states, natural phenomena, directions, adjectives, making things, words to describe time, and religious practices.

Why these categories specifically? The most commonly used words in a language are the most functional and critical for communications, making it unlikely to radically change, get rid of, or replace these words on a regular basis. Think about this: Why would we change the words for *I, me, you, mother, son, year,* etc. That's why many of the oldest words in the English language also happen to be common words and vice versa, dating back to the time of the Indo-Europeans and having not been or minimally changed for six millennia.

For example, here is the English and PIE side by side: work (*werĝ-), door (*dʰwer), light (*leuk-, also the root of Lucifer—"light bearer"), water (*wódr̥), murder (*mer-), sweat (*sweid-), salt(*sal-), nose (*nas-), heart/core/cardio (*k̂erd-), and we (*wei) to name a few. These people eventually spread their language, culture, religion, and their genetics across Eurasia from Russia and Ukraine, to Northern India and

Iran, to Western China, to Spain, Turkey, the British Isles, and the North of Europe.

It is also worth noting that the modern religion of Hinduism, and the ancient pagan religions of Rome, Greece, the Vikings, pre-Christian Anglo-Saxons, the Irish, and the Celts among others all derive from a religion practiced by the Indo-Europeans. A religion that honored a "sky father" with cattle worship, the instrumental role of horses, the sun as a central deity, and a creation story of twin brothers who initiated the first sacrifices to the sky father god.

In ancient India, this god was known as "Dyaus Pita," literally "sky father." In ancient Greece he was known as "Zeus Pater" and in Rome "Deus Pater" or "djous piter" later transformed to "Jupiter." The same goes for the Germanic people who had "Tyr, Tir, or Tiwaz" (for which Tuesday in English is named, just as Wednesday is Woden's or Odin's Day, Thursday is Thor's Day, and Friday is Frigga's Day)—all deriving from the same understanding and language of a people far gone. The parallels are endless and if you want to explore this further, I recommend *Survive the Jive* on YouTube.

I could say much more about these people, their religion, and their language, but I can't without going into too much detail of this fascinating ancient culture that influenced the entire world unlike no other could have a whole book dedicated to them. In fact, many books, papers, and online documentaries about this topic I have referred to greatly by scholars have taken this to be their life work. I am merely here to relay this information for my own satisfaction of blowing your mind. Language barriers can divide us, but isn't it quite the thought that half the world's languages today were at one point all one language spoken by a tiny tribe in the middle of the wilderness? It is similar in mind-blowing factor as the fact that all humans originate from a small population in Africa hundreds of thousands of years ago.

OTHER FUNKY LANGUAGE FAMILIES

So, if 50 percent of the world's population speak a language of a common origin, where do some of the other major world languages come from?

English is the most widely spoken language worldwide in terms of total speakers (primary and secondary speakers) with 370 million primary speakers and 894 million secondary speakers, but Mandarin Chinese has the most primary speakers of all languages with a whopping 921 million native speakers (and 198 million secondary speakers).

Mandarin is clearly a humongous language that belongs to an even bigger language family: the Sino-Tibetan family. This family includes Sinitic/Chinese (Mandarin, Jin, Wu, Hui, Gan, Xiang, Hakka, and others), the Tibetic languages (the family of languages spoken in Tibet), Lolo-Burmese, Karenic, Bodo-Garo, Kuki-Chin, Meitei, Tamangic, Bai, and Jing-pho-Luish. These language groups subdivide further into unique, individual languages, which in themselves include hundreds, if not thousands, of dialects.

In North Africa and the Middle East, there is another widely spoken language family known as the Afro-Asiatic languages. You might not have ever heard of it, but you undoubtedly know— rather, have heard of—Arabic, Aramaic, Hebrew, and Berber. which are languages in that greater tree. Afro-Asiatic languages originated from Proto-Afro-Asiatic, and split into the subdivisions of Chadic, Berber, Semitic, Egyptian (yes, what the ancient Egyptians spoke and conveyed with hieroglyphics), Cushitic, and Omotic. Within Semitic you have Hebrew, Canaanite, Aramaic (language of Jesus Christ), the many dialects of Arabic, new and old, and the European language of Maltese. Maltese is a strange creature because it is a combination of the Tunisian dialect of Arabic and Italian due to bizarre historical circumstances.

There are so many other language families across the world including the Americas and Pacific islands, but I simply do not have the time, space, or know-how to relay all this information to you. You are probably on information overload as it is.

TAKEAWAYS

1. Languages that seem to have no relation to each other have a good chance of having a common ancestor. Depending on how long ago the linguistic split occurred and how geographically close its modern speakers are can help you to determine how close the languages may be.

2. When learning a second language, picking languages closer to your native one may make fluency more quickly attainable through efficiency; however, this can be easily overdone.

3. If you learn multiple languages at a time, it is best to pick languages in a family and understand the differences and the rules on how to change words from one language to another so you can maximize your versatility and learning potential.

CHAPTER 8

Slang Gang

SLANG, DIALECTS, AND LANGUAGES ARE LITTLE DIFFERENT

In my discussion with the Ohio State University doctoral candidate Ke Lin, I truly had my eyes opened about how vast the field of linguistics is. Ke was able to distill many of the complex themes and concepts in the science of linguistics into spectacular summary sentences. When describing the difference between a language and a dialect, she gave me a detailed technical interview and then provided the simple quote: "The difference between a dialect and a language is that a language has an army and navy."

Essentially, a language and dialect can be the same thing, truly. The difference is that one is politically recognized as a language and the other is not (think how Czech and Slovak are called different languages but are mutually intelligible to the extent they are really dialects of one language; they are separated only by political borders). By extent, slang seems as if it could be a dialect, and perhaps it is, but finds itself in every dialect and every language. A language within a language. What slang dialect do you speak?

HINGLISH AND FRANGLAIS

Slang can be individual words or an entire way of speaking. Slang, in some sense, is an improper way of speaking, deviating from the academic and formal standards of a language. This makes me wonder what a pidgin language is. No, not a pigeon language. I am not talking about squawks and chirps, but rather impromptu languages created by combining elements of two or more languages.

If you live in the US, I guarantee you have heard of Spanglish, a combination of Spanish and English. In Uganda, a highly modified form of English is influenced by local culture and other languages; you get Uglish (that's what Ugandans call it—I am merely the messenger). Hindi and English? Hinglish.

The names for these pidgin languages are portmanteaus, reflective of their combined nature. If English's name reflected its multilingual nature, we might call it Anglonagaelatinell-nicodancais (Anglic-gaelic (Celtic)-Latin-Greek-Danish (Old Norse)-French).

Jokes aside... Well, that joke aside, when I was a part of the CFA Research Challenge Team, five of us had unique backgrounds: two Ohioans, one Brazilian, one Canadian, and one Haitian. The Haitian is my friend Elioth previously mentioned. We got to the point in our financial analysis of a metals and mining company where we did not know how to do a very specific type of valuation calculation formula in Excel, so we got onto YouTube on the hunt for tutorial videos. We looked and there was but a sole video, and that one video was by an Indian man. We were open to what the man had to say, but we quickly found out the man's accent and Hinglish were so thick that the combined linguistic and financial knowledge of a Canadian, a Haitian, a Brazilian, and two Americans, our truly international coalition, could not cut through. The two of us Americans likely canceled out the multilingual brain power of our international friends.

Between my best friend Adam and myself, we spoke English primarily and French secondarily. When we both were practicing at the same time, more often than not, we would have full conversations in French, which devolved into *Franglais*, a pidgin language combining French and English. When in Albania, I encountered a Frenchman named Sacha. He spoke broken English and my French was out of practice so, without conscious decision, we broke into Franglais.

NEWFIES, NOT THE DOGS

So, I have a lot of Newfie friends. Like a ton. A big cluster. Back in the days of middle school and high school when the majority of time was filled with inconsequential Minecraft playing for hours on end. I met a group of video game-loving Newfies by accidentally stumbling on a Canadian Minecraft server. If you didn't know, I am not talking about the dog breed; I am talking about the people who live on the island of Newfoundland on the Atlantic side of Canada that shares the Gulf of Saint Lawrence with Nova Scotia, New Brunswick, and Quebec, and is a little northeast of Maine. Again, the *people*, not the dogs.

In normal conversation I thought they sounded just like me, a midwestern Ohioan with the occasional country twang. Yet, when the mining and the crafting got too intense or we were playing a combat game mode where the stakes couldn't be higher, their speech patterns and accent completely shifted into something I had never heard. My reaction was not too dissimilar then, as if I was racing my car down the highway, and my Newfie friend Sydney grabbed the gear shifter and put the whole car into reverse. The heart and gut-wrenching sound of the transmission, gears, and engine blowing to pieces that you are imagining is exactly how my brain felt when I heard Newfies speak in their true accent for the first time. Not a feeling of disgust, but one of awe and utter amazement wrapped in a burrito of confusion. How can someone who sounded so normal all this time turn into a barely comprehensible, drunken Scottish sailor? To quote a Newfie proverb of unknown origin, "It puts a knot in my gut and a tear in my eye."

DEFINITION:
Slang

"a type of language that consists of words and phrases that are regarded as very informal, are more common in speech than writing, and are typically restricted to a particular context or group of people"

— OXFORD LANGUAGES

Some definitions even go so far as to specify that slang is created to create exclusive groups with the purpose of excluding others and to form a strong group identity.

Unsurprisingly, linguists disagree... end of sentence. No, linguists disagree on a formal definition of slang and what qualifies as slang. In the 1964 United States Supreme Court case *Jacobellis v. Ohio*, Justice Potter Stewart when describing obscenity, and more accurately hardcore pornography, said, "I shall not today attempt further to define the kinds of material I understand to be embraced within that shorthand description, and perhaps I could never succeed in intelligibly doing so. But *I know it when I see it.*" Although he was talking about pornography, I believe the concept still holds. I cannot put my finger on slang but, hey, *I know it when I see it!*

If we think of slang as being something that enhances a group identity and creates a feeling of exclusiveness, that builds a pretty good picture for what it is and why we use it. Even if you are some high and mighty, heavily educated individual who *only* speaks proper English, you still use slang. Everyone has their idiosyncrasies in the way they talk and generally communicate. If put to the test, you could probably do an imitation of a close friend or relative in the way they speak, what words and phrases they use, and their general mannerisms. Even more so, we change our ways of speaking depending on who we talk to. You probably don't talk to your parents or grandparents the same way you talk to your best friend, your sibling, your boss, your employees, or your significant other. However, if you are talking to your brother and your uncle the same way because they are the same person, you've got bigger problems than communication. Aside, inside jokes are the epitome of slang. You and your bestie could say some word or phrase, and you would instantly know what the other is exactly trying to say.

Slang takes the textbook language and applies cultural incites. I believe the slang of a language creates the biggest barriers when learning the language of a culture you are not entirely familiar with. Textbooks and traditional language courses will often teach you the textbook phrases, questions, and responses. Depending on how formal or informal the language is, what people actually use and how they use it changes. When I began learning French for myself outside of the classroom, I quickly discovered that no Frenchman in their right mind would say, "*Comme ci, comme ca*" (Like this, like that) if they wanted to say, "I'm okay." You'd actually say "*Bof!*" which needs no explanation; the word sounds how the person feels.

In American English when we want to affirm or deny something, we, of course, could not be so straightforward as saying "yes!" or "no." As a wonderful reel by @athena.illustrations on Instagram pointed out: Yeah means yeah. No means no. No yeah means sure. Yeah no means no. Yeah no for sure means yeah. Yeah yeah yeah means no. Yeah no yeah means I'm willing to do it. No yeah no means there is no way I'm doing it.

CURSING, CUSSING, SWEARING, BLASPHEMING, EXPLETIVES, AND PROFANITY

Another form of speech that violates social norms are curse words, as I will call them.

Have you ever wondered why some words are *bad*? Comparable to slang, curse words generally are unacceptable forms of speech when used in public or for a formal occasion. Although government regulations have been made more slack for what words can and cannot be used on television and radio, words are still bleeped out. The irony is that these expletives run free on the internet, and a child, who the regulations are designed to protect, can and is easily exposed to a multitude of profane content including curse words which the regulators do not and cannot practically monitor, censor, or ban.

Aside from slang and general profane content, aside from the growing acceptance of certain swear words, why is it that certain *bad words* pack such a punch? Why do these specific words pack such a punch, even for the sailors among us?

Swear words are embedded in all languages, even from the most pious and pure communities. As a co-worker of mine told me once: "My friend who left the Amish didn't retain any of her traditional upbringing... except for one thing. Any time a non-Amish person pissed her off she would not hesitate to swear at them in German." As you will see, the traditionally religious Quebecois and Islamic societies are neither an exception.

At first glance, it may seem as if curse words are comparable to any other word: just squiggles on a paper with an assigned meaning. But how the brain processes curse words is different than other languages. The brain processes and produces language in several parts of the brain, mostly in the left hemisphere of the cortex (the outer layer that performs higher level processes and thinking), but when the brain is damaged on the left in these areas and not the right, sometimes the ability to swear can remain where the ability to speak is gone.

THE FOUR FS

Odd, isn't it? It is as if swearing isn't language, or at least how we know it. Cursing is not like any other part of language because it is produced and comprehended first in the limbic system of the human brain. For those not caught up on their neuroanatomy, the limbic system is often called the "emotional brain," which is associated with a far older, more instinctual mammalian structure shared with our animal cousins and distant ancestors of eons past. The psychologist Karl Pribram famously described the limbic system as being bound by "Four Fs": "Feeding, Fleeing, Fighting, and… Sex." If you think of a curse word, it likely fits into one of these emotional categories.

When we curse, it is often involuntarily prompted. When we hear or read a curse word, it is always involuntary, because before we process it as a word like any other, it goes directly to our limbic system to provoke an emotional response, specifically one of negative emotion.

Swearing, of course, can be used to intensify something, e.g., "That was *f***ing* delicious" as opposed to "That was very delicious." But it is always limbic. These specific distinctions between normal speaking and listening language and that of swearing is important when understanding the brain, especially as it relates to conditions such as Tourette's syndrome where involuntary swearing can occur (Crain, 2018).

THE FIVE TABOOS

Do you remember that Canadian American psychologist and linguist I mentioned back early on in the book? Well, he's back. I love his work, and when researching the topic of the psychology of swearing, I genuinely was not looking for his work. Lo and behold, his role as a science communicator caused him to show up first and foremost.

Regardless, Pinker has put a considerable amount of thought into the psychology of swearing and he, himself, has done the research. In his categorization of curse words, he observes that regardless of culture or language, those words talk about five major categories:

1. The supernatural/religious
2. Bodily effluvia and organs
3. Disease, death, and infirmity
4. Sexuality
5. Disfavored peoples and groups

With the supernatural/religious curse words, many of them have lost their potency in the West as it has shifted away from a traditional religious culture to a seemingly secular society. Despite this historic shift in the West, religious curse words still hold currency, even among the most lapsed atheists, e.g., *Jesus Christ, lord, hell, damn, heavens, God,* or the classic French *sacre bleu!* or Quebecois *tabarnak, câlice,* and *baptême* (Paskevics, 2017). In Islamic societies, God is invoked in all manner of ways: *wallahi, mashallah,* and other phrases, although these are not blatant or strong curses.

Why religious language for swearing? When *emotions of awe, fear, or confusion* surrounding the supernatural are invoked, a religiously minded people would instinctively go to the concepts they are/were familiar with.

It goes without saying that cursing often is related to parts of the body, organs, and that which comes from the body. Why? Excreted materials, fluids, organs, and body parts in certain contexts can easily and instinctively incite the *emotion of disgust*. Why? The aforementioned skein are vectors of disease. An emotional outcry, an evolved feeling of disgust at such things would save pre-modern humans who had limited medical know-how, and it would serve you, dear reader, to wash your filthy hands.

Curse words are not just those coarse words used in the height of an instant, but they are also words that perhaps draw too much emotion or gravity to a situation that would cast *emotion of grief and morbidity*. Even words like *cancer* and *die* or even *suffer* are not used lightly, especially in writing about a particular person. One would scan the obituary to find that someone *passed away*, not of cancer, but of a *long illness* or of *complications*, *old age*, or *natural causes*. These are all euphemisms for the more painful reality. Older curses even saw malicious wishes such as *a plague on both your houses!* or *a pox on you!*

Sexuality and the body are the most obvious categories of cursing. Sexuality is a subject rife with emotions, but not all are negative as you might have observed. Nonetheless, the curse words related to sexuality stem from those negative aspects that solicit deep and traumatic associations such as exploitation, incest, illegitimacy, spousal abuse, infidelity, desertion, feuding, harassment, cuckoldry, and rape. Any of these horrific subjects when dwelt on for any span bode not simply disgust but an *emotion of revulsion*.

Ultimately, some of the most contentious curse words deal directly with the dispossessed and marginalized peoples and groups. Words to describe infidels, cripples, enemies, subordinated people, outcasts, and the mentally disabled. Despite making up a small percentage of swears commonly used, these are often the most potent as these conjure *emotions of hatred and contempt* often nested in a historical context of depravity and atrocity. One does not have to go and cannot go further with that point than with the *N-word* in the context of American English (Pinker, 2009).

URBAN DICTIONARY

There is a great irony in academic language research. Professors, graduate students, volunteer compilers, and linguists devote their entire life to developing comprehensive indexes, cataloging word after word, phrase after phrase, creating precise definitions, and tracing roots and prevalence throughout history. Meanwhile, someone starts a website such as *urbandictionary.com*, where anyone can contribute, and lo and behold, emerges the largest catalog of slang terms in the English language. When you crowdsource any project, you are bound to have a wealth of knowledge (and idiocy) spring forth like a broken fire hydrant on a hot summer day. Or, in the perspective of the more pompous among us: a flooded septic sewer system backing up into the streets and homes of everyone in sight and smell.

Knowing slang and curse words can make a huge difference in how you are received within another culture or language community. Some cultures invite all manner of profanity, in others it could get you in serious harm. Knowing profanity, even if you are not going to use it (and err on the side of not using it if you are ever unsure), knowing what is profane can help in not mispronouncing similarly pronounced words.

Now that we have defiled the hallowed, it's time to get into the concrete steps and specific tactics of learning a language.

TAKEAWAYS

1. When communicating with someone who speaks a different language you are not fully fluent in, and likewise to you, create a pidgin language by attempting to speak their language while filling in the gaps with English or with words they might more easily recognize. This is not ideal, but you will quickly learn foreign words and so they will lead to a convergence of understanding. Perfect for getting out of a pinch. Stumbling is okay.

2. Swearing or hearing curse words activates a primitive part of the brain involuntarily, a different area processes other parts of language.

3. Learning curse words in a foreign tongue is tempting, and it is better to know them than not to avoid unnecessary conflict, know when you are being insulted, or even threatened.

4. Knowing a degree of slang in any study language will allow you to more easily communicate with foreign speakers, especially younger ones. In a language like French, slang can be so prevalent as to become normal speech. If you are studying French, look into Verlan.

PART III

CHAPTER 9

Embracing the Inner Child

BABIES ARE SCHOLARS, ADULTS ARE DUNCES?

"Yeah! By the time we learn a language in school, we are in high school. By then, it's too late!" If you're American and you ever talked to someone else about language classes and education in America, either you have heard a phrase along those lines or you were the one to say it. Admittedly, I've said that phrase before... several times. And guess what? It's WRONG.

"Best time to learn a language is when you're a kid," is a common refrain, and although this is true, it is not an absolute truth. Of course, learning a language as a child through your development and growing up is going to be a great way to learn, but think about it this way: Who do you know who has grown up not having learned at least one language? "Well, my brother's pretty dumb; he can barely speak Engl—"

Yeah, I've never heard that one before. It is worth reflecting on the idea that we teens and adults struggle so much more with learning a language than a baby who doesn't even know a single language.

Let me say that again: A baby or toddler has an easier time learning their first language (without any language experience at all) than a full-grown adult who knows *at least* one language. On paper, it *should* be easier for us adolescents and adults, but it sure seems like it isn't.

Think about it. Everyone learns a language; they learn the language of their family or the language of their social environment (school, friend group, town, workplace, etc.). So, I will concede that it is *easiest* or perhaps the most *convenient* to learn as a child. But if you are truly interested in acquiring another language besides the ones you already speak, consider for a moment that it might not be the sole fact that the baby/child is a baby that they learn language, but rather *how* they learn a language. Consider that for a moment: What does a baby do to learn a new language? What are the conditions that surround the child that make it ideal in learning a language?

WHY DO BABIES SEEM TO LEARN BETTER?

As Joseph Everett, host of the YouTube channel "What I've Learned," points out in his video "How to Learn a Language: INPUT (Why most methods don't work)," as babies we do not naturally learn English or any other tongue by our parents showing us flash cards when we are infants, or them going over grammar like *subject-object-verb* versus *subject-verb-object* orders.

What makes the brain such a unique part of the body is that it has a characteristic to it called "neuroplasticity." What this means is the brain can change its "wiring" and its actual anatomical structure under influence of environmental stimuli, cognitive demand, and behavioral experience.

Okay, how about in English? The actual shape and configuration of the brain is altered and our environment and the decisions we make can change that structure (*What I've Learned*, 2018). Our brain is like Play-Doh: We can shape it, mold it, and transform it. Just don't leave it out to dry or eat it. Fun to play with, but not so much to eat.

There is a common understanding that comes from psychology that says what happens when we are babies and children affect our whole life. Who our parents are, how they raised us, past traumas or life lessons, etc. We are forged by our childhood. Our babyhood, if you will.

LISTENING IN BABYHOOD

When we are infants and children, our brain is developing at an extremely rapid rate with our body, growing in size but also building the foundation of the experiences we will have for the rest of our lives. Think about it as laying the foundation for a building that will be continuously added upon for years and years.

Children possess an increased neuroplasticity because there is so much potential of direction you could go when you have a fresh start. That first language(s) you learn becomes a deep part of your psychological makeup.

Also, most of what babies do are three things: babble and listen and watch. My parents, particularly my mother, told me I was a terrible listener (she still does). Because of that, I think my parents did not think I was listening at all, so I got to learn all sorts of fun swear words at an early age. I knew not to use these newfound words (around them), but they figured that at a certain age I was able to understand them, so they stopped swearing like sailors... for a while. Certainly not out of malice, but that's how they talk. So, if you're reading this now, Mom and Dad, I was always listening.

Listening constitutes a major part of how children learn, and truth be told, how language is learned. Wanting to get my French right so I would not be wasting my time, I took time to research how other people were learning languages and to see what the statistics and research literature had to say about the best learning methods. Exposing yourself to different audio is extremely useful, as listening helps you get a proper understanding of how a language sounds with pronunciation, and it can provide context to help construct the logic of the language and figure out what is going on in a specific conversation or monologue.

Listening, paired with visuals and scenes that play out in real life or on television screens, iPads, or picture books help establish a secondary layer to language learning. Here, a more focused context can be given to the baby allowing for multiple types of sensory input (visual and auditory) that combine to form this context. We learn through context.

A word (or character) spoken or written means absolutely nothing without an assigned meaning. The letters/characters

C, A, and T are meaningless drawings, and the sound that we would pronounce "cat" is also just a sound without the *context* of what a cat is. The *catness* of the cat is not in the language, but the context of the language placed next to a furry feline.

If I raised a child who had no exposure to English or any other language, who was illiterate and did not know what a cat was, and I showed them a paper with the word "cat" and said "cat," the child would likely be confused. If anything, the child would learn that the piece of paper or paper with the etches on it was the cat, which, of course, is not correct. If I wanted to teach the child what a cat was, I would not do any of that, but I would find a cat or a picture of one and say "cat" and use it in the context of an appropriate sentence. And only maybe after some time would I show them how to write the word "cat," which symbolizes the cat along with the phonics of how to pronounce each letter.

To help build context, it is also important to show contrasts, so in time I would introduce them to other animals and their names, because if I do not establish that context, we might run into the situation I had with the paper, and the child would perhaps think "cat" means animal.

Listening and observing is a key component to the most important method of acquiring a language: that is, INPUT. Luckily for you, there's a whole chapter on the keystone to language acquisition.

GOO GOO GAH GAH

If you have ever looked at a language even slightly different than English, you quickly notice that the sounds other cultures use in their tongue may be similar but very different from any sound you ever normally use. Consider the Russian letter "Щ," which is pronounced "shch." Or the nasal "m" and "n" sounds found in the following French: *Je ne me sens pas bien.* The way "r" and "l" are pronounced in foreign languages can vary widely and is often tricky for English natives, and the English "r" is likewise tricky for foreign speakers. The two "th" sounds in English are notoriously difficult for English as a second language learners. Yes, English has two "th" sounds. Think of "the" versus "thud." English itself has even lost sounds like the guttural "gh" or "ch" found in words like "van Gogh" and "loch," and instead replaced them with softer, more pleasant, or silent pronunciations such as *laugh*, *through*, and both pronunciations of *slough* (Laurence, 2013).

How can the sounds we use be so divergent from language to language?

There is a limited range of sounds humans can make with our vocal cords, about 150 total. English has roughly forty-four. These most basic units of sounds are called phonemes, and phonemes when combined are the basis of words (Bainbridge, 2021). Phonemes cannot be divided any further into separate sounds.

It just so happens to be that babies babble in *all* phonemes, and thus have the potential to use any or all by default in the language(s) they will first be exposed to. This is the opposite of how language acquisition is commonly thought.

It is commonly thought that we learn how to pronounce sounds and words first, but in actuality, by listening through context babies are subconsciously discerning what phonemes belong to their language and which do not. The ones not used are babbled less and less, and forgotten, or rather, fall out of practice.

Babbling is an innate ability to do a probing of sorts of their linguistic environment. It is shooting in the dark until certain sounds stick, then are practiced more frequently until more sophisticated language is slowly acquired. It is not that babies know how to speak every language or have a mental index of all sounds; it is more so that they are *capable* of fumbling in every way possible with their mouth, tongue, and lips. Baby mice have little to no motor capabilities, so they use their tiny legs and paws to slowly club the ground in every which way until they can map their environment onto their brain and muscles. Language in human babies is very much the same. Creating a map of the environment through fumbling, tumbling, spitting, buzzing, screaming, cooing, and babbling.

Trial by error has a huge impact, as the only language a baby knows is the input of what they are exposed to and their attempts to mimic it in a brain that has not had full exposure to other languages.

Children are innately curious, and asking questions prompts new territory of understanding that includes new words, concepts, and phrases.

A SIDE NOTE ON THE NECESSITY OF LANGUAGE AND SOCIALIZATION

There is also the pressure of socialization. It is critical for a child to socialize rapidly within the first four years of their life, as the consequence of a lack of socialization after this point often results in a lifetime of disconnect, immaturity, loneliness, and many other characteristics attributable to those who cannot properly socialize, as brilliantly explained both in the 2010 textbook *Sociology: Understanding and Changing the Social World* and as explained by psychologist Dr. Jordan Peterson in his 2017 lecture "Personality 17: Biology and Traits: Agreeableness." An inability for a child to properly communicate and act with its peers is what it means to be anti-social.

For the unsocialized, unconventional and socially unacceptable and socially unsophisticated tactics like anger, aggression, lying, cheating, hitting, intimidation, and stealing are often used in place of learned communication and conflict resolution skills. Contrary to common sense, aggression is the default for many toddlers, but socialization is the process of learning language skills both verbally and behaviorally. It is commonly accepted that humans are innately good, and it is society/culture that corrupts, but this is horrifically inaccurate and the opposite of the truth. As alluded to in previous chapters, society and culture rightfully exist to constrain individuals in their aggression and fascination with infinite complexity in order to free us from the animalistic aspects of human nature.

Language is a component of the socialization process, not only learning a language, but also what to say when and where, how to say it, and the things that should not be said or acted out in certain scenarios and the exceptions for when they are. Articulate language skills are the alternative to aggression and violence. As language and articulation become more sophisticated, we are able to avoid violence through debate, dialogue, argumentation, and negotiation. War and civil strife often follow the breakdown of reciprocal communication. Individuals have to engage in communication.

THE FACTORS THAT HINDER ADULT LANGUAGE EDUCATION

The factors that hold back adults have less to do with barriers and more about their brain being not so "plastic" as children's. But anyone can still learn a language without that plasticity. The barriers have less to do with a change in the brain and more with an allocation of time. The typical child has what seems like endless free time, if we look back at our own childhoods or from a parent's perspective. When we become adults with a career, a job, a family, tests, children, bills, responsibilities, etc., it can seem like free time is only a myth. A romantic notion of our past concocted by nostalgia. Rest assured; it still exists.

Balancing all those commitments, responsibilities, and hobbies is difficult for the average adult, but it comes down to allocating that time. As mentioned earlier, it is not about you having time or not; it is about the internal struggle within yourself deciding whether you are *willing* to make the time. As well as the matter of whether you value your time at all.

Some parents make the time for their children and others don't; everyone knows this. The same concept applies to all other aspects that occupy time. Truly, all manners of existing. As an adult, it becomes more difficult to find that space of time to carve out, but if it is something you *truly* want, you will make time for it. So, either you convince yourself or you don't. You take the time, *or* you don't. How you use your time is a reflection of how it is you think you should exist. Time management is existential and a catalyst to individuation.

FORMING YOUR ADULT-BABY OPTIMAL LEARNING ENVIRONMENT

Not to be confused with man-child basement dwelling, your adult-baby optimal learning environment is a set of conditions you create around you both in terms of time spent and where it is spent to maximize language immersion as an adult.

Language fluency is not something you just hit, but rather is a gradient that can be expanded upon. When I first met my friend Dominika, she was fluent in English with a strong accent, but I could understand her 80 percent of the time. Nevertheless, after speaking over Skype and her studying in school and watching American shows like *The Walking Dead*, gradually over the course of two years, her English improved significantly. Having met her four years ago, I can confidently say her English abilities now are worlds apart from where they were. Immersion and consistency work.

The point is, because many Americans lack such a rigid but orienting structure to learning our own language, which typically comes in the form of grammar (as well as our lack of exposure to other languages), we fail to see the gradual efforts and goal setting that need to be made in order for us to attain fluency and to continually build upon what we already know. What you know today is merely the groundwork for what you will know tomorrow. The present moment is ever the foundation of the future.

When we grow up in the world learning our first language, we just do it.

We don't really think about it as a scientific and educational experience in the same way we first encounter the periodic table of elements or the biological distinctions of a plant, an animal, and fungi, or how we memorize formulas and proofs with concerted effort as we do in trig, geometry, and statistics.

AMERICAN IMMERSION

In America, we learn via immersion where we are raised by American English speakers (generally), we grow up in schools or communities with people who predominantly speak English, and then English/Literature classes in school assist in sharpening our fluency.

All of my own proficiency in English was forged in childhood. I spent years of my youth reading Star Wars articles online on Wookieepedia hours before school started, reading loads of story books, having my dad read books to me before bed, hanging out with friends, watching countless hours of YouTube, and being exposed to documentaries on ancient Egypt expanded my knowledge beyond the typical. My bizarre interests exposed me to a broad stroke of the English language, which oddly enough strengthened my proficiency.

Through middle school and high school, my writing and comprehension skills were refined and forged (thank you, Mrs. Thomas, Ms. Hurley, Mrs. Pernod, and Ms. Pavkov).

Mrs. Pernod, my tenth and eleventh grade literature teacher, was able to carve out time in our class schedule to teach us etymology and grammar away from state-mandated studying for state-mandated testing, which, in turn, produced state-mandated frustration, teacher and student alike. However, at the time, I was regrettably not interested in grammar, which probably arose from my adolescent inclination to resist any new ways of understanding what I "already knew."

Coming from this American experience (and the experience of countries where native languages spoken are not taught in classrooms) where language is largely absorbed and not taught, we lose a sense of how we learned what we did, when we learned it, and how and if continual development is existing. Whatever language you speak natively, as long as you have continual exposure to other speakers or forms of media in that language, you are expanding your understanding and usage.

HAVE A GOOD TEACHER

Eventually in high school I realized that my love for creative storytelling could be expressed through writing better than any other medium. Thus, English classes became my favorite because of the way we were taught. Admittedly, having the right teacher made all the difference. I will never forget how Mrs. Pernod taught our classes. She would convey extremely important literary concepts and themes by having us do hands-on activities and take field trips. That gave us broader understandings of the world, while greatly expanding our vocabulary and grammatical command of the English language.

She would not simply tell us definitions of words and have us memorize them or drone through grammar lectures; rather, she would give us context to their usage. For example, it is important to understand the culture and history of western civilization to understand words, phrases, idioms, and cultural references throughout English. So, Mrs. Pernod would teach us the epics of Greek and Roman mythology, and literature from the Judeo-Christian tradition, while comparing texts like the Bible and Quran.

This way we understood those references, such as *Apollo 11*, or that cereal literally means "of Ceres," or who Hercules was, why we have words like narcissist, echo, exodus, genesis, odyssey, siren, tenebrous, fortune, atlas, orthodox, hallowed, theist, jovial, martial, music, hypnosis, volcano, chaos, panic, chronology, morphine, nemesis, Hades, phobia, tantalize, what the heck an "Oedipus complex" was (that was a particularly eyebrow-raising and eye-gauging unit to cover), or all the pop culture references and imitations of stories like *The Odyssey* and those with in the Bible.

Every quarter or so, we would try to see a play as a class, work our lessons around it thereby making relevant what is taught in the classroom. I remember we toured a mosque in our section on the literary and cultural influences of Abrahamic religions, all while reading Khaleed Hosseni's *Kite Runner*. From there, our final research papers and presentations were intertwined with our experiences, and trustingly, allowing us to choose our own topic so long as it fit within the objectives of the class. This wasn't some boring year-long lecture about grammar; it was a holistic education about the English language, its historical development, how it currently is developing, why it matters to us, and how it can be a fun process.

By making the context of our language relevant (establishing an English language learning environment), Mrs. Pernod definitely eroded away many of my stubborn and prejudiced convictions I had against the only language I spoke, while opening my eyes to the larger world. This allowed me to become more aware of the world beyond the United States and to stoke the fires of my passion for writing, which is the very reason you, the reader, are reading this right now.

With all that, how do we form a holistic language learning environment that gives us the benefits of learning as an adult with the ease of a baby child?

YOU ARE YOUR BIGGEST JUDGE

You are your biggest judge. Stop being such a tyrannical judge to yourself. I do not care so much whether you are super judgmental of others or overly accepting of the actions of others to a fault, because as it pertains to language learning, the judgment that will affect your progress and desire to continue with a language is your own. As in all things judged, you must be fair to yourself. Often, we treat our pets and our friends better than we treat ourselves. Yet, *our* individual fear of what we *think* others will think of us is the problem, not the reality of others judging us negatively. It is our *perception* of a judgment that strikes us down, not actual judgment external to us from someone else. We judge ourselves with the anticipation that others will judge us. The anxiety and anticipation are a two-sided coin. The anxiety is often worse than what actually ends up happening.

It is commonly known that the number one fear people have is not sharks, not death, not even clowns or dark spaces, or dark spaces with clowns, but public speaking. It all comes down to the anxiety of being judged, which stems from an ancient evolutionary fear of doing something so horrific or embarrassing that you could be cast out into the wilderness to die.

I am a classic introvert. I do enjoy socializing with others, but the more I do, the more I need to recharge. Public speaking has always been a fear of mine but having countless opportunities whether it be a Walmart greeter, giving academic presentations, participating in policy debates, or making a YouTube channel has all helped me to enjoy that anxiety, that anticipation. I get that stage fright, but that is part of the fun, putting myself in the proverbial fire and withstanding it. Because once you're in, the fun begins.

Humans are wired to get anxious engaging in big choices, which include speaking to others. Our distant hunter-gatherer ancestors evolved in an environment where groups of others, perhaps from another tribe could mean war, disease, death, destruction, and chaos. Today, talking to strangers does not often carry those risks, but the germaphobes among us keep that ancestral tradition alive.

TAKE THE RISK TO SPEAK

When practicing your speaking skills with others, know they are not going to judge you negatively. What I've found in my own language learning with French, Czech, and Farsi, and interviewing countless people who have learned other languages, people will not judge you harshly (unless you ask them to). Think on it. They see you are not only trying to do something incredibly challenging, but that you are also making an effort to meet them more than halfway by speaking *their* language. When I used very broken Czech/Slovak here in the States, those I spoke to were elated that I made the effort, and the same goes for my family friends in Czechia. Some places like parts of France and Italy expect you to speak in their language. So long as you try, they are happy even if it sounds like you are being strangled.

Babies don't so harshly judge themselves. As far as I understand, babies cannot blame themselves for trying and neither should you. A baby who judges itself to the point of being paralyzed by anxiety for fear of the world is a baby who never will learn any language, will never attempt a math equation, will never attempt to walk, or will never venture beyond baby food. *See?*

When we first come into the world, it is innate for us to first venture and explore and then learn from the consequences. We try to eat the dryer lint, we attempt to climb up furniture, we get caught almost sticking the fork in the electrical socket. It is better to ask for forgiveness than for permission. Get in the practice of speaking in your native language with strangers to build up confidence, then with your target language when the opportunity presents itself.

Also, consider this: If you are traveling to a foreign country and you need help asking for directions or you are ordering off the menu or reserving a hotel room, the embarrassment you will have is not at all a negative because chances are, you will never see that person ever again. We become embarrassed because there is an implication for a social consequence because we evolved in such small communities where actions are not forgotten. In the modern world, these social consequences are minimized to negligible levels... at least embarrassment. You are your biggest judge, but let that be a force for good. Use that judgment to mentally track where you made mistakes and how you can improve upon them.

You are your biggest judge, so be curious like a baby and babble. The hardest thing a baby does by their own will is stand up and take that first step. When are you going to take yours?

CHAPTER 10

Zipf, Nada, Nothing

THE INVOLVED GET INVOLVED

Those who find *some* success often find a lot of success. Seeing success, or winning once, makes a tremendous task so much easier to complete, making winning again and continuous achievement more likely. This is why it seems like those who do well in something continue to do well in something else. They are able to see the whole project through and focus on that consistent, persistent pursuit. To taste success is a major motivator for many people.

Travelers are hardly satisfied with one amazing experience abroad; the best athletes do not quit after one good game. Success is not a singular instance, but a pattern. As the ancient Chinese philosopher Confucius said, "Success depends upon previous preparation, and without such preparation there is sure to be failure."

It's about the war, not the battle.

American inventor and futurist Ray Kurzweil discussed in his 1999 book *The Age of Spiritual Machines* that evolutionary systems, particularly technological advancements, can be charted as exponential returns—or, "the law of accelerating returns." This can be applied to language when we look at what we know about the rule with many names: Pareto, Zipf, and the 80/20 rules. Here is the principle: To know a few things, perhaps a few difficult things, is to create a fundamental understanding of the language (which makes up a tiny portion of that language), which then propels us forward in easily acquiring the rest.

Master the difficult first 20 percent and the remaining 80 percent will be easy peasy, lemon squeezy. If you are visualizing this as a graph, imagine the horizontal (x) axis is progression of time, and the vertical (y) axis is percentage of language understood. As you go from left to right along time, you begin with just a tiny percentage of your target language understood. This will keep a relatively flat line persisting for some time, only gradually increasing by a few percent. BUT, as soon as you hit a certain point in time the percentage jumps up, and soon the line is no longer a steady slope but a line that skyrockets. Your returns will be exponential. Master the fundamentals, and all else will follow.

This principle applies to so much else in life. When you start a business, chances are you will have minimal returns for months and even years. If what you are selling or providing is something valuable to the customer and you reinvest the profits back into the company, that value will be recognized in time. Assuming you stick with it, chances are you will start experiencing those returns.

What I find absolutely fascinating and enthralling is that at the heart of learning any language is a universal principle that strikes to the core of what it means to be human, beyond just learning a language. Focus on the few important details, and all else will make sense. Focus on the many unimportant details, and the fundamentals will make no sense.

THE MYSTERIOUS PATTERN

The idea of the 80/20 rule has become more pervasive throughout the decades. The origin of the rule as presently articulated comes from the 1999 book *The 80/20 Principle: The Secret to Achieving More with Less* by Richard Koch. I believe the description of the book encapsulates the principle well: "Eighty percent of all our results in business and in life stem from a mere twenty percent of our efforts."#‹

Yes. You read that correctly: Roughly twenty percent of our effort gives us eighty percent of our results, our output, our productivity. Now before, perhaps, you write off this aphorism as another strange self-help guru, business developer, entrepreneurial sham as it sounds, I want to encourage you to consider that the book's author was observing something far beyond our modern grasp of the principle.

The 80/20 principle is a concept, or rather a pattern, that manifests itself in many ways, across cultures and throughout time and thus has many names. Here are a few of its names in its many forms: the Pareto Principle, law of the vital few, Zipf's law, principle of factor sparsity, Matthew Principle, law of accelerating returns. The reason I say it is specifically a *pattern* is because I believe the universe is arranged and continually arranges itself in intelligible patterns. For the same reason the universe has laws of physics and nature, those laws arrange Being into specific patterns such as the Golden Ratio and prime numbers, and the 80/20 principle is just one of these patterns.

PATTERN MANIFEST

Before this turns too quickly into a philosophy book, let's look at where this mathematical pattern appears.

In the late-1800s Italy, the economist Vilfredo Pareto when observing population data noted that roughly 80 percent of the land of Italy was owned by merely 20 percent of the population. Conversely, that meant that 20 percent of the remaining land was owned by roughly 80 percent, or majority of Italians. The principle crops up most often in distribution of economic activities, such as resources, money, or even uneconomic subjects such as arrangement of furniture in a room. Let's go down that rabbit hole.

All who have fundraised or are in that business quickly note that the majority of their funds are raised by a tiny minority of contributors, and vice versa—the majority of donors constitute the minority of total funds. I have heard of this before and can attest to it myself, as the majority of funds raised that made this book possible came from a small percentage of total donors.

To continue, restaurants may make 85 percent of their revenue in 15 percent of the time they are open. The bulk of road traffic happens during only a few hours of the total day, that is to say: rush hour. Twenty percent of peapods in a garden produce roughly 80 percent of peas. In criminology, 80 percent of the crimes are committed by 20 percent of the population. In the environment, 80 percent of pollution is released by 20 percent of factories.

In business, 20 percent of customers are responsible for 80 percent of business conducted. In marketing, 80 percent of sales come from 20 percent of advertisements, and 80 percent of sales come from 20 percent of the sales team. In investing and finance, approximately 80 percent of stock portfolio growth may come from the few 20 percent of the holdings within that portfolio. In customer service, 80 percent of complaints originate from 20 percent of customers.

How about this: If you have a smartphone, you likely have more apps than you need. If you disagree, you'll find it harder to disagree with the fact that the apps we use most often are a small portion of all apps on our phone. You may have fifty apps and only use ten of them frequently. I'd say that's a reasonable assumption. Turn that into a percentage, and you get an 80/20 distribution.

In a different and more ancient way of articulating this pattern, or more accurately the driving force of this pattern, the Gospel of Mark reads, "For to him who has will more be given; and from him who has not, even what he has will be taken away." That is from the Bible, Mark 4:25, 2,000 years ago this principle was deeply understood. And we can observe the pattern in even older, more applicable themes to language acquisition.

RULE OF LEAST EFFORT

Another quite useful and appealing way of wording this ancient pattern is "the principle of least effort." When learning a language, that sounds good doesn't it? I am sure you are up for the challenge to acquiring a language, but why not maximize the benefits with minimal effort necessary?

In communicating and languages more broadly, being able to convey the most amount of information with the least amount of effort is a rule as opposed to an exception. Many languages have inflections which show who or what is being talked about based on the pronunciation and/or spelling of the verb such as the Spanish *camino, I walk* from the verb root *caminar, to walk*. This simplifies how much needs to be said. Another way of simplification is to do what English did centuries ago and drop inflection altogether and use the same verb with a different pronoun: *I walk, you walk, we walk, he/she/it walks*.

There is no better example of simplification than contractions, namely *goodbye*, which is a compressed version of *God Be with You/Ye*. *Adios* and *adieu* in Spanish and French are exactly the same: *a dios vos acomiendo* or *a dieu vous commant* (*I commend you to God*).

All language is inevitably bound by this balancing act of communicating articulately in a pithy manner. To illustrate, when the 1,000 most common words in a language are internalized, most of the language is cut out for you. One thousand strategic words will give you near-comprehensive coverage of words used. That being so, even yet an infinitely smaller 1 percent of that 1,000 can cover the breadth of the lexicon. How so?

Twenty-five percent of *all* the words used in English are *the*, *be, to, of, and, a, in, that, have*, and *I*. Ten words make up 25 percent of what you say. What do I mean by this? In any given book written in modern English, any paragraph spoken, any text typed, any advertisement, magazine, warning label, any conversation falls into this distribution with a narrow margin of error. You can attempt to break out of this, yet this would require heavily concerted effort, which most of any language does not need for everyday application. More than likely, you would fall into a similar distribution with different words. You cannot get far without fundamental vocabulary that connect concepts. It quite literally is the backbone of English, and this principle extends to the foundation of all other languages.

ENTER ZIPF

The principle of least effort was developed and articulated clearly by George Kingsley Zipf in his 1949 work *Human Behavior and the Principle of Least Effort: An Introduction to Human Ecology.*

Not only does he outline minimal effort being a principle of communication as a result of behavioral biology; he claims the distribution infers a ranking of word frequency directly related to percentage or fraction used. What does he mean?

Every single word in any language can be ranked by its usage frequency, such as the prior mentioned *the* in English, which would rank number one. *Be* would be rank two, the word *to* would be rank three, and so on. Let's turn this into an equation.

Wolfram Alpha, the world-famous math problem search engine named after its CEO Stephen Wolfram (mathematician, computer scientist, and theoretical physicist extraordinaire), states:

> *"Zipf's law states that in a corpus of a language, the frequency of a word is inversely proportional to its rank in the global list of words after sorting by decreasing frequency." (Wolfram, 2021)*

You can place the ranking of the word's frequency as a denominator in a fraction under "1," and that is how frequent the word is in use relative to the most used word in that language. Simply put, one over its rank. For instance, if we take the second most frequent word in English, that being the word *be*, we can say that *be* occurs half as often in English as *the*. Extrapolate this and the third rank is one-third as often, the fourth is one-fourth as often, etc. Likewise, we can take the word *philosopher* which is the 5,208th most common word and we then know it is used 1/5,208th as common as *the*.

This strange relationship typifies the importance of focusing on the critical vocabulary, not because the other words and phrases are not important but because you will almost never use them. If you need to know obscure words, often knowing those common ones will be far more than enough of a tool to inquire and acquire specific language.

This principle extends not only to entire languages, but to any sizable collection of words such as a book, an article, a TV show, or social media profile. There are even written languages undecipherable to modern man that, despite being unknown, still have word frequency that follows this Zipfy pattern.

The rule when applied to language states that 20 percent of words are used 80 percent of the time and the remaining 80 percent of words are only used 20 percent of the time. Thus, to learn most of the functional vocabulary used in a language, the learner need only memorize the meaning, usage, context, and variability of that small set of vocab. Depending on who I asked, interviewed, or researched, different numbers range from 200, 400, 500, 1,000, and 4,000 words.

HOW 80/20 APPLIES TO LANGUAGE LEARNING

When you break down all the aspects of learning a language—the grammar, the vocabulary, the pronunciation, the spelling, the word order, etc.—you will find, depending wholly on which language you are learning, that learning some of these equally integral portions will have greater impact on your speaking ability. For instance, if you determine that the three most important aspects you will focus on to learn your target language are grammar, vocabulary, and conversation, and you spend equal time each, you will quickly discover that of those three, some will have greater impact on the others.

Let's say you pour 80 percent of your efforts into grammar. A noble pursuit, not for the faint of heart. What will become apparent when you then go into conversation with native speakers is that you will probably struggle to navigate conversations because you lack a strong vocabulary and collection of important phrases. Conversation and listening is the best way to refine actual usage, but if you go into the conversation not having any vocabulary or know-how of how to ask for clarification or specificity, grammar is useless.

Don't get me wrong, grammar is crucial for full immersion and avoiding miscommunication, but slightly erroneous grammar in most languages can still be understood by native speakers. For instance, phrases like "He like sport" or "Can I has cheeseburger?" are perfectly intelligible despite being wrong.

As thoroughly covered, the ten most common words in English make up 25 percent of all words used. Just as one-third of your life will be spent sleeping, one-fourth of words you speak or hear fall into a narrow boundary. Isn't that so counterintuitive to how we think about language? Memorizing endless lists of nouns, verbs, and adjectives compared to understanding the "essentials."

Why these common words are used so frequently depends on a variety of factors, such as explaining relationships between different things (*of, and, to, in*...) or specifying which thing you are talking about (*that, the*), talking about the person behind your life (*I*), and verbs, action words to illustrate what you *are* and what your condition *is* and what you possess (*be, have*).

Language, simply put, is a way to describe the human condition in a way it can be relayed to other people and understood. The distribution of word frequency arises naturally, but its natural cause arises from a balance between wanting to communicate a message in a way that strikes a balance between the minimal amount of explanation on our side as possible and, with that, of providing as much detail as possible.

LANGUAGE THAT PAINTS THE WORLD

To go on a well-meaning tangent, it is so extraordinarily amazing what the purpose of language is when we dive deep down into it. Here we are, living in our own minds, thinking our own thoughts without anyone else being able to see in and read our minds. Sometime many years ago, our ancestors began using sounds from our throat and mouth to paint an invisible picture with sound waves, which is then received in the ears and interpreted by the brain. Our vocal cords are the paint brush, the breathable air is our canvas, and our ears are our eyes (say that ten times quickly) that see what has been made manifest that, moments ago, did not exist.

We use the same or similar words often because we live in families, cultures, and societies all bound by consistent and reoccurring themes. These all in turn reflect the universal human condition. We speak so others can understand us and our experiences and perspectives, but we write so we might carry our message beyond the present to be shared with someone in the future.

The odd part of this is that we often write, not for the same reason we speak (to be understood by others), but so our future self can understand what the present is recording onto paper or into text. Language's original purpose was to communicate with others, with the invention of writing transforming into a way to communicate with ourselves to understand more thoroughly what we have experienced or heard. We take notes in class to better understand concepts, or we create grocery lists, Post-it notes, and to-do lists to better order our life, turning written word into an extension of memory. We write to remember, but also so we do not have to remember.

This is precisely what is meant by the ancient Greek concept of *pharmakon*. The word *pharmakon* literally means "drug." It is used in the context that a drug or medicine aids human healing but often at the expense of health elsewhere in the body such as innumerable side effects and dependency (Pageau, 2021). This concept is often applied to technology: With every innovation, we are relieved of some burden, but a new dependency and necessity is created with the abolition of another.

WRITING IN THE TRANSCENDENT

Right here, with writing, we have uncovered something uniquely human, which is our ability to contend with the future. Whether consciously understood or not, humans in action at least understand there is a future, and our future self is not the same as our present or past self—not the same sometimes to the extent that our present and future self are as different as you reading this book and me, the person writing this book. I know for a fact that the person I was when I wrote down the first few sentences that would turn into the first piece of content for this book is not the same person writing this paragraph, and will definitely not be the same person when this is published and in your hands, reading this very line.

In fact, unless there is some massive Orwellian book burning, this book will exist throughout my life and beyond it. That's the beauty of history; it often is thought to begin with the advent of writing because we are able to understand what the ancients jotted down, whether it was for us or not—most often not. This book is not primarily intended to be a history book, but in the future, it could be read to understand who I was, but more importantly, the time I lived in. It is an odd and emotionally provoking thought to think that you, the reader, may be reading this just months after publication, or a few years, or even decades if not hundreds of years later. I couldn't write a book about language without at least entertaining this idea. Discussing and contemplating philosophy is one of my greatest passions, and the philosophy of language is by no means sparse.

HOW MANY WORDS DO YOU NEED TO KNOW TO BE FLUENT IN YOUR LANGUAGE?

Back to word ranking. You can attempt to universally rank level of language fluency based on a certain number of words to some avail. If fluency is what you want, make that your goal. However, note that reaching the different benchmarks of language learning have different implications. By shooting for at least conversational level, you will be able to move in any direction for your needs. FluentU is a treasure trove of language blogs, list articles, and tips, techniques, and resources to help learn languages to fluency (Gibbons, 2021). On their website they create tiers for the levels of fluency:

- Functional Beginner: 250–500 words
- Conversational: 1,000–3,000 words
- Advanced: 4,000–10,000 words
- Fluent: 10,000+ words
- Native: 10,000–30,000+ words

Quite frankly, I think this is a pretty good generalization or summary of what is needed for each level. I have seen these tiers play out in my own language learning. When I was learning Czech, I, by no means, had the goal of becoming fluent; I wished to grasp enough to understand the very basics when I would be gabbing with my Czech friend and visiting her family. With Czech, I primarily used Duolingo and some flash cards to acquire the bare bones basics. This roughly included 200 words, several dozen short phrases, mostly questions, and cultural incites like toasts.

TOAST OR BE TOAST
Learning to toast should always be on the top of your list as it helps to strengthen new bonds and show your desire for the well-being of others, as the word or phrase used in many languages for toasting often means "to good health," "to your health," or simply "health." In Afrikaans you say *Gesondheid*, in French we say *Santé!* or *À votre santé*, *Skål* in Swedish, in Yiddish *Sei gesund*, *iechyd da* in Welsh, *Egészségedre* in Hungarian, and *Å'kålè ma'luna* in Hawai'ian. In Czechia when I would use *Na Zdravi* when a new glass of alcohol was poured out, I was met with ear-to-ear smiles and cheers. I guess it Czeched out.

In Czech I knew my numbers, simple question phrases, some random nouns and adjectives and some useful phrases like "Jak se jmenuješ?" (What is your name?), some phrases quite odd "Mám rád maso" (I like meat), some good for driving... I suppose: "Nepodařilo se mu vzdát" (He failed to yield). And others are just downright rude: "Odejít od ní k mladší ženě" (Leave her for a younger woman).

Moving to conversational, I believe this is the best position to be in as a beginner, because it is a reasonable goal that is absolutely attainable in a short amount of time. It also gives you a lot of room to maneuver. I believe this is where I stand with Spanish, even though it has been over a year since I have actively practiced with it on a regular basis. I can have basic conversations, ask the important questions, and understand a summary of what is being said.

Even though I am closer to fluency in French than Spanish, I can understand Spanish words and phrases more often because the pronunciation system is more straightforward and limited than the complex rules of French phonetics. The sounds used commonly in Spanish are more similar to English than those found in French.

Getting yourself to a conversational level can take about three months of moderate practice every day, and even in a month or less with intensive everyday practice with large exposure to the language. To get to this level in Spanish, I spent nearly five years of elementary school learning the numbers, basic questions, and pronunciations. Two semesters of college Spanish helped me a lot with sentence structure, general grammar, conjugations, speech practice, and subject-specific language.

Words are concepts. Think about the number of concepts you need to know in a particular school subject and subsequent chapters to be able to navigate a conversation on that subject and pass the test. Of course, this is not a direct comparison, but the principle remains the same. Entertain me: In a typical chapter of high school science or social studies, you might have roughly twenty to thirty terms. Say you are learning about plant cells in a biology class. You'll cover concepts like the *cell wall*, the *cell membrane*, the *cytoplasm*, *Golgi bodies*, *chloroplast*, *vacuoles*, the *nucleus*, and you cannot forget the *endoplasmic reticulum*... just to name a few.

You learn what each concept means, what they are, what they do, what their relationship is with the other terms, and eventually you will build on this information when you go into the following chapters talking about plants as a whole. How we learn language, *concepts*, in specific subjects is not just an allegory for learning language; this *is* learning language. To learn a little is better than to know nothing, and those few words give you room to pivot. Ask yourself: What few words, concepts, and phrases do I need to know to be able to communicate in a variety of topics?

WHAT YOU RESIST PERSISTS

> "What you resist not only persists, but will grow in size."

—CARL JUNG, SWISS DEPTH PSYCHOLOGIST

Let's go back to Zipf and the 80/20 principle, briefly. Often when foreign language is taught in schools and independently, teachers and students focus on vocabulary that is a selection of the few hundred or thousand most common words along with random word sets such as zoo animals, obscure foods, or subject specific.

However, because the absolute essential words and phrases are not focused on at the very beginning, novice speakers often struggle to communicate outside of specific scenarios, thus how much they can learn is stifled. It is like giving a handyman a wrench to drive nails: Yes, a wrench can beat nails into wood, but it is going to be sloppy, ineffective, a time sync with slow or little to no return.

We can resist learning the heart of a language, but we will inevitably be forced to confront it via context. We are inevitably defined by what it is we oppose and avoid, by actively (or unwittingly) creating opposition we are building a foundation of resistance upon that which is opposed. That sounds a bit symbolic and metaphorical, but symbolism is the best way to understand this concept.

It is best to use context standing in the symbolic core of a language, bringing in the rest of the language from the shrinking margins than it is to know the scarcely used margins of a language to acquire the core. Metaphorically, it is the equivalent to using a fish in your hand to catch a boat and a net instead of using a boat and a net to catch a fish. Start from the core and work your way out.

ZIPFINESS SHOWS ENGLISH ORIGINS

English is a Germanic language *because* the set of words used most often are almost entirely Germanic. Of the fifty most commonly used words in English, only one is of non-Germanic origin. That word is "use" which comes from Latin via French and ranks in the forties. Despite there being thousands of words in English from French and from Latin through French, or just plain old Latin, as well as plenty of other Romance roots, the most commonly used words are Germanic.

The irony is that if you tally the number of Germanic words compared to Romantic words in the English language, thousands more have Latin roots than Germanic ones. Approximately 26 percent of English words have a Germanic origin (Old English, Middle English, Dutch, Old Norse), and far more come from Romance languages. Roughly 29 percent of English vocab comes from Latin and 29 percent comes from French including Anglo-Norman, for a grand total of 58 percent from Romance origins. Yet, roughly 50 to 80 percent of the words used in any given sentence are made up of the one hundred most commonly used words in English, and a vast majority of those common words have Germanic origins.

This is a testament to the origins of English. Old English, the language of Alfred the Great, Saint Bede the Venerable, and used in literary classics of *Beowulf*, *The Dream of the Rood*, *The Anglo-Saxon Chronicle*, *The Seafarer*, and *The Wanderer* [1] was a language distinct from modern English in that it is unintelligible to modern ears. To illustrate, here is a portion of the *Lord's Prayer* in Old, Middle, and Modern English:

OLD ENGLISH

Fæder ure þu þe eart on heofonum; Si þin nama gehalgod to becume þin gewurþe ðin willa on eorðan swa swa on heofonum.

MIDDLE ENGLISH

Oure fadir that in heuenes, halewid be thi name; thi kyngdoom come to; be thi wille don, in erthe as in heuene.

MODERN ENGLISH (LITERAL TRANSLATION FROM OLD ENGLISH)

Father our thou that in heavens be thy name hallowed come thy kingdom be-done thy will on earth as in heavens.

MODERN ENGLISH

Our Father who art in Heaven hallowed be thy name; thy kingdom come, thy will be done, on Earth as it is in Heaven. (Living Hour, 2021)

The most common words you use in a day and everyone who speaks English in a day are not that interesting. In fact, they are more functional words than anything. With that said, what is the most commonly used word in the entire English language? The… yes. It's *the*. It makes sense if you ponder on it. Now you're definitely going to have a hard time not noticing the number of times *the* is used, particularly in the book that is focused on *the* idea of learning *the* language of your dreams.

I'll leave you with this:

"There are approximately 1,010,300 words in the English language, but I could never string enough words together to properly explain how much I want to hit you with a chair."
—ALEXANDER HAMILTON TO THOMAS JEFFERSON

Perhaps our Founding Fathers should have tried the Zipf method.

This chapter was heavily inspired by the god of educational and nerdy YouTube, Michael Stevens in his video "The Zipf Mystery." Michael is the producer of VSauce and co-host of *Brain Candy Live* with Adam Savage. In 2017, I had the opportunity to watch them live. I'll never forget how short Michael is.

TAKEAWAYS

1. The involved get involved and success often finds those who have had success before. In your language journey, define your big picture so that you can "win the war." Uncover what are the basics of your target language so you can leverage those basics for long-term growth.

2. Constantly familiarize yourself with the 100, 200, 500, and 1,000 most used words and phrases and how they relate to each other so that you have a core to pivot in any direction to and from.

3. Internalize the absolute basics of a language at the very beginning of your journey to the point those basics become nearly or as second nature as your primary language. How to ask basic questions like *what, when, who,*

where, what is this, why, and *how much* need to become deep-seated.

4. Memorizing cultural phrases and toasts is a great way to reciprocate hospitality, generosity, and fellowship. Wishing someone good health, expressing gratitude, or greeting someone in their own tongue is always a show of good faith and is more often than not met with kindness beyond customary politeness in return.

5. Zipf's Law and the 80/20 principle teach us that communication is about conciseness and precision: efficiency by all means. Most language used is an extremely small percentage of total vocabulary. Do not overcomplicate where complexity is not required in a given language.

6. Never start learning a language by practicing uncommon parts of a language. Initially practice what is common to the language, especially the vocabulary and rules that are used in nearly all contexts.

7. English is the perfect case study of Zipf's Law, as the majority of English words are non-Germanic, yet the majority of words in a given sentence are of Germanic origin.

FOOTNOTE:

[1] *The Wanderer* is an elegy originally written in Old English by an unknown author. It is a poem told by the subject of the prose *eardstapa* (Earth stepper/wanderer) who recounts better times as a member of his lord's war band, tells of his present exile over a cold terrain, and meditates on the virtues of fortitude and his own faith in God. The narrator is a survivor of a battle that killed his lord, friends, kinsmen, and displaced him from home. I note this short epic poem, only 115 lines, because it was one of several texts that the

Medievalist scholar, J.R.R. Tolkien translated himself and took as major inspiration for his famous works of *The Hobbit* and *The Lord of The Rings*, which have undeniably shaken the West to its core both as entertainment, philosophy, religious expression, and literature.

CHAPTER 11

Door-Wedging

ONE TRIP TO CARRY THEM ALL

Have you ever been unloading a car full of groceries into your house, taking out the trash, or perhaps carrying something heavy in and out of a building? Having to open and reopen the door because there is either no one to hold the door or the door automatically shuts? We've all been there. We put a loaded grocery bag on every finger, with five more slid up both of our arms, to get to the door to realize it's locked, or it's shut and your fingers are too busy flexing with what little energy remains for you to turn the door knob.

What would make the single trip we are attempting from the car with all the groceries to the house so much easier is if the door stayed open! How about a *door wedge*? You know that piece of rather archaic technology that you jam under the open door so it remains ajar? You can buy one, you can carve one from wood, you could use a folded newspaper, a brick, whatever! Just something to hold the damn thing open.

Okay, Max. Why are we talking about doorjambs? Short answer: because doorjambs are a good tool to open our minds and keep them open, so we can learn language faster, more effectively, and seamlessly. No, I am not suggesting you take a door-wedge and hammer it into your head. In fact, I highly urge you to not let this book cause you to do anything of the sort.

Rather, a door wedge is a Zipfy tool. It's a metaphorical tool to help us maximize our language input in conjunction with Zipf's Law/Pareto coefficient/the 80/20 rule. It's a tool, or tool kit, of language "must-haves" and basics in order to maximize all the rest of acquiring a target language. More specifically, a door wedge is the 20 percent (often times less) in the 80/20 rule.

DOOR WEDGING

In the last chapter, I went into detail on the Zipfy phenomena. I mentioned that it can and should be used as a basis to language acquisition by applying it to vocabulary use, but how else can it be used? Door wedge is a noun, a *thing*, but let's turn it into an *action*, a verb.

Door wedging. When beginning the language acquisition process, we need to start door wedging as soon as possible.

A mistake in learning a language is to focus on the things that will not have as great of an impact early on. Doubling down on grammar will only yield a knowledge of the rules of a language without anything to apply the rules to. When speaking a foreign language, it is far more important to get out the words you are trying to say in the wrong order or form than it is to only be able to construct perfect tiny little nondescript sentences that have masterful grammar. Have some humility. You want to be able to communicate ideas and intentions as soon as possible. The grammar will naturally come through listening and correction.

With that said, we know of one great way to door wedge: memorize the most used words, anywhere from the 300 to 1,000 most common. I also mentioned you should use flash cards to help with memorization. That seems antiquated, doesn't it? Old fashioned, pre-internet, archaic, but highly effective when you use a special flash card method. You thought you knew everything when it came to writing on the front and back of notecards, didn't you? Let's go into it.

FLASHCARDS—MEANINGFUL ASSOCIATION

Human memory is often compared to a library or video log, where our past is recorded to accuracy. However, our memory is often inaccurate, vague for most of the happenings of the day, and abstract. Memory is not as simple as hitting the record button and playing back what we saw and heard to accuracy. Why?

Memory cuts corners and memories can even change because the purpose of memory is to learn from the past to carve out a better future. Turning points, brushes with death, wise words from an elder, association with previous events, celebration, and periods of mourning are crucial to remember to repeat successes, avoid tragedy, and maneuver through chaos, disease, and death when they inevitably strike. Things that are not important or do not fall into a pattern most conducive to remembering are simply not recorded as well or at all.

Flashcards can help. Obviously. To repeatedly expose yourself to the same concept will grow your familiarity with it. However, what flash cards often lack are meaningful association and spaced repetition.

Meaningful association is when we are presented with a word and can immediately associate it with a concept, word, or person we already know. Jim Kwik, the brain coach with a fantastically trained memory, uses meaningful association to remember people's names. Not just a person or two, but he can (and you can) memorize dozens of names as he hears them. How? When someone tells him their name, he immediately makes an association in his mind. Jack? Jack and the Beanstalk. Ruthie? Ruthie Toothie. Leonard? Leonard Nemoy. Steve? Steve doesn't deceive. Kai? Kai, nice to meet you. It can be a rhyme, a reference to someone else with that name, what they are wearing, or something about their personality. Anything. The same goes for words.

When you are going through your deck of cards, visualize the action or thing. If it is a connecting word like *like, as, to, from, in*, make some association even if it is thinking of an example phrase where it is used. For example, the French word *dans* means *in*. Visualize a person waving from *in* the house. *Dans la maison. Dans une voiture. J'étais dans le magasin.*

FLASHCARDS—SPACED REPETITION

Now don't use just any old flashcard decks. Again, flashcards seem to have some obvious utility as many online sites such as Quizlet and Anki have decks you can make and use from other people about any topic. Nevertheless, the app Anki uses a research-backed memorization technique called spaced repetition. If you are a law or medical student, I guarantee you have run across this term and perhaps you use it.

When using a typical flashcard deck, you might place the cards you get correct in one pile that you do not touch again for that session. The ones you get wrong you place in a second pile to repeat over and over again until you start getting them correct. Good! But not good enough. This method does not maximize memorization potential. Over time, this will end up costing you a lot of time.

So, what is spaced repetition? E-student.org puts it guilelessly:

Spaced repetition is a memory technique that involves reviewing and recalling information at optimal spacing intervals until the information is learned at a sufficient level. (Tamm, 2021)

Optimal spacing between the same cards reviewed over again keeps the material fresh in the brain so you can use active recall as opposed to having to expend extensive energy recalling something locked away in the vaults of the mind or uselessly repeating words so fresh in your memory they do not need to be recalled. It also does not repeat the same word over consecutively. It utilizes the "theory of disuse," which means we tend to memorize something more strongly when we forget about it partially but it is reviewed before it is entirely forgotten. It is a sweet spot. For a visual representation, search for the "Ebbinghaus Forgetting Curve" (Shrestha, 2017).

Spaced repetition is complex, which is why most people who practice with the method use apps, programs, and websites that already have it implemented via algorithm. Doing it with physical cards is not advisable. Use programs such as Anki and SuperMemo. This method is so effective and widespread, formerly unhelpful apps such as Duolingo have implemented their own spaced repetition algorithms which have exceedingly improved their effectiveness and educational value.

But what, other than vocabulary, should we know off the bat?

Here are a few: alphabet/writing system, common question phrases, common phrases, how to form a question, basic cultural concepts.

I outline these below.

WRITING SYSTEM—LEARN TO READ AND WRITE THE SCRIPT

Fortunately for anglophones and many European language speakers, most languages have a Latin form of a writing system even if the language is not primarily in a Latin script

(Latin script, meaning the writing system/alphabet derives from Latin as opposed to a writing system like Russian Cyrillic, which is based off the Greek alphabet).

Before you start taking classes or teaching yourself a language, do a little bit of research to see a language's orthography, that is, how it is written and what script they use.

Do they use an alphabet [1] where one character/letter represents one sound?

Aa Bb Cc Dd Ef Gg

Do they use a syllabary where one character represents one syllable?

Bo Bee Ba Boo Bew Bi Beh

Do they use an abjad (discussed in the introduction)?

Do they use glyphs or pictograms where the character/symbol represents an idea and not simply a sound like Chinese or Egyptian hieroglyphics?

Do not rely on the English Latin script, as you will find that native speakers have different pronunciations associated with letters you thought you were familiar with. Many languages have unique sounds that English does not have at all. On top of that, English uses the same letters for different sounds. For example, the L in "cool" is a different sound from the L in "like." These hidden features can sabotage us if we use our own writing system as a crutch.

Furthermore, even for French with a script remarkably similar to English, pronunciation is far different! Take the English word "pain" and the French word "pain." One hurts; the other is quite tasty.

Mastering the way a language is written and the way a language sounds from the beginning will save you heaps of energy. If you do not prioritize this from the beginning, you will expend copious amounts of time distracted from your studies simply to relearn what should have been learned from square one.

More on this further on in the pronunciation section.

HOW TO FORM QUESTIONS

"The important thing is not to stop questioning. Curiosity has its own reason for existence."

—ALBERT EINSTEIN (1955).

Beyond absorbing the context of our surroundings as will be discussed in the chapter "Embracing the Inner Child," the way we learn is by being curious, and the way we manifest that curiosity is by asking questions. You will not get far in any language without the ability to ask questions.

Asking questions is the means by which you learn the rest of the language.

If you are stuck with an aspect of your language, knowing how to ask questions will help you to look up resources that can help you. A search query in your target language will give better results than if you typed it in English.

Every language is unique in how it forms questions. Question words such as "who, what, when, where, how, how much, how many, why, that, and which" are crucial. English is rather versatile in regards to where you put these words in the sentence. "Where are we going?" "We are going where now?" Other languages demand you put them at the beginning or another specific part of the sentence. Some languages only require a statement to add a question mark, whereas others require complete restructuring.

Memorize the basic question words and phrases, where they go in the sentence, and teach yourself how to turn a statement into a question and vice versa. This practice of going back and forth between question and statement will not only help you form statements and questions, but also help you understand basic grammar and the versatility (or lack thereof) of the language.

Don't stop asking questions!

BASIC CULTURAL CONCEPTS

In Iranian culture there is a concept called taarof (تعارف). Taarof is a form of civility or etiquette that helps bring about social balance in a culture that can be extremely hierarchical. It has a functional purpose, as you can see, but it also acts as a sort of ritual politeness.

If you were to go to Iran and you were about to pay your taxi driver, when you hand him the money, he may politely decline payment. For me, a native Ohioan, I would be off put and, depending on the situation, heed his advice. But to the unknowing foreigner, his polite decline is part of the cultural ritual of taarof. This custom would then have you insist on paying him, to which he may decline, but surely, by a third insistence he will kindly accept. Shopkeepers and restaurant owners may also say to you, "Be my guest," but that doesn't mean you're getting that meal for free. It is a form of hospitality for Iranians to show genuine intentions through a common politeness, as contradictory as that may seem to the unaccustomed.

Taarof also extends to invitations you receive, where you are expected to decline at least twice, and if you can truly come to what you are invited to, you may accept on the third. It kind of sounds like that annoying couple from high school who both would refuse to hang up after being on the phone for any length of time. "You hang up," "No you hang up," "No! you hang up!" However, taarof is far more admirable. This custom extends to all echelons of Iranian culture, so failure to know this one minuscule-seeming custom will dictate your interactions with everyone you would encounter where Iranian custom is being practiced.

It is not enough to know how to speak, read, write, or hear a language; it is critical to know how all of that may be used practically.

Language is a facet of culture, and both help form and influence each other in a never-ending cycle as thoroughly discussed in the chapter "Foundation of Linguistics." Cultural attitudes, characteristics, traditions, norms, habits, and customs will show up in how a language functionally works. This is why it is extremely helpful to do a quick read-up on the culture that uses your language, even down to the dialect.

If you are learning American English as opposed to UK English, it's best to read up on American culture, a snippet of America's history. If you are learning Egyptian Arabic, it would be helpful to know a bit about modern Egyptian history and cultural practices. Cantonese? Better study up on Guangzhou Chinese culture.

That seems like a lot, but as with Taarof, it can be as simple as one concept. It doesn't have to be extensive, perhaps one or two articles on customs or cultural concepts. Then you will have a much better understanding of the culture, but also the language. Better yet, if you know someone from a particular culture, ask them!

If you are going to a country during one of their holidays or cultural festivals, it would behoove you to do some research on that specific holiday. Going to Serbia over Orthodox Christmas may be as simple as learning relevant phrases like "Srećan Božić!" (Merry Christmas). Or, if you are in Iran, Afghanistan, or Tajikistan over the Persian new year, "Nowruz mubarak!" would bring plenty of smiles.

I am no cultural relativist; it goes against every fiber of my stubbornly moralist being. Nevertheless, an ancient Greek historian named Herodotus who was—by coincidence—born in the Persian Empire (Persian = Iranian), famously said "custom is king." An attitude I find useful when abroad.

PRELIMINARY TAKEAWAYS

1. Do brief, preliminary research on the culture that created your language.
2. Pick out and attempt to understand two to five cultural concepts.
3. Learn basic phrases related to relevant cultural events (holidays, weddings, funerals, festivals).

PRONUNCIATION

When I was learning Farsi, I had a lot of trouble finding reliable online resources for beginners beyond lists of basic phrases and suspect apps. So, what I did was search for an introductory textbook to the language. I intended to find a textbook that you might find in a language class, but I found something even better. I uncovered an interactive workbook called *Farsi (Persian) For Beginners* by Saeid Atoofi, PhD.

It was quite different from the typical language textbook or guidebook. For example, in the first chapter I learned a few basic phrases, a slew of key words, four letters transcribed into the Farsi-Arabic alphabet, writing practice, a key cultural concept, and a guide to basic pronunciation. A perfect balance of academic literacy and practical cultural fluency.

With that same Farsi book came an accompanying CD with pronunciation guides and example conversations that you first listen to, then you follow along in the book. (It's so important to be able to hear how a language sounds naturally! I cannot stress this enough.) Each chapter was put in simple terms and had the student do a variety of small tasks, slowly introducing different aspects of the language.

This book was amazing overall. However, it needs to be said that it would not be nearly as practical, if it did not come with the CD, and thus, the listening portion. When we think of pronunciation, we often think of reading text aloud, getting in practice of speaking it. Nevertheless, this is not the best way to form pronunciation. As it comes down to most language learning, comprehensive input via listening is the best way to learn pronunciation. By listening to how the language is spoken, picking up on subtle differences, and seeing how sounds can change, our minds become adapted to the "pronunciation software," making it much easier to then try it ourselves.

Never use a textbook to learn how to pronounce something. Yes, you probably will be able to get a good approximation of the sound, and maybe even be 100 percent correct. But compared to listening, a textbook is only giving you half the advantage. With listening, not only do you have a good understanding of the pronunciation to practice from, but you're also getting a more comprehensive understanding of other aspects of a language beyond pronunciation—such as sentence structure, cadence, tone, variation, etc. A textbook is for learning about a language, not speaking one.

READING RAMBO

Once you establish a good groundwork for learning a language by understanding the essential but basic cultural concepts and the most common vocab, phrases, and questions, use all that knowledge and turn it into applied knowledge, i.e., wisdom. Leverage what you have, like that door wedge, to unlock a whole new wave of content.

How? Well, how do you learn vocabulary in your native language, let's say English as a teen and adult? Or really any age past understanding basic language skills? READ! I find that the best, most obvious wisdom is the most often overlooked and thus taken for granted, so don't over complicate it. You may have had a teacher or parent tell you, "Reading is the best way to boost vocabulary." I believe it is! Reading, or input in general, is how you take what you know and extrapolate it out to what you don't know, using context to fill in the gaps.

This does not mean you need to pick up a book. Rather, expose your eyes to reading in your target language as much as possible. If you are not a time traveler from the past, you are probably reading this entrenched in an age where smartphones or some other technology has consumed the human race. If you have a smartphone, switch your phone over from English to your target language. If you are pretty accustomed to your phone, you will know how to use it through muscle memory. You will understand what a lot of messages and buttons say without knowing the language. Over the course of weeks and months, you will have amassed a whole new set of vocabulary by passively reading short blurbs in another language.

If you are on social media, follow hashtags and accounts that pertain to your target language and culture. For me, I followed hashtags like #citation, which is French for "quotes." Look up famous people, YouTubers, music artists, athletes, gamers who are from that culture. Chances are that their social media accounts are in their native language. This is great for exposure to the language, but also practical slang, phrases, and generally understanding the culture and humor of that culture. Humor (or lack thereof) is crucial in understanding a culture, and that shows in language. British humor varies from American humor, and American humor is worlds apart from Chinese or Russian humor.

If you want to become fluent, and if you want to speed up the process, become a Reading Rambo. Sitting down to read books is not for everyone, but if you can, desire to, or are willing to, I cannot recommend it enough. Even though you are not hearing the language being spoken to you and you may be missing out on pronunciation keys, the very act of looking at a book and reading line by line, word for word, you are internalizing the structure and logic of the language and your brain is subconsciously putting the pieces together for the words you don't understand.

Better yet, pronounce what you are reading out loud and what is in your head, but make sure you have a good understanding of the pronunciation system (also known as the phonics).

If there are words or phrases that are truly beyond you, write them down, and move on to see if the following sentences can't piece together what is going on. Context clues will at least give you hints, even if not exact definitions. The more you read, the more you will see this word, and the wider exposure you have to the language, culturally specific idioms and phrases will crop up in due time.

I have been using the short book *L'Étranger* (*The Foreigner*) by Albert Camus to expose myself to French in context. This book is especially useful as Albert Camus is a famous French philosopher and writer in and out of France and the

French-speaking world and has greatly influenced French culture. This gives me an inlet to the modern language and culture.

If you were learning Ancient Greek, the *Iliad* and *Odyssey*, the Bible, or *Oedipus Rex* would be difficult books, but great for the same reason *The Foreigner* is, establishing the culture and the practical use of French. If you were learning Japanese, perhaps the works by Kōbō Abe and Yukio Mishima.

If you are looking for a less daunting task and you do not have previous experience with learning a foreign language, search online or at libraries for "readers." Readers are short books designed to help language learners with the fundamentals of a language. Readers can be blatantly called "readers," or you could pick them up in the form of children's books or young adult novels. Of these, you will find no shortage.

Even try searching up books or stories you are familiar with. Your knowledge of the context will make it far easier to understand what is being said, how it is being said, and why it is structured in such a way. It's like a cheat code without putting you at a disadvantage. This same principle applies to other forms of media. Watch your favorite movie in Russian if you know it by heart in English.

MEDIA RARE

You don't have to know a language to use media in that language. In fact, most people who speak English are illiterate to most media types out there in English. Not because we English speakers are dumb but because so much content is out there it would be impossible to consume even a fraction of one percent of all news, music, TV, video games, radio, blog posts, forums, live streams, and podcast content in our lifetime or all of our lifetimes. On top of that, many forms of media have a learning curve. We barely understand the media we are bombarded with so there shouldn't be anything stopping you from tuning into media in another language.

TAKEAWAYS

1. Door wedges are tools to make language acquisition exponential: Learn the critical basics in each area of a language through reading, listening, and spaced repetition to allow for less important knowledge to be freely learned.

2. Identify what writing and pronunciation systems are used in your target language; knowing what sounds are the same and different from your native language is crucial for communication; mastering the script and diction early on will save you the time and effort of having to continually re-learn later on.

3. Memorize basic questions and learn how to form questions; questions are the means by which you will acquire advanced knowledge specific to your needs early on. The more questions you ask from the outset, the less you will be taken off guard at critical junctures.

4. Every language is nested within the culture it emerged from and helped create, be cognizant of this by endeavoring to understand cultural concepts such as customs, how to address different people, figures of speech, role of religion, sports, and colloquial icons.

5. Listen to real conversations as this approach will show you how the language is pronounced, but also how these

can change when the speaker wants to convey a particular tone, attitude, or place emphasis on a certain topic. Think of how melodic conversations are with family and close friends, this exists in other cultures and in diverse ways.

6. Find simple books in your target language even if you do not fully understand what is being said. Books are condensed forms of language, and reading will give you a wide variety of context to operate with.

7. Picking popular books within a language will help you understand the language, the context of the culture, and also what is contributing to the culture and language. Older books can help establish understanding on cultural mindsets, origins, and principles where newer reads can help you understand popular language and foresight of a culture's course.

FOOTNOTE:

[1] The word "alphabet" comes from the name of the first two letters of the Greek Alphabet which were "alpha" and "beta." Likewise, an abjad which is entirely (or mostly) consonants comes from the first four letters of the Arabic alphabet/abjad which is a, b, j, and d.

CHAPTER 12

Inputting-Output

———

LISTEN TO THIS

In the early stages of writing this book, I did not write at all. In fact, most of the first few months of the authoring process was strategy and preparation. No writing. Rather, I looked into my network and asked droves of people about the topic of language acquisition, how to learn a language, and language education in the States. I interviewed friends, family members, multilinguals, international students, teachers, linguists, and professionals in their respective fields, language related or not. I wanted to gather as much information to pinpoint the trends, the frustrations, the success stories, and the adventures so many people undertake.

I *listened* to the input before I acted out what I thought I already knew. Turns out, I learned a lot. So, my advice to you? *Listen.*

In an early conversation with my friend Emily Ghazoul, she hit on a massively important point:

"I'm the type that can read Spanish pretty well. I can listen to it, and I pretty much know what's going on. But when it comes to me actually speaking it, I get shy with my accent, or I don't know how to construct certain words or conjugate certain words. I even saw when I was in Italy for a study abroad, even the May-mester, that one month, I came out really understanding a lot of conversation and really starting to kind of put together my own sentences in just a short amount of time just because of the immersion."

Immersion. Therein lies a secret to be told. The key to learning a language to fluency (and fast) lies in that word "immersion," and I think we all know this with how popular study abroad or foreign exchange programs have become. To immerse oneself in the culture, and thereby the language, is the key—but this key derives from a more fundamental principle. You've come this far so I might as well tell you what it is: input. That's it! Plain and simple. Comprehensible input.

Okay, Max. But what the heck does that mean? What is comprehensible input?

COMPREHENSIBLE INPUT
The second language education scholar Stephen Krashen is well known within linguistics for pushing the idea of *comprehensible input*. In one of his lectures, he raised his hand and pointed to it, saying:

"Das ist meine Hand. Fristenzidast hand?"

I have a feeling you understood what he is attempting to say to you. He went on to explain:

"In my opinion, we all acquire language the same way. We acquire language in one way and one way only, when we understand messages, or when we understand what we read. We call this comprehensible input."

He goes on:

"We've tried everything else. We tried grammar teaching drills and exercises, computers, but the only thing that seems to count is getting messages you understand, comprehensible input."

Essentially:

"[A]nything that helps make input comprehensible—pictures, knowledge of the world, realia, helps language acquisition."

In other words, by establishing the context of a message being communicated even if we do not know the words, that context of pictures, a setting, recognizable key words, the way the speakers are dressed, or anything else may help us to establish that crucial context.

Conversely, think about attempting to learn Japanese by listening to a Japanese radio show that you do not know the subject or have no context to draw from. You might recognize the odd word, but not enough to fill in with context because you do not have any comprehensible input. It's just gibberish to you.

Now imagine watching a Japanese TV show where the input of language of speaking and subtitles is accompanied with context: that being the actors or animations doing something provides context.

A baby may come to understand what "Happy Birthday" or "surprise" or "birthday cake" mean, not by listening to the radio but by watching her first surprise birthday party unfold before her very eyes as her family sings "happy birthday."

ENLARGING OUR EXPOSURE

Consuming a foreign language in context is *the* way to learn a language, and there is no way around it.

Speaking is fantastic to hone in your pronunciations but it is useless if you are not getting feedback and receiving new *input*.

The role of input may have to do with a mathematical concept used in statistics called the *law of large numbers*. Roughly, this states that the more information you have, the more numbers being put into a system, the more accurate the answer will be. For example, the average age of an American will be far more accurate if you use census data that shows nearly all 330 million Americans as opposed to polling 1,000 people, 300 people, or five of your friends.

By growing a sample of a whole population (the language with all its vocabulary and phrases and contexts), you begin to take in more parts that make up that whole, thus making it more representative of that whole. If you are learning a language, the broader exposure you have to the language over time, thus the more accurate your fluency will be.

Luckily, as we discussed in the previous chapters on Zipfian distributions and door wedging, the number of words you need to learn to cover a large portion of your target language is small. When you master and continue to practice the core vocabulary, input will not only help you improve the base vocabulary, but it will also help you shrink the margins of what you do not know. Even if you are studying specialized or technical jargon, the core vocab remains largely the same.

Think of learning a language like stepping into a dark room. Pitch black. No light gets in. At first you can't *see* anything but bring a tiny candle and you'd be surprised at how much of the room is illuminated. There are still dark corners that wade in and out to the candle's flicker. In time you might decide to bring in a flashlight to illuminate those dark corners, but eventually your desire to want the whole room lit and bright will cause you to install a ceiling light. Little shade escapes the light's reach.

By practicing more, and giving yourself continual exposure, more of the language opens up to you. You will find that this process is exponential. Learning new words and phrases opens up entire sentences you couldn't understand before.

INCREASING INPUT
How do you increase this input and what does it look like?

Would you believe me if I said you can learn a language to fluency without ever having to speak it? Probably not. So, you probably wouldn't believe me if I said you can learn Japanese just by watching anime, news, and Japanese game shows. Guess what? You can! In fact, much of the world that learns a foreign language does so through media. The more I interview and research the subject of language learning, the more I hear of people learning English through watching American television shows. The funniest part about learning a language is you don't even need to study grammar too much at all (although, it is helpful).

For example, my friend Phil Kopatz is getting his masters in Russian history; a part of that is to learn Russian. So, what does he do? He studies Russian with flashcards and notes in the traditional way, but he also watches Russian television shows. And, in fact, his Russian tutor learned English to fluency entirely by watching American shows on Netflix.

I have another friend named Suchi Sherpa from Nepal, and she told me the way she and other Nepalese learned English and Hindi was by watching English television and Bollywood productions from India. It sounds silly, but it does make sense. When you cultivate an environment where you are exposed to comprehensible input, your brain has two options: Let's make sense and piece this puzzle together in front of us or otherwise we can watch TV for the pretty pictures and ignore any narrative. Human perception is designed to understand the world as a narrative. "All the world's a stage," as Shakespeare famously wrote, and we are the actors.

You're probably thinking, "So I've been studying grammar and memorizing the colors of the rainbow, and the objects of the classroom for all those years in high school just for some chump to tell me I'd be better off watching Spanish soap operas?" Yes. That is exactly what I'm saying.

FOUR PRINCIPLES OF ACQUIRING A LANGUAGE TO FLUENCY

In doing research for this book, I found many different approaches to learning a language, with many similar methods but also some widely different. In investigating comprehensive input, I found four solid principles I really could not agree with more, so I've included them with my own commentary. These principles were outlined on the *What I've Learned* YouTube Channel in their video, "How to Learn a Language: INPUT (Why most methods don't work)":

1. acquire languages through context
2. maximize input
3. listen and pronounce
4. make sure the experience of learning is positive

FOUR PRINCIPLES BREAKDOWN

1. **Acquire languages through context**
   a. Language is contextual; this applies both to itself and other languages, which is why word-for-word translation will often not work after a certain point. Word order is a part of grammar and for example it can alter the meaning in different languages. If you watch or listen to shows/podcasts in your target language, over time you will naturally notice the patterns words are used in. New words will constantly pop up, but just as how we use context clues to figure out new words in English, the same applies for foreign languages.

Look not only at what is said for context, but what is happening in the scene? Who is speaking? What is the tone? Where have you heard this before, if at all?

2. **Maximize input**

   a. The more patterns you realize over a shorter period of time, the more of a language you will understand. Podcasts, TV shows, music, and even flashcards are a great way to actively learn words and phrases, and also to utilize passive methods. If you are in a car and typically listen to music or the radio, tune into a channel for your target language. For my morning commutes to university, I used to listen to French pop as I reviewed my day ahead in my head. Change your phone or computer over to your target language; you intuitively know how to use most of your phone from muscle memory, but having it labeled in a different language causes you to pick up common and import words, which are especially relevant in the internet age.

3. **Listen and pronounce**

   a. When you are watching a show, throw on the subtitles, but make sure they are in your target language. That way you can both see the word as it is spelled as it is being said while piggybacking on the visual context of the show or movie. This improves reading both in speed and comprehension as well as associating words written with words spoken, getting rid of any incongruity between the written and spoken language. The nearly 2,000-year-old Chinese proverb by Xunzi summarizes this perfectly: "What I hear, I forget. What I see, I remember. What I do, I understand."

   b. Pronunciation is a stumbling block for many second language learners, but it does not have to be. Use the shadow or shadowing method! When you are watching a video or show mirror how the person speaking is moving their mouth as they pronounce. First do this before trying the sound, getting the shape of the mouth, lips, teeth, and tongue gradually to how native speakers have it. Then work in the pronunciation aloud. Repeat as much as you can. Many videos online can show you how to pronounce specific sounds. When I was learning basic Serbian, I had to learn the slight pronunciation differences between "C," "Ć," and "Č" which all sound extraordinarily similar but are crucially different. What I did was find a video on the pronunciation and slowly worked through mirroring the speaker. Most of a language you can learn simply by comprehensible input, but pronunciation should be practiced in tandem because of the diversity of sounds in different languages. This also doubles the efficiency of doing input and shadowing all in one.

4. **Make sure the experience of learning is positive**

   a. This book was created for people who more or less wanted to acquire a language for their own enjoyment or those around them. Learning a language is difficult. That's the truth. But do not mistake the difficulty of the process with a boring or frustrating negative experience. Have a positive goal for why you want to acquire this language. Have a positive disposition to the language and its culture. What genres of shows, podcasts, and music do you like? Find those in your target language. Make the experience relevant to your interests. Watch your favorite movie dubbed in the target language. Translate your favorite songs both in your native tongue and the one you are acquiring.

Have conversations with family, friends, or strangers in your target language. If you are a gamer, change the language setting to your target language. Join the part of social media in your target language. Go to a language meet up. Talk to a native speaker casually or as a tutor (services like iTalki are great for this). Cook using a foreign recipe in a foreign language. Keep a journal. I did this with French and even when my grammar was atrocious, it got me *thinking* about what I normally do BUT in FRENCH. How cool is that? Learn a tongue twister, joke, riddle, or rhyme. Write a story. Go on a date with a native speaker (*Joy of Languages*, 2017). Talk to a cat, give it a pat, even if it doesn't talk back (Peterson, 2018).

b. Remember Suchi who I mentioned above? She learned English in two ways: by watching English television and by learning it in the classroom. She told me that she enjoyed watching TV much more than the class setting, especially because of the strict teachers in the class. Any time she or any other student tried speaking with each other in their native Nepali in English class they were asked to expose their knuckles and have them whacked with a ruler. Oh, you don't know how to answer in English? WHACK! You're chatting with your friends in Nepali? WHACK! That certainly does not sound like a positive experience.

A SIDENOTE ON READING

In my initial research, I found a lot of different techniques to learning a language, and I really was not expecting a secret key to learning any language. Yet I found one. Obviously: input. And then I found another. I assumed there were general tasks you needed to do like practice a lot with flash cards and get practice speaking, but there are other ways to rapidly accelerate your language fluency.

The first key was input.

The second key was input via reading.

If you have no experience with a language and you pick up a book to read to acquire that language, you will definitely struggle to understand anything. However, if you have used input and the other methods I have laid out to learn the basics of a language, picking up a simple book in your target language becomes a different story.

What I did with French is teach myself the basics: the most common words and phrases, simple grammar, and colloquialisms to understand the French mindset. Once I did this, I picked up a short and simple book by the famous French absurdist and existentialist philosopher Albert Camus. The book was called *L'Étranger* or in English: *The Foreigner* or *The Stranger*. Camus' writing style uses simple, plain language that anyone of any age can understand, assuming they know a rudimentary amount of French, which I did and only took me a few months to get to.

That tiny bit of French I mustered was enough to understand the book, as I had established a necessary amount of *context* of the language to fill in the blanks for words I perhaps didn't know. Just as if we did not understand a word or phrase in English, we use context clues to make good guesses. That association and investigation is how we learn from the unknown. It is how we acquire language at any meaningful rate.

Reading as comprehensible input is invaluable to boost existing language knowledge. Books are generally highly curated, dense catalogs of information, often able to relay more information than movies. Practicing reading is also one of the best ways to build up vocabulary and will obviously boost your reading speed. Pick up a "reader" or a simple book, even children's books, to increase your language learning.

THE HIERARCHY OF INPUT

Let me ask you this, would you rather *study* a language or *learn* a language?

There is a difference and I know you picked up on a difference. Chances are you might've cringed a little bit when I said *study* because of its association with boredom, long hours reading books or practicing flashcards for tests. For me, I thought of long nights in college hitting the books for political science quizzes and exams, where even if I spent a good amount of time studying, it was all up to the roll of the dice of that day. There is a hierarchy to input: studying, learning, and acquisition. In that order from least to greatest as follows below.

STUDYING

Studying is as I alluded to. It is the memorizing of facts about a certain subject, reading on that subject, and going to school for that subject. Studying in the context of language would be, for example, to take a class on the Japanese language and observe the purpose and differences between the three writing systems of Kanji, Hiranga, and Katanka, and when to use the は *wa* topic and subject が *ga* particles in grammar. You may memorize a fairly large set of vocabulary including numbers and phrases, which are useful, but it is a survey of the subject, a shallow look.

LEARNING

Learning is similar in that it builds on the technical aspect of studying, nevertheless it goes further in the development of knowledge or a skill *by* studying, being taught, and practicing through experience. It is a larger experience that is the process of attaining that knowledge of, say, Japanese. For example, you would do all mentioned above, but you would also be taught, perhaps by a native speaker, and given opportunities to practice what you have learned in conversation and speeches, or you may even be immersed in a setting where only Japanese is spoken, whether that be a trip to Kyoto and Osaka or taking a class where only Japanese can be used. (Hopefully no knuckle whacking.)

ACQUISITION

Acquisition, the third and supreme on our hierarchy of comprehensible input, on the other hand is the position of being able to understand what is being taught to you or what you are teaching yourself through listening, watching, reading, and interacting. The difference between learning and acquisition is the difference between automatically getting a joke and having someone explain to you why the joke was funny. At the point where a joke needs to be explained to me or I need to explain the joke to someone else, that's when it stops being funny. So, why approach language by explaining everything with the hope of understanding foreign and complex abstractions when we can simply understand it by acquisition?

Yes, of course, you want to learn that language you've had your heart set on throughout this book, but if you want to maximize your time and effort, gain fluency, all the while enjoying the process, acquisition through comprehensible input is your best bet when used as a foundation for your journey. You need to change your mindset from studying to learning and from learning to acquisition. Acquisition is better than studying and learning, but it also includes them. Acquisition is holistic.

SUMMARY

I'll leave you with this quote.

> "*We acquire language in only one way: When we understand messages, that's it. We've tried everything else. We've tried teaching grammar, we've tried having students memorize vocabulary, we've had people memorize dialogues, sit in front of machines, next we'll try electric shock... We've tried everything. But the only thing that works, the only thing that counts, is giving people messages they understand: What we now call comprehensible input. We acquire language when we understand WHAT people tell us, WHAT is said, not HOW it's said, but WHAT is said.*"
>
> —DR. STEPHEN KRASHEN

CHAPTER 13

A Healthy Body Is a Healthy Mind

———

This chapter is to help guide you in creating the conditions outside of the mind and in the body that will give you a *sharp* mind to acquire languages with.

SOUL, MIND, BODY

Where are you? Who are you? Are you your body? Are you your soul? Are you your mind, your psyche, your spirit, your thought processes? Are you the brain behind your eyes piloting your body? Are you the body and not the brain or the brain and not the body? Are you one and not the other or are they all the same?

We so often think that the happenings of the mind are oh-so separate from the business of the body.

Perhaps it is an American cultural idea to compartmentalize or, perhaps, modern secular society having more or less disregarded the idea of an immortal soul separate from the body that has shoe-horned the idea of the mind in its place. A mind as a sort of rational soul that inhabits the body but is distinct from that body.

We mistakenly think, "I am in a body," and not properly say, "I am a body." I'd hope you are some-body, if not you would be no-body, and who wants to be nobody? You would be just somebody that I used to know.

This would make sense as the secular culture of the day triumphantly holds up rationality above religion, faith, or even intuition/gut feeling while also demonstrating no clear understanding of what those three terms actually mean or the value they bring while still unknowingly being beholden to all three as traditionally conceptualized. The scientific secular perspective sees the religious and traditional as it does and as it must because that modern position's strength and weakness requires the removal or separation of the human from the equation in order to limit bias. Yet the human variable is essential in a broader understanding of the world, as the human perspective is the only perspective we have, even when we observe the results science produces.

Nonetheless, I have observed that in the society I have grown up in, we separate the mind and the body as two distinct, unrelated parts of the human person.

That the mind is in its own compartment of the person and the body is in an unconnected portion, unrelated. Or in some perceptions, that the mind is the "pilot" of the body that hides in the brain just behind the eyes.

The body is a place of physicality; it's the shell the mind inhabits. The mind is like the soul—amorphous, conceptual, and full of ideas. I think these concepts are overlooked, and the more you think about how we typically think about the mind and body, I believe you see how bizarre and unfounded the conception of a compartmentalized mind and body is.

The bottom line is that the mind and the body are not so separate, nor do they occupy completely different domains. Rather, they are inextricably linked because the mind arises from the body because it is generated within the brain, the center of the nervous system that stretches to all parts of the body. And let me tell you, the brain is most certainly a part of the body. I am not trying to reduce the mind or body to simple biological machines or say that the mind is a floaty soul. Quite the opposite! Rather, these two concepts and aspects are connected. All a critical understanding for improving the rate of language acquisition.

HEALTHY BODY, HEALTHY MIND

"Gym is a sacred place which
makes your life feel worth existing
by putting effort of care into the
home of your soul called body!"

—MUNIA KHAN

Your physical health directly affects your mental health. Why? Your mind's health is a function of what's going on in the body: drugs, alcohol, bad diets, poor sleep, and little to no exercise will cripple your mental health especially if you already struggle with mental stability or are high in the psychological trait of neuroticism. The great news is that you can drastically improve your mental health, focus, and ability to acquire a new language no matter your mental condition. We do this by making a series of tiny changes; eliminating one, multiple or all areas of your life that harm your health and personal development, and *crucially*, replace them with an even better habit or task (Huberman, 2021).

We all know this intrinsically, but it needs to be said because how well you learn a language and your likeliness to stick with it depends on those factors of how *you* treat your mind and body.

What you do to the mind is reflected in the body and what you do to the body is reflected in the mind. Don't believe me?

DIET
I am not here to tell you what to eat. I wouldn't be so authoritative… in that regard. But I will tell you what you absolutely should not put in your body. Diet is the foundation of healthy habits. What you put in your body is either helping you, hurting you, or only addressing the surface level symptoms of being hurt.

SPIKES
During the time you are awake, you likely feel a bit more tired around midday into the afternoon or a few hours after waking. This is a dip in your mental and physical energy

levels that occurs naturally, called a postprandial dip. However, this is majorly exacerbated by your diet. If you eat a carb-heavy lunch with simple carbs like bread, pasta, and sugar (desserts, sodas, candy), you will prolong this slump and make it a deeper valley compared to your mountain peaks of energy. You can lose several hours of productivity every day just by these slumps.

We've all been there. I used to dread having afternoon classes in high school and university because I could barely keep myself awake after lunch, even when the classes were entertaining. Combined with exhausting heat, it was a done deal. No wonder afternoon is naptime for little kids and cultures in extremely hot climates, (e.g., *siestas, riposo, inemuri,* power naps).

These energy spikes followed by slumps also exacerbate symptoms of anxiety.

Afternoons for most people have downtime that would be well spent practicing language, but when beholden to these slumps, you may lose focus, fall asleep, or be completely unmotivated.

SOLUTION

Those slumps, or postprandial dips, are actually mild hypoglycemia—hypoglycemia being the scary medical term meaning an abnormal dip in blood sugar, which is often followed by lethargy, clumsiness, difficulty speaking, confusion, and even in extreme cases: seizures, loss of consciousness, and death. Okay, now that I've scared you, know that those last few symptoms are not *as* common.

Decrease the amount of refined and simple carbohydrates you have for breakfast or lunch (whichever is your first meal), and wait until dinner or don't have them at all. Also, eat more leafy greens, proteins, and fats before eating carbs in a meal to reduce the energy spike that will be followed by a massive crash.

Never eat refined sweets or sweets by themselves or on an empty stomach, always after a meal. To also reduce the spikes after meals, take a short walk, this helps digestion, and subsequently the reduction of energy spikes and slumps. These energy or blood sugar spikes that then prompt insulin spikes over time are the cause and/or exacerbation of the constellation of diseases known as metabolic syndrome and insulin resistance, which include conditions such as type 2 diabetes, acne, erectile dysfunction, high blood pressure, psoriasis, obesity, morbid obesity, heart disease, and may be linked to the development of Alzheimer's.

When you picked up this book on language, did you think you were going to get a crash course in proper diet and exercise? When I picked up the metaphorical pen to write this book, I didn't think so either.

COFFEE AND CAFFEINE

Hi. My name is Max Kelbly, and I am formally addicted to caffeine. Caffeine has the modern world in its grip. Caffeine is the most prevalent psychoactive drug in the world. Approximately 80 percent of the entire world population drinks a caffeinated beverage each and every day.

In America alone, sixty-eight million Americans (roughly 20 percent of the US population) drink *at least* three cups of coffee a day. Eighty-five percent of American adults consume some form of caffeine daily, and in 2009, 354.5 million gallons of energy drinks were sold. That's roughly 537 Olympic-sized swimming pools (*Health Research Fund*, 2021). I can only imagine what that number is now, twelve years later!

This is not purely a Western phenomenon as caffeine consumption in the form of coffee, tea, soda, chocolate, pain relieving drugs, and energy drinks is ever present. If you visit nearly any country across the globe and it doesn't have a coffee culture, it almost certainly has a tea culture. Some countries like Canada, Saudi Arabia, and Ukraine are torn right down the center of this divide, both having lots of tea and coffee drinkers (Desilver, 2013).

Caffeine clearly has a negative side to it as it creates sleeplessness when consumed too close to bedtime, it has been shown to increase stress and anxiety when taken in large doses, can disrupt your digestion, has been observed to induce rhabdomyolysis in large quantities (the breakdown of muscle into the bloodstream increasing risk of kidney failure), high blood pressure, rapid heart rate, fatigue, and having to go to the bathroom too often and urgently (Spritzler, 2017).

Nevertheless, after I've given you a fright once more, in moderation caffeine *can* be used to help your language studying ability for two main reasons: 1) its nootropic properties and 2) social and cultural associations that come with caffeinated beverages.

Again, you're probably thinking, "What is a nootropic? He definitely made up another word!" Not this time.

1) Nootropic: A nootropic is a substance that can enhance mental/brain function, like helping memory, learning, and overall function of the brain (Tomen, 2021).

With that definition, you probably can see pretty quickly how caffeine can fit in that category. [1]

Caffeine boosts concentration, alertness, reaction time, even memory, and to my surprise, mood.

Clearly, caffeine is going to make your brain run faster, but if you are practicing with language and you already enjoy caffeine, I would try combining them. When you're doing a practice task like flashcard memorization caffeine is perfect when consumed within an hour window of beginning practice. Going through flashcards is not always exciting, but caffeine will help you to make connections faster, making more connections in a shorter amount of time, and with its mood-enhancing effects it will give you a rosier disposition toward the activity. According to the website Nootropics Expert:

"Caffeine improves mood within an hour of consumption. Because it increases the density of GABA receptors, potentiates, dopamine, and causes some serotonin receptors to be more responsive." (Tomen, 2021)

Now that's science!

MORNING CUP

Before work or school, I like to carve out about two hours before I leave to pray, exercise, shower, and do small habitual tasks that I know will be much harder to get myself to do after I get home in the evening when I'm exhausted. Language practice is one of them.

I sit down at the dining room table, hair still a mess from the shower and face still red from exercise and take a crack at my basic language study. AH! But not without a bit of caffeine. I brew a cup of green tea, which is not nearly as strong as coffee both in caffeine, acidity, or flavor, and kick-start my brain for the day. Practicing language flash cards with that smooth delivery of caffeine *after* I have been up for a while makes the rest of the day move more rhythmically. It's enough for a nudge of momentum without being pushed off a cliff.

However, many people who use caffeine use it detrimentally by conditioning themselves to use caffeine as a drug to wake up. We all have that friend that shows up to first class or work that says, "I *need* my morning cup of coffee." That may be you.

We can still get our "morning cup" while allowing our body to naturally wake up. Wait two to four hours after you wake up and then have coffee. It's the same principle as not having a carb-heavy meal in the morning: you don't want to super-charge the first few hours just to crash before noon. If you take caffeine when you get up, go for decaf… or try out green or white tea, or a black tea mix. A million flavors are out there. A little bit of caffeine upon waking up will give you an extra bit of momentum… a full cup of coffee is going to crash your day before it even starts, necessitating another cup… and another. A cup of coffee has ninety-five milligrams of caffeine, whereas green tea has only twenty to forty-five milligrams of the psychoactive drug (Wartenberg, 2019).

THE SOCIAL ASPECT OF CAFFEINE

Whether it's coffee or tea, nearly every culture around the world has formed a social association with caffeinated beverages. Throughout many places in Europe, Africa, the Middle East, South and Central America, and Asia, you will encounter cafés where locals (and travelers) socialize, smoke a cigarette, or watch football (soccer for all the Yankees). In many of those same places and elsewhere you can find teahouses.

ALBANIA—HIDDEN CAFÉ CAPITAL OF THE WORLD

I am a travel junkie, on top of a caffeine junkie, and I most recently traveled to Albania—one of the only countries fully open to the outside world amid this coronavirus pandemic. To my surprise, as I wandered around the bustling, pluvial capital city of Tirana, I quickly noticed how deep coffee culture had implanted itself.

On every marble and concrete street corner were cafés packed from the early morning well into the evening with locals of all ages and backgrounds. On every street between each corner café there were a few more wedged in-between or even next to one another in the amalgamated mix of enchanting Italian and brutalist communist architecture. Albania, a tiny, too-often-forgotten country across the turquoise sea from Italy has the most coffee houses per capita in the world. The tiny country nestled between the Adriatic Sea and the Balkans has 654 coffee houses per 100,000 people. That's one coffee house for every 152 people. To compare, imagine if New York City had 54,000 cafés not including restaurants, which, in reality, NYC *only* has an estimated 26,000 restaurants, whereas Albanian coffee shops are ever growing (Haas, 2017).

Sitting around a table with a cup of coffee (or tea) is quite possibly the most natural way of learning a language because it puts you in a situation where ordering your drink will likely have to be done in the native language. Without a doubt, you will hear locals around you talking in their tongue giving you a chance to consciously and unconsciously pick up new insights. And, if you are meeting someone it is a relaxing place for a chat, or even a rambunctious get-together. Plus, a little bit of caffeine helps roll a conversation and having a drink in hand takes the pressure off of having to speak the whole time.

In Albania, I met a lot of generous and genuinely fun people such as Xhuliano, a jolly but rough motorcycle mechanic (pronounced the same as the Italian name Juliano) who showed me around Gjirokaster, the city of stone. Or Boris, an Albanian teacher and tour guide who studied in the same field as I did at an American University in the United States. I met most people at cafés and hostels. Every country I have been to has had a caffeinated social element. The Netherlands, Czech Republic, and Italy were all about cafés, whereas in Uganda every day at 4 p.m. was "teatime" where we sat around, socializing to the tune of sipping tea and munching on biscuits.

If you aren't traveling to a country (or in your own country or province), diversify *where* you are practicing language. Go to a café, coffee shop, or tea house, and practice flash cards or meet up with a tutor (in person or over video).

EXERCISE

Despite the prevalent misconception that our mind and body are wholly different compartments of what makes us *us*, a growing amount of evidence suggests physical activity has fantastic cognitive benefits, and specifically when it comes to learning a language. Allow me to first explain from my lived experience (anecdotal evidence) and branch off to tell you the excellent story the research has to tell.

STRUGGLE TO READ

Since early on in college I struggled to quickly read books, academic articles, and quickly come up with answers to math questions. I used to be a speed reader back in middle school and could read upwards of 350 words per minute, but I lost that through high school. Then I hit a wall with reading in college, struggling to read 150 words per minute and sometimes I would take five minutes to get through a single page. Even at the beginning of writing this book, I was still struggling to read at a pace I deemed acceptable.

However, in the last few months I have used several concerted methods to bring my reading speed back up to pace for my age and beyond. I use tactics such as using a pen as a pacer guide that traces under words. I listen to non-lyrical music to block out my "inner voice" or subvocalization which causes us to read slower (at the pace of which we speak), I use my peripheral vision to capture the words at the edge of the page, and most importantly, I pair cycling with reading. I sit on a stationary bike and read.

What all those above tactics have in common is that they cause me to block out the world around me and focus on what I am doing. They narrow my focus, which is exactly what we need to do in order to make the most out of our time acquiring a new language. Since then, even when I read without pairing it with exercise, my reading speed *and* comprehension have increased dramatically.

WHAT THE STUDIES SAY ABOUT EXERCISE AND LANGUAGE LEARNING

In a study by Winter and colleagues titled, "High Impact Running Improves Learning," the researchers took a look at three different groups of people: those who do high intensity anaerobic sprints, those who do forty minutes of low intensive running, and those who are sedentary for fifteen minutes. After each group performs their physical activity (or the last group who sits around) they had to perform a vocabulary memorization task. Both immediately and in the long-term study, those who just finished the most intense workout were the best equipped to learn new vocab and to comprehend it faster. And not by a tiny margin, but by 20 percent faster

(Winter et al, 2007). Let's say it took thirty minutes to get down some vocab, now it would only take you twenty-four minutes. You save yourself six minutes a day studying while also benefiting your body.

Now that is for vocab after working out. How about language learning overall and how about during exercise?

Depending on what kind of exercise you are doing, your ability to include another task into it may be easier or harder. Podcasts and music in a foreign language can be used in most exercises, whereas reading a book, doing flashcards, watching Netflix, or playing a memorization game may be possible on a stationary bike, elliptical, or treadmill (Lyons, 2021).

A study by Liu and colleagues found that practicing a language (or learning something new of that language) is far more effective when undergoing physical activity than if you were sitting down learning a language with no physical activity (Liu et al, 2017). So, if you find that you can match language learning with your exercise, take a chance and pair them together.

There's the evidence, but why might pairing exercise and language learning help the latter?

The previously mentioned study offers three possibilities based on the body of research: "by slowing down age-related cognitive decline, by allowing efficient allocation of attention, and by improving executive control functions."

They went on, "By and large, physical activity is supposed on the one hand to favor synaptic plasticity and on the other hand to increase the availability of specific neurotrophic substances in the brain, such as BDNF (brain-derived neurotrophic factor) that facilitate learning."

In other words, exercise helps make the brain more "plastic" or readily available to learn or make changes as well as release brain chemicals that all help with thinking, memory, and learning (Liu et al, 2017).

Overall, the findings in these studies can be summarized by what one of the researchers, Dr. Simone Sulpizio said to *The New York Times*:

"We are not suggesting that schools or teachers buy lots of bicycles... A simpler take-home message may be that instruction should be flanked by physical activity. Sitting for hours and hours without moving is not the best way to learn." (Reynolds, 2017)

Another suggestion is to take exercise classes in a foreign language. How? Prior to the 2020 pandemic but also accelerated by it was the growing prevalence of online fitness courses be it Peloton, yoga, Pilates, calisthenics, etc. (Lyons, 2021). To engage our minds, we need to move our bodies.

UNFOCUS

I *just* got done telling you about the importance of diet, caffeine, and exercise to focus. Moreover, this entire book I have been telling you (and will continue to tell you) to *focus* on your goals and *focus* on specific ways of studying language. Nevertheless, no matter how big or small, or long or short term your language goal, taking moments to "unfocus" are critical to engage in *deep focus*.

The internet's new favorite neurobiologist, Professor Andrew Huberman emphasizes the importance of "unfocusing." That is to say, we need to bring ourselves to a place of deep relaxation before going into hyper-focused mode *if* we are to get the most out of that session.

Going on a walk causes transient hypofrontality, which turns down the dials on the more demanding parts of the brain, funnily enough including language. In some sense, you have to get out of your mind to come back and truly use it. Just as types of thinking vary widely across individuals, you now understand you can induce such different ways of thinking in yourself.

A super relaxed state can be induced by napping, prayer, meditation, yoga, going on a walk, taking a shower, or any activity where your mental engagement—your thinking—is not being demanded. Think about it (or don't), many people's best thoughts and ideas come from going on walks, showers, or being in a state of meditation. Thirty minutes of unfocusing can prepare you for two hours of deep focus.

Huberman also talks about how *now* is the best time for our brains to learn a new skill (nudge nudge, cough cough, perhaps a language) because of people's heightened arousal around uncertainty. He said this in reference to the Lockdowns in 2020 and with all the developments around the Pandemic, but any time of uncertainty will do. The combination of heightened stress/focus (these two concepts are interlinked) and the increased availability of sleep (many working at home, going to school online, or unemployment) has created the perfect storm. Focus/stress and lots of sleep can create neuroplasticity, related to the above-mentioned synaptic plasticity, which is our brain's rapid ability to literally change its structure to adapt to new skills and frontiers (Huberman, 2021).

CLARITY AND CLEARING THE FOG

All this is to say your ability to mentally perform when you need your brain the most relies so heavily on your physiological state. If you do not listen to signs of discomfort or distraction, these thoughts and feelings will cloud your mind.

Likewise, if you participate in behavior like drinking, eating junk food, or ignoring your need for sleep, you will reap the rewards in your mental state. Clarity is another word for mental sharpness. In my life, I have become obsessed with self-development. As in, improving who I am to myself and in relation to others so that I can be the best man I can possibly be. This is what Matthew McConoughey calls "egotistical utilitarianism." With this, I really see this constant battle between choices that will produce mental clarity, or conversely, mental fogginess, and uncharitable behavior.

THE ECONOMY OF CHOICE

Junior year of college, I had to take an economics class as a major requirement. I wasn't an economics major, but I still looked forward to the course. Going in, I loved economic philosophy, which stems from debating with friends and other political science majors over the merits and detriments of Austrian, Keynesian, Marxian, and Chicago schools of economics. I had the expectation that the class was going to be all about numbers, charts, formulas, and mathematical concepts, and it was, but that's not at all how it began.

When Professor Chen introduced economics, she broke all my preconceived notions of the lofty subject when she asked, "What is economics the science of?" I thought, "Well, maybe it's the study of all transactions in an economy. Or money in general. How does it circulate?"

She answered, "The basis of economics is that it is the science of how people make decisions. What choices people make and why do they make them." Human behavior lies at the base of what economics is. An economy is simply the collection of human choices in a given area or network.

Ever since she instilled that concept in our class and emphasized it through case study after case study, I cannot help but to think about how *everything* we do in life comes down to the decisions we make. Choice. Whether you believe in free will or not, the fact is we at *minimum* have the illusion of choice in our lives. It is a biological fact that human perception is organized in a way where we must construct hierarchies of value based on each and every choice we make in that we prioritize what we pay attention to in a subconscious rank order (Peterson, 1999).

DECISIONS, DECISIONS

A livery stable owner from renaissance England would sell his horses to his clients. He gave them one option, which was, "purchase the horse in the stall closest to the door, or not buy any horse at all." He famously would say to his customers, "Take it, or leave it," inventing the common phrase.

In a world of increasingly plentiful options we are often given more than just the two options of "take it or leave it," but I cannot overstate how important it is to put yourself in the frame of mind of "will participating in this choice improve my life or of those around me, or will it diminish it?" and to the specifics of this book "will skipping, shortening, or doing something else other than practicing language today help me achieve my goals?"

The world is not black and white, but when it comes to making decisions, you either eat the donut or you don't. You either binge drink or you don't. You either workout or you don't. There is a duality to life. The existence of one thing implies its absence. Light to dark. Day to night. Alive or dead. Second language or no language. One day you will die, and whether you reach the end of your life full of regrets from opportunities not taken is wholly up to you in the present moment. The fact you are reading this indicates to me that you want to change or improve your habits, and thus your choices, so why not follow through? The attention you give is the attention you will receive.

TAKEAWAYS

1. You are a body. Somebody. You are just as much your body as you are your mind. The mind and body are inseparably linked and thus the health of the body will, without fail, affect the health of the brain and thus the mind. Take care of your body by eating properly and exercising, your brain will thank you.

2. When we pair language practice with other actions such as exercise or caffeine ingestion, we can increase the rate and effectiveness by which we learn. Do not confuse this with multitasking, as that practice requires constantly shifting attention while producing the opposite of productivity by doing so. Pairing practices should be done when one activity encourages the focus of the other.

3. If you want to improve your reading speed listen to white-noise or non-lyrical music to block out your "inner-voice" so you do not subvocalize in your head what you are reading. We can read far faster than we can speak. Use a pacer such as a pen or finger just as one would have pacer for training to become a better runner.

4. Unfocusing is as important as focusing. Limit the time you spend practicing and take frequent breaks where your brain is not heavily engaged if at all such as taking a silent walk, talking to a roommate, taking a quick nap, prayer, meditation, exercise, or taking a shower.

5. Become an Egotistical Altruist. If your pursuit of a new language is hurting you or others around you, something is horribly wrong. Create practices that make both the pursuit and fruit of your language acquisition beneficial for you and for others.

6. Life and languages come down to choice. What you make time for is a direct cause of what you will see in your

results. Choose wisely how you divide your time and what you do with that time. The attention you give is the attention you will receive.

FOOTNOTE:

Footnote [1] Fun language fact: Nootropic is a "neologism" or newly created word by Romanian psychologist Dr. Corneliu Giurgea; the word comes from Greek *nous*, or "mind" and *trepein* "to bend."

CHAPTER 14

Digging Your Teeth In an Extra Mile: Goals and Routines

————

LEARNING A LANGUAGE IS PERSONAL DEVELOPMENT

Language learning needs to be tailored to the needs of the differing students and the objectives of teaching a language. I wrote this book not just so you can learn a language and be done with it; rather, I want to give you the proper tools that will make the best out of the time you use. Language learning that is productive, efficient, useful, and enjoyable. Why make the process harder or more convoluted if it does not serve you learning that language?

If you are not familiar with personal development and self-help, I am sure you can see the connection between developing yourself into a better person and how those methods can be applied. If you are not familiar with these subjects allow me to broach and bridge them. These are terms most people hear on a daily basis, but little explanation is often given.

Self-help, personal development, personality development, personal growth, and self-improvement are a jumble of the similar words and concepts mixed together often used to mean the same thing, yet they are notably different.

The most important categories are *self-help* and *personal development*. Just by saying them out loud, you notice they immediately have slightly different associations with them.

Self-help deals with a near obsession with solving a characteristic or personal flaw that, in the perspective of the person doing the self-help, needs to be fixed.

Personal development refers more to an acceptance of who you are as you are right now, while also engaging in a concerted effort to improve characteristics, learn a skill, increase knowledge, improve health, or engage in any other habit for lifelong change (Scuderi, 2014).

The key difference is not the first word *self* or *development* (because they both obviously deal with us and start and end with us) but the key word is *help* and *development* (Scuderi, 2021). I associate *help* with a sense of urgency and a need to rescue, and *development* with a more gradual, positive experience. This is not to say one is better than the other because they both have their specific uses.

For me, learning a language has come part and parcel with my commitment to personal development.

After a monumental realization in my life a few years ago, I clung to self-help understanding that my attitude toward life was unacceptable. I had a bleak outlook on my future prospects. I was heading in the direction of overdependence on others, not because I was incapable, but because I had no proper aim, no structure, and no courage to set myself right.

Realization alone opened the doors to self-help, to immediately stop and evaluate my life, to chart out where I was, where I was headed if I didn't get my life in order, and where I could be if I fulfill my potential. So often we cling to what is familiar and comfortable, unaware of the fact that those very comforts are what cause us to stagnate and regress.

Self-help was getting out of the hole I was digging for myself, but personal development was the commitment and willingness to engage in new, constructive habits that would leave me better off today than I was yesterday so long as I continuously engaged with these new, positive habits.

These habits are an anchor that would make sure I kept on my path.

THE RULE OF HUMBLE ACTION

Now, before I break down goal setting, I cannot go further without telling you perhaps the NUMBER ONE rule when learning a language. The rule actually has very little to do with learning a language at all. This simple but difficult-to-follow rule is called the "Rule of Humble Action." Confused? Allow me to explain.

Have you ever met someone who told you they were writing a book, perhaps over the span of years and they never publish it? Of course. Everyone knows *that* person. Most people know multiple of those people, and one might even be your friend. If you have not heard this before, in the writing community it is commonly cited that 97 percent of people who start writing a book do not finish or go on to publishing. That means only 3 percent of people who attempt to write a book go onward to publish. Why is that?

One might say a lack of perseverance weeds out many who just won't make the time or effort needed. Others might say that many people do not know how to write a publishing level book, which is possible. But I believe the answer hides in plain sight.

LANGUAGES ARE LIKE BOOKS

Writing a book and learning a language to fluency are two difficult tasks, especially when it is your first time doing so. Yet, as the neurobiologist Andrew Huberman pointed out on the Lex Fridman podcast, when the reward of praise of pursuing something like learning a language or writing a book outweighs the pleasure one would derive from completing that task, our brains lose the incentive to pursue the project.

When you tell people around you that you are trying to learn a language to fluency, just as if you were writing a book, you will most likely get praise. If you have tried and failed to learn a language before, you probably have reaped the praise for *writing your book* so to say, without finishing it.

HIDDEN PRAISE

So, what's the solution?

Praise is such an odd creature. Many of us spend much of our lives seeking praise or validation from others to fulfill our very human need of having a sense of social belonging, but the pursuit of seeking praise is always fruitless. Why? Once you work to receive praise and you get it, that good feeling quickly goes away, leaving you to do something else to get more praise and validation. It is vain glory: a lust for something that cannot be fully obtained as the imagination sees it. If a portion is had, it cannot fulfill because it does not meet lasting necessities, physical, psychological, spiritual, or otherwise.

The solution is to avoid praise and validation throughout your time acquiring your language. How? Make this a personal project, a sort of hobby that you keep to yourself like reading a book series, learning to cook, taking music lessons (or teaching yourself), or working on your car. If you are to include others in your venture, it should be people who are eager to teach and from whom you are eager to learn.

In the *Lord of the Rings* trilogy, Aragorn, the man destined to become king, learns all the necessary skills and experiences to become a benevolent king by being in exile, living and working away from his people. Or think of Harry Potter becoming a wizard at Hogwarts *away* from his loved ones and the muggle life he was accustomed to in England. Or, if you will, Anakin and Luke Skywalker leaving their desert lives where their duties were clear and instead going and being trained as warrior wizards, Jedi Knights, so they could fully realize their gifts tied to their destiny. It was the cunning of Odysseus that revealed him as a brilliant tactician, not in his comfortable palace in his home of Ithaka, but in the field of battle devising the Trojan Horse and applying his ingenuity to be harnessed, refined, and mastered so he might return home.

The tasks of reading a full book and mastering a language and many more require a considerable amount of mental time and effort to complete, but we do these tasks without boasting about it or looking for that validation. Of course, you should absolutely enjoy the learning process and involve others who want to achieve the same awesome goal as you, but the more praise and validation you avoid, the more you will be pursuing this goal for the right reasons.

Be humble about it, but don't hide it either. This is not something to be ashamed of after all. It is a skill to be proud of, but preferably when you have something to show for it. When you inevitably receive praise for pursuing a language, kindly thank that person and do not take too much credit outwardly and crucially, inwardly. The job is not yet done. Improvement necessitates completion of what one sets out to do. In other words, keeping your word is what facilitates growth, and with genuine growth comes maturity. You are as mature as you are faithful to your word. If you start something, finish it.

As a rough formula the Rule of Humble Action could be explained as: Your goal *minus* praise received *equals* amount of action taken toward your goal.

TWO TYPES OF LANGUAGE GOAL SETTING

The absolute basis of learning a language that you do not yet know starts in individualized goal setting. I can give you specific tactics and areas you should focus on, but they are all worthless if you approach language aimlessly.

The only "aimless" language learning is that of how you learned your first language—immersion, and constant input—but if you're reading this, you probably are not seeking to live out the rest of your life in some small Filipino fishing village to learn Tagalog aimlessly, and you might not have the time or resources to do so. Let's set concrete goals.

The process of learning a language effectively really relies on the fundamentals of self-development: goal setting. Finding your mission, passion, and purpose. Understanding that purpose. Planning and executing. Gradual improvements over time as opposed to monumental changes at the drop of a hat.

There are two roads you can take when learning a language in terms of time:

1. Rapid Learning
2. Gradual Spaced Learning

RAPID LEARNING

In Rapid Learning, you are trying to learn a language as fast as possible. This could include intensive and repetitive study of the absolute basic phrases, words, and questions, immediately tackling foreign books/movies, and speaking in the target language with natives ASAP. A person in the rapid learning category is likely urgently preparing for a trip or event when use of the target language is needed or preferred.

This category makes me think of the *Star Trek: Enterprise* episode "Darmok," in which Captain Jean Luc Picard, played by Sir Patrick Stewart, has to rapidly learn phrases of an alien language to exact precision in a frustrating and dizzyingly brief amount of time. You observed this austere, confident captain buckle and get nervous and jittery, not from commanding a spaceship of hundreds of people, but because he had to practice a language under pressure (not too dissimilar from learning key Dutch phrases in the Amsterdam airport). If he were to fail to pronounce exactly what needed to be pronounced, what he said could be taken as a sign of hostility, rudeness, and an act of war!

Captain Picard's demeanor is an exact reflection of what it can feel like to learn a language in a short amount of time before you will need to use it.

Rapid learning can occur when someone is dropped into a culture where the language is completely foreign to them, by necessity they are able to pick up the language through a rigorous example of trial and error. The absolute necessities are prioritized. Here, the learner needs to know x amount of a language by y deadline.

GRADUAL SPACED LEARNING

In Gradual Spaced Learning, the learner wants to become conversational or fluent but does not have much of a time constraint. This person likely wants to incorporate the language over time. This reflects how language is taught in schools where it is not expected for students to be fluent, even after years. It also reflects a more natural progression similar to how children learn languages: over time, by experience, through context. Not nearly as much pressure.

Which of these two categories best fits you? Figure out which category you best belong to and choose one. When you do that, schedule out how much time you are going to want to practice every day. No matter what category you are in, do not set yourself up for burnout! For long term goals it is better to err on the side of less time each day, say, fifteen minutes as opposed to one hour, but still carve out the time.

Ask yourself: What is the bare minimum amount of time I am willing to practice language? That is your baseline and your goal, to practice that amount and attempt to exceed it daily. Then ask: What is the maximum amount of time you can—that you are mentally capable of without dipping into your mental energy for the next day—practice every day? This is your cap. If you want sustainability of your habits day after day, you must never exceed this cap. How much you practice can vary, but should remain at or above your baseline and never exceed your cap. These vary widely from person to person. Caps and baselines can be extremely close or enormously widespread. The amount you engage in your habitual, normal, ritual practice sessions should always be limited within the baseline and cap range and should err on the side of your baseline. Keep a timer going so as to not exceed or underperform.

EFFORTLESS HABITS

Habits drive who we are. The purpose of habits is to make our lives easier. Our brains are complex things, but if we had to make a concerted effort in absolutely everything we do, thinking through each process as if we were learning it the first time, we would be exhausted before lunch time.

Imagine if every time we brush our teeth, we had to learn the movements to brush and the motions through the mouth.

Imagine if every time you got dressed for the day, you not only had to learn how to put that specific shirt on and pants or a dress, but how to put on these types of articles of clothes on in general. Think back to being a kid how it was difficult learning—even with adult assistance—how to put on clothes, brush teeth, tie shoes, write, and even go to the bathroom. Even walking... if your memory is that sharp and robust.

Our body (which includes the brain) has evolved to create habits to essentially automate our most basic processes, making life flow more seamlessly and not waste time relearning how to do something. Forming good habits are crucial to becoming fluent in any language. As the Arabic idiom goes, "التكرار يعلّم الحمار" (it-tikraar yiʒallim il-humaar) This translates roughly to, "Repetition can teach even a donkey," or as we say in English without *directly* calling someone an ass, "Practice makes perfect." But why? Why does practice make perfect?

Consider this: Do you have to make a concerted effort to remember how to pronounce words and phrases in your native language every time you speak? Do you have to actively draw from memory each word you are going to use as you are forming a sentence, or do you have an idea and express it verbally in the form of a sentence?

Humans routinize everything from how to open a door, to walking, to eating, to even our reactions to what others say. I believe in free will, but I also recognize that most of what we do as humans is *preordained* by the habits we create and the social environments we are exposed to.

This instinctual muscle memory comes by many names: consistency, habits, quirks, and second nature (Merriam-Webster, 2021). Other words we might associate with this, and are definitely connected are: ritual, practice, pattern, fashion, tradition, custom, and way. We all have our daily rituals, our family traditions, our personality quirks, our speaking habits, and things that come to us as second nature. They are all habits made by practice, and if these habits catch on, they become fashionable. Broadly speaking, culture creates language, and culture is an amalgamation of habits, *traditions*, people consistently participate in.

Like the words "omen," which has a bad connotation, and "natural," which has a generally positive connotation, the word "habit" has a certain connotation that is seemingly bad. Yet, all three of these examples can be either good or bad depending on the context. Make good habits; break bad habits.

HABITS FOR COMFORT

Have you ever lived or worked with someone who lived by their wristwatch? Who would be at the same place at the same time every day? Or a coworker or classmate who would bring or buy the same thing every day for lunch without fail?

When I worked in a jam, jellies, and preserves factory warehouse as a forklift driver, I worked under a man who, at first, perplexed me. Being the youngest and most inexperienced on the team, and not caring otherwise, I was rather flexible when I would take my breaks, typically going around the convenience of our shipment schedule. However, I noticed that a coworker of mine always came out of the dock office, looked up at the clock, then down to his wristwatch, sometimes waiting, and then walking off. Always around the same time of day. It took me a few days to realize he was leaving exactly at 10:45 for lunch. It didn't matter what was going on or how busy we were; 10:45 was his lunch.

Clocking out, he was always first in line with his wristwatch resting on top the time clock, the two perfectly synced, punching his timecard in a few seconds before 3:22 p.m., the earliest we could clock out so that when he pressed "enter" he would be clocked out at 3:22 p.m. to the second!

I was amazed at this man's ability to work like a clock. He got everything done he needed to, and he conformed to his strict schedule. For this very reason, people can appeal to habits as a form of order and comfort in their life. Life is an uncertain place, but being able to control little things *precisely* how you want them to be is a way of calling order and thus comfort into your life. A sense of control over one's life.

Although not heavy-handed on the habits, people who drive maliciously and viciously on the highway often do this for the same reason. Life may be uncertain in most aspects, but controlling and manipulating others on the highway gives that crazy driver a sense of control in their own life even if it means shaking their fist, cutting you off, and screaming at others while their window is rolled up.

HABITS FOR COMFORT TURNED ADDICTION

For my coworker, his extreme conformity to his desire for control and comfort through habits was not so disruptive to himself or other people. However, clinging to a habit for comfort can be detrimental when you replace going to lunch at 10:45 every day with drinking every night, going shopping regularly to the detriment of your finances, eating beyond your fill most meals, or becoming undetachable from media: social media, the news, TV, porn, video games, or even books.

Habits are a tricky business because we know that in good things doing it once is not sufficient. Hard work is showing up repeatedly day after day. When it comes to bad habits, we ignore this logic and tell ourselves, "This is a one-time thing," or "I have control; I can stop whenever." Yet, we know intrinsically that if it's ultimately good for us (a good habit) or it feels good (the ability for it to form an addiction when repeated), our brains will turn it into a habit. Habits can be comforting to the point of self-destruction.

I covered this more in the chapter "A Healthy Body is a Healthy Mind."

"You are nothing but your habits."

—ACHARYA PRASHANT

CORONAVIRUS: DESTROYER AND MAKER OF HABITS

For most of this book, I have appropriately shied away from talking about that massive event that took over the whole of 2020 for fear of dating this book and casting it into immediate irrelevancy. Yet it is an event that happened and for this clear-cut discussion of habits I can think of no more unambiguous example in my own life than the obvious effect of the pandemic on daily routine.

During the initial Ohio coronavirus lockdowns in March 2020, I knew the obliteration of my normal school itinerary and not having a work schedule could create chaos if I did not form a routine promptly. (I knew this from my aimless and irresponsible summers in high school with little to no obligations, limitations, and consequently next to no accomplishments). In lockdown, I made a habit of practicing a set amount of French every day, which allowed me to learn a lot of French swiftly, but it also helped anchor the rest of my life in ritual. Fifty flashcards in the *morning* and fifty in the *evening before bed.*

Even when we think we can set out a bunch of items on our day's "to do list," the chances of getting it done and not wasting hours during the day on things we don't care about are slim without morning and evening routines to anchor everything else. Anchoring the productive, social, and trivial, into the bland but necessary.

Creating a meaningful language routine that suits you—be it three minutes, five minutes, twenty minutes, or an hour—gives enough of an anchor to the day that slipping into aimlessness becomes more difficult than working up the will to practice the new language.

I am neither a therapist nor a doctor, and I will not be prescribing you a language to learn to help rescue you from your inner demons itching and clawing at your soul to see daylight. Rather, use personal development methods to bolster your language learning abilities, which will practically engage you in the consistent persistent pursuit of learning a language. This will intrinsically improve your communication skills of speaking, writing, and listening, while sharpening your mind and opening you to new perspectives (Pratama, 2017).

CREATING MORNING AND EVENING ROUTINES

Acquiring a new language requires a bit of self-mastery and discipline. Ugh. That sounds hard, I know. Discipline can seem terrible or even painful to many, myself included, but truly it is not about pain or rigid conformity. Rather, it's simply about showing up.

Woody Allen famously said, "Eighty percent of success is showing up." (Eighty percent is a number that often occurs.)

Similarly, "Showing up is essential. Showing up is consistently powerful. Showing up consistently with a positive outlook is even more powerful" from Jeff Olson.

And I certainly can't leave Stephan Hawking out of the equation: "Half the battle is showing up."

I know what you're thinking: "So what, you're going to make me get up early and practice flash cards?" No, not necessarily. I am an early riser and I do believe there is an advantage to getting up early, but an even bigger advantage than that is simply creating a routine around the first hour or two immediately after you wake up—regardless of whether you wake up at 4 a.m., 10 a.m., or even 2 p.m. Really, any time.

Every person's morning routine is different but there is a basic framework, especially for language learning:

1. Wake up and immediately get out of bed
2. Wash your face and drink something stimulating
3. Review today's goals laid out the prior evening
4. Stretch
5. Mantra, prayer, or meditation
6. Task: *Insert language learning here*
7. Get ready for the rest of the day

The hardest part about doing something is working up the will to do it. Leave yourself with no other options, and you are forced into committing to what needs to be done. This is why our ancestors have so many profound struggles they were able to overcome. They were left with the option of do this extremely difficult task or... perish! Sounds rough, but it's true. Extremely difficult tasks are not intrinsically hard to do; we just have so many easy outs in the modern world that we are paralyzed by the cornucopia of choice. Too many distractions.

If you're not using your phone for practice, hide it away. Put your phone in another room, lock it in your car, or throw it on your roof! If you are practicing alone, go to a place where you can't be interrupted. Limit the number of items on your desk. Everything you are not using to study at that moment is a distraction. A clean desk, study environment, and room is a reflection of a focused, uncluttered mind.

Have a specific place in your house or corner of your room dedicated to studying and studying *only*. To become more productive and constructive, it is wise to separate out different focuses of our lives into different rooms or stations. This is why we build houses with a bathroom, a kitchen, a laundry room, an office, a bedroom, a porch, and a living room. Much of the technology that causes disruptions is because the technology such as laptops, TVs, and smartphones often serve many and unspecified purposes that cannot be so easily separated by different rooms: entertainment, social connection, education, business, work. We separate out functions to rooms to keep ourselves mentally organized. Quite odd, isn't it? By organizing our physical environment, we organize our psychological mind space and make it more bearable to live with ourselves and others.

CREATIVELY DISORGANIZED

I am a highly disorganized and creative man which is due to being in the ninety-eighth percentile of people with the psychological "Big Five" trait: openness to experience. I naturally don't like rigid borders, boundaries, hierarchies, accepting the way things have been done are the way things will be, or organization. I function better when I can freely create new ideas, experiment with them or start new ventures constantly. But, I recognize there is a balance. So, after my dad and I painted my room, I sketched out different plans for my new bedroom layout that would allow me to work creatively, productively by adding in some constraint, organization, and boundaries with specific rules for the specified zones.

My office space, which included a computer desk and bookshelf, was carved out in the corner between my two windows. The rules for that location: workspace only, no eating, get up and away if you are taking a break, and absolutely no phone. In the other corner was my closet. Pretty straightforward. In the opposite corner, I placed a chair with a tiny table next to it for reading and studying only. The rules and purpose of the zone: reading books, letters, or studying language, absolutely no phone (unless doing spaced repetition flashcards or listening to language podcasts). In the middle against the back wall, I have my bed jutting out forming a natural border that separates either side of the room. What physical boundaries will you create to create psychological distinctions between language acquisition and other activities?

I have seen a concern from many different people with different motives—a concern that discipline, organization, and creating boundaries can stifle creativity. Yes! That is a totally acceptable and plausible concern. Excessive order can stifle the chaos necessary for creativity and growth, but you still need organization. In fact, by creating appropriate rules and boundaries, you can actually create a mental and physical space free enough from distraction that creativity can flourish.

Creativity is a necessity, if not in you, in others you surround yourself with. Our proclivity to be creative, or inversely, conscientious is innate in the constitution of our individual personalities. I have a hypothesis that much of self-help is geared to or appeals to personality types high in trait openness/creativity because their sporadic nature to be interested in everything can be smothering and requires much of what self-help offers: goal setting, discipline, organization, habits.

If you are afraid of losing your creative autonomy by setting restrictions on yourself, let me help you see it from a different perspective. Voluntarily adopting, *creating* rules by which you operate will allow you to be challenged to truly harness your ingenuity. Too often is it thought that absolute freedom fosters creativity; rather, it is restricting possibility, distraction, resources, time, and attention that forces the mind to become exceedingly innovative with what is given before its eyes (Starfire, 2021). Think MacGyver.

When you use time limitations and a limited knowledge with a new language, it will force your brain to find patterns and construct intelligible sentences in your target language. It is the obstacle; it is the constraint that gives you no other option than to concoct a solution. This is why when a problem is found, the solution often becomes obvious. How can you knowingly solve a problem if you have not identified the cause, the problem?

MISCONCEPTIONS AND CAUTIONS

Willpower Is NOT Finite

To bust a common misconception, willpower/ego depletion is not like gas in a gas tank. The antidote to impulse is always forethought, planning ahead: It is easier to deny the chocolate cake by not buying it as opposed to it being at the end of your fork. Hack back external triggers to distraction, reshaping your environment as to not, well, distract yourself! It's hard to be distracted in a room with nothing in it except white walls.

If you struggle with a specific goal on your own, create pacts with others to create accountability for those goals. It is good to reward yourself for completing hitting the mark, but it is also important to reprimand yourself in a way that doesn't harm you. By including others in on your goals, especially people with similar or the same goals, you keep each other accountable. Failure means disappointment, success means social reward, but both have support and necessary consequences built in.

DO I NEED MOTIVATION?

Needing motivation is a modern myth. A lot of external motivation (music, motivational speeches, pep talks) are important, but to form a dependency on it is one of the greatest weaknesses. Why? Because it gives us an out, an excuse, when we don't have it. Also, it can be a distraction to what I mentioned above. It is used to cut through our abundance of options to make us guilty for making all decisions but the right one, but in reality, we need to limit ourselves to only making the right option, the one we planned for. Not the impulse.

UNSUSTAINABLE GOALS

The desire for long breaks from school is the desire that unites all kinds of college students, and students in general. Most love seeing their friends every day but cannot wait for that week-long spring break, that three- or four-month summer, or nearly all of December. For me, it was the winter break of my junior year of college I was so envious of. When early December 2019 rolled around, I was physically and mentally drained from school, having been enrolled in eighteen or more credit hours, leading Dead Philosophers Society, participating in student government, and dipping my toes (or my whole body) into about four other student organizations and clubs on top of working with university dining services.

Not having my campus café job or a mountain of schoolwork freed up nearly all of my time. Looking back, I probably will never have such a big swath of absolute free time in my life, but hey, that's life. I used this free time to turn to self-mastery and self-development. It was time to put the pedal to the metal, the nose to the grindstone, and stay on the treadmill to take a break from the monotony of school to build new and lasting habits.

In the morning, I would get up at 4:30 a.m. (yes, you heard me right—I was insane, a lunatic even), immediately get dressed and do morning cardio, either running or biking in the snow.

Right after, I would strip down to shorts, drenched in cold sweat and freezer-burnt BO, and do calisthenics training in my apartment living room. Pushups, dips, planks, mountain climbers, Russian twists, etc. Then I would get a rinse and get ready for the real kicker: three hours of language learning. Yeah, as you could probably tell, I traded endless days of schoolwork and caffeine-fueled writing and study sessions at night for a new form of physical and mental absurdity. It wasn't sustainable. (Pro tip: When studying a language, make sure you have habits, but more importantly, make sure those habits are sustainable for your personality, schedule, and level of commitment.)

I applaud anyone who devotes time for daily, habitual language practice. If you are focused on one language, that will most likely work great in the long term. Yet, if you did what I did, you might find some trouble. Instead of picking one language, or even two that were similar—maybe French and Spanish because they are both similar romance languages—I picked not two, not three, but four. Ya know, just to make sure every single one of my bases was covered.

Spanish was fun, but not that fun alone, so I threw in French because of the similarities and my prior experience and recent trip to France. Then I also threw in German to make sure I maximized learning languages similar to my own (English). Lastly, I didn't want to leave the poor Slavic languages out of the European bunch, so I picked up Russian. Four different languages, three different language families, two different alphabets, and one overly ambitious wannabe polyglot. After about two and a half weeks into this routine, I found that I was mentally drained by the time I would move onto non-language tasks that involved critical thinking or even physical activity tasks.

I didn't realize it then, but I expended my willpower on far too many things at once in one day, even before I got to the other important tasks like working on writing, prayer, spending time with friends and family. Correction, it was not my will power that was expended, rather it was my focus was too diffusely split between far too many large, unspecific, and unsustainable goals. My attention was maximized with no room for mental unfocus and rest. Yes, you can work a little bit on a lot of things, but if you spread yourself too thin, you will find you are exhausted from seeing such little progress in so many things, as opposed to seeing a lot of gradual progress in a few things. Compound your success.

If you are to have goals, you must have sustainable goals.

SET SMALL GOALS

When we get that massive motivation to sit down and learn a language because it will precipitate our hopes and dreams, we often lose sight of the short term. Most people don't have the time to study language for three hours out of the day. Nor, I would argue, would this be an effective way of learning for most people. Setting small *daily* and *weekly* goals is a way to make the process less frustrating, more conducive to most busy schedules, and more tangible overall.

If you study for three hours on Monday and review the material on Tuesday, you'll realize that you did not retain a good portion of what you "learned." Probably not even 50 percent. If you continue this, you will be spending more time reviewing than letting things settle in the mind. This sort of momentous level of studying to produce a marginal return the following day will discourage you. Massacring your endurance to learn that language.

On the contrary, say that you take fifteen minutes with flashcards to learn ten new words on Monday. On Tuesday, you review those same words for five minutes, then spend the next ten minutes learning ten new words. You probably didn't get 100 percent right on Tuesday, but it certainly wouldn't be as low as 50 percent. With each day you take a little time reviewing a small number of words and adding new ones. By the end of the second week, you will at minimum have been exposed to 140 new words (ten words x seven days x two weeks). It is highly unlikely you will know all these by heart at the two-week mark, but you will be pretty close. Also consider that when you compound this over an even longer time, you will have exposure to those words over and over, solidifying their meaning. When you hit one month, those 140 words will be part of the new total of 280. At that point you will have practiced that 140 twice as many times as when you did at the two-week mark, and because they become easier and more integrated into your memory and vocabulary, you will spend less time with them, leaving a lot of your daily practice time to new vocab.

The core idea is to set small or attainable goals that balance your level of knowledge of the language with the amount of time you are willing to set aside for language learning, along with making sure you won't become burnt out over the long haul. Depending on your goals, your time, and your personality you could vary from practicing ten new words a day, to listening to three foreign podcasts a week, to taking an hour-long language class every day. When goal-setting, the key is consistency and sustainability.

SET FUN GOALS

People who care about what it is that they are doing in life always tend to be more passionate in their work and joyful overall. We all know someone who loves their job or hobby to an almost unreal level, and that love, that passion, causes them to excel at what they do. We want to curate this level of passion for our target language. Otherwise, what is the point of learning it? Misery is a sure-fire way to fizzle out.

It is important to pay attention to where we focus and invest our time during the day and not so much what we say we hope to invest our time in. Our mind thinks it knows exactly what our passions are, but where we invest our time often reveals this for us. Actions speak louder than words. Action dictates belief, words only confirm or lie about our belief.

IT'S ABOUT TIME

What is it that you spend most of your time with? Do you read a lot of news articles, magazines? Do you watch a lot of Netflix? Do you often study for school with friends? Do you always exercise with music or podcasts on? Do you binge-watch on a regular basis? Do you spend free time scrolling through Instagram and Twitter, reading threads or laughing internally at memes? Chances are, I caught 95 percent of you with those questions alone. Lo and behold, you can take every single one of those habits you enjoy or find comfort in and transform it into a language learning experience you enjoy.

If you have a basic grip of a language, take a look at a Wikipedia page, news article, or Snapchat reel in your target language. You won't understand all of it, but by knowing the absolute basics, the general idea will be apparent to you and your brain fills in the rest you don't know via context.

If you watch a lot of streamed content, find a show or movie in your language. Netflix and Amazon Prime have tons of foreign films of all genres in their subscription base. Recently I have started to learn Serbian for an upcoming trip. There are only eleven million Serbs in the world, and only about twenty-one million speakers (for reference, two billion people speak English) worldwide. To my surprise, over fifty television series and movies are on Amazon Prime alone not including those films available for rent! I love political thrillers like House of Cards, so during my journey to learn French, I watched Netflix's *Marseilles*, all about the political intrigue of the Southern French city of, well, Marseilles. Your local library is sure to have content of all sorts for a target language, book or movie.

Music and podcasts have to be the easiest, *wu wei, laissez-faire* way of learning a language *passively*. In the age of the internet, there is no shortage of international music to choose from. On top of that, if it's a song and it exists, there are likely a website or dozens that have the lyrics written out for you, sometimes even translated side by side.

For social media, the simple answer is to follow accounts that are in a different language. Following #frenchlearning or #learnfrench filled my Instagram feed with hilarious, easy to understand memes, French quotes, pronunciation videos, and verb charts. Find some celebrities and influencers who speak and post in that language. Curate your feed, and generally, what you are exposed to, so you are immersed in your target language.

DEADLINES, REWARDS, AND PUNISHMENTS

Goals without deadlines are hardly attainable. Goals without a plan of action are daydreams.

If learning a language was like building a house, your goals would be the foundation, your action plan (what you will specifically do to achieve your goals) would be the walls, and deadlines would be the roof over your head. Within that framework you have in essence maximized your protection (minimized the risk of not completing your goal).

Learning a language is difficult for a million and one reasons, but a key difficulty is that it is so hard to see our progression as we attempt to use quantifiable measurements on growth that cannot be easily quantified.

Fluency is not marked by someone saying, "I know all 53,088 words and 209 grammar rules by heart. That makes me a master!" Language proficiency can be categorized in tiers and often is for government testing and private employment, but these are still not wholly quantitative, or numbers based. Language is something so broad and fluid, objective to the student but subjective to the speaker. Because of this difficulty in seeing a progression, it can be easy to be discouraged by the progress made.

As told earlier on in the chapter "Hope Yet," language is not forgotten and even taking a break of several years, and even decades, what you learned is still there. You can't unlearn a language via any nonsurgical maneuver.

TAKEAWAYS

1. Language acquisition is a form of personal development. Treat it and curate the process as if it were to improve your life and those around you because it will, in due time.
2. Create baselines and caps to define the range of time you are willing and able to commit for daily language practice.
3. The Rule of Humble Action requires you to work diligently but quietly when acquiring a new language. Do not seek praise before the work is done and you are conversational, or even fluent. Even then, it does not serve to boast out of vainglory. The rule can be summarized by the equation: Your goal *minus* praise received *equals* amount of action taken toward your goal.
4. Creating limitations, restrictions, discipline, and organization are crucial to obtaining goals and can force necessary ingenuity required for figuring language out.
5. Rearrange your physical space such as your desk, room, or office to be clutter-free. Allocate specific areas and rooms for specific tasks with rules of what is allowed there and what is forbidden. Removing distraction and excessive disorganization in physical space will create greater organization and clarity of thought in the psychological space.

6. Avoid unsustainable goals. It is better to consistently practice for a few minutes a day for years, than for hours every day for only two weeks. No matter how ambitious or competent you are, err on the side of small goals while also frequently asking yourself: Am I underperforming?

7. Instead of praise from loved ones, reward yourself proportionally to the goal you achieved, but also lay out consequences ahead of time for not meeting your own expectations. Create accountability groups with those of common goals for appropriate praise and appropriate reprimand. Learning how to help others with their goals in this group will force you to see solutions to your similar goals.

FOOTNOTE:

[1] Initially, we can see personal development as a tool that starts and ends with ourselves, and although that is partly true a major critique I have of the whole self-help/self-development industry and community is the hyper-focus on the self to the point of selfishness and neglect of one's relationships and social obligations. You can go so far in improving yourself by yourself, but you hit a wall when this crusade for self-improvement gets to the point of pushing out the social dimension of "the self." "No man is an island," as John Donne's saying goes. If we treat others as "toxic," any interaction we have can be expected to be poisonous. The irony is that true self-improvement happens when you do selfless acts for others and pursue higher goals outside of yourself. An act of kindness toward another without expectation of anything in return will even make you feel better than the same act for yourself. Why? Your future self you seek to improve and another person are equally strangers to who you are in the

present, but your future self cannot interact with you in the present. "Grant that I may not so much seek to be consoled as to console; to be understood, as to understand; to be loved, as to love; for it is in giving that we receive, it is in pardoning that we are pardoned..." —Saint Francis of Assisi

Acknowledgments

———

This book was conceived unexpectedly at the dawn of the COVID-19 pandemic and completed throughout that turbulent time for all the world, possible only by a plethora of factors all being true at a particular moment in life. Again, a perfect storm. Through the power of the internet, primarily, an amazing community came together for this book to be possible. This work was feasible only by the support of family, friends, strangers, donors, and all manner of generous souls.

The content of this book outside personal anecdotes relied on research, much of which came from interviews and conversations I had with dozens of language learners, polyglots, professionals, and academics. I want to thank those willing to be interviewed: Elioth Bernard, Yi-hsuan Rebecca Tsai, Samara Kaloun, Jadelyn Milburn, Madelyn Goins, Madalyn Staudt, Bahador Alast, Suchitra Sherpa, Germinal Van, Ke Lin, Mateo Gomez Mita, Emily Ghazoul, Phil Kopatz, Sandra Chzhan, Cade Lloyd, Drew Shields, Joshua McGrath, Mark Koester, and Nathaniel Drew. Due to reasonable limitations, I was not able to include all conversations and all content from those chats; nonetheless, they all fueled the book in its final form.

DONORS

My gratitude to the author community who went beyond in funding this project. Thank you to my best friend Adam Satterfield, who characteristically bought the book first. Thank you to Francesca Ciraci, Nathaniel Chwalik, Laura DeGrandis, Mary Anne Baucco, Maria Catherine Wells, Katherine Deibel, Josh Steiner, Annette Kelbly, Mare Edmundson, Michael James Chalfant, Jeff Satterfield, Ian A Kelbly, Rachael Geiger, Adrienne Moch, James Kelbly, Peggy Dolensky, Tina O'Grady, Debra Schluter, Aciel Muheisen, Concetta Peterson, Paul Hamilton, Ariel Tsai, Rita Malloy, Kimberly Kelbly, Therese Marie Ozbolt, Bradley Bynum, Hannah Lesko, Morgan McKeon, Sandra Guelker, David DeGrandis, Edward Battig, PJ Suso, Samantha Schmucker, Jim Garris, Jane Garris, Colin Stoll, Vince Suso, Kirsten Attwood, Sydney Knapman, Eugenia Johnson-Whitt, Jarrett Sims, Matt Lundell, Keenan Fentress, Julia Bonneau, Katie Baucco, Rebecca Cabe, Sarah Cannon, Nick Romano, Paul DeGrandis, Michael Sproull, Andrew Bebesi, Clay Troup, Jared Cline, Vera Carter, Dimitri Giavis, Lucas Schaffer, Reece Human, Lindsey Craft, Julia Losasso, Evie Aaron, and Hannah Kasper. Many donors are listed throughout the acknowledgments for their manifold ways of assistance.

Special recognition to Mary Catherine DeGrandis and Patrick Denny for financing a substantial portion of the fundraising goal. The two of you boosted this project beyond the bounds of expectation, for which you have my gratitude.

BETA READING/DEVELOPMENT

Keeping one's word is invaluable without exception in writing. To all who read, edited, revised, and suggested the drafts and manuscript. Thank you to my dear friends, Phil Kopatz, MaryBeth Edmundson, Nathaniel Chwalik, and Clay Troup for Beta Reading the many manuscript drafts. Thank you to my high school English teacher, Brianne Pernod, for magnifying my love for writing, the English language, symbolism, and storytelling. Without her creative and rigorous influence in the classroom, a book written and a book read by my hands and my eyes would not have happened.

Thank you to my developmental editor Angela Ivey, acquiring editor Alexa Tanen, marketing and revisions editor Janice Riley, and the many dozens of editors, wranglers, speakers, coaches, and facilitators at New Degree Press, with marked thanks to Eric Koester, who introduced me to the Creator Institute, the much-needed framework for getting a book from pen to paper.

FAMILY AND FRIENDS

My family has holistically contributed to my development as an author, but most importantly, has given me the example of how to live the good life, steering me away from physical, mental, psychological, spiritual, and moral harm and treachery by their vice and virtue. To my father and mother, George Eli Kelbly Jr. and Ruthie DeGrandis Kelbly. To my grandparents, George Eli Kelbly Sr. and Karen Kelbly, whom I am honored to have the opportunity to read my work. To the rest of my family who constitute the bulk of my support already mentioned.

So many exchanges led to this book, and if I have not mentioned you, let it be known I acknowledge your support. I have never received so much support for any other endeavor in my life. To list all those who have cheered me on and positively impacted me to write and stick with this book, I would have to fill a book strictly with names. Cheers and best regards.

APPENDIX A

Reading Comprehension Tips

———

1. Be Curious
   a. When there is something in the reading you do not understand, make a mental note, or write it down on paper. Come back to the question when you have finished reading.
   b. Ask yourself questions like "What did the author mean by...?" "What does this word mean?" "Why did the author write this?" "How does x concept relate to z concept?"
   c. If you don't understand certain words, make a mental note of where they were in the section, and come back when you are done to see if you understand them. If you are still unsure based on context, type the word into Google. A big benefit of reading comprehension is learning new words.
2. Note Recurring Themes
   a. Is there a word or phrase the author keeps using? When you are finished with the section, make a list of

these recurring words, phrases, or ideas. Chances are they are the main themes and concepts of the reading.

3. Limit the notes you take UNTIL you are at the END of a section

   a. To improve memorization it is extremely helpful to wait to take notes until you are completely finished with the chapter or section. This may sound ineffective, but it actually works really well for recalling what you read, and thus, reading comprehension.

   b. When you have finished reading the section or chapter, write down everything that you remember into a short summary. Give yourself time to let it come back. You'll be surprised how much you retain!

   c. If you are typing your notes, put them into a font you're not used to. This creates an association between the words you type and the font it's in, which makes a mental link or memory.

   d. Plus, the process of recalling and writing a tiny summary helps solidify your understanding.

> "Repetition is the mother of learning, the father of action, which makes it the architect of accomplishment."
>
> —ZIG ZIGLER, AUTHOR, SALESMAN, & MOTIVATIONAL SPEAKER

4. Pace yourself and getting yourself to read—study in practice

   a. It is common for students, or any reader, to put off reading and to think they will sit down for several hours and finish the assignment in one go... I've been there. Doesn't work.

b. When reading, set a timer for twenty-five minutes. Read for twenty-five minutes, then take a five-minute break NOT reading (stretch, walk, talk to a roommate) then go back to reading for another twenty-five minutes, then break, and repeat. The human brain begins to lose focus after twenty-five minutes, making any time after that not nearly as productive as it could be. If you read for five hours without break, you are only getting twenty-five minutes of productive work, and the remaining four and half hours are not nearly as productive as they can be. This twenty-five on, five off rule applies to all mental focus activities: working out, writing, video games, puzzles, reading, or learning a language.

c. If you have a big reading assignment due in a few weeks, schedule out when you'll read and for how long. Plan out the specifics of how you read too, example: "I'll read five pages a day for two weeks." Use the twenty-five-minutes-or-less rule to your advantage. Set aside up to twenty-five minutes a day to knock out reading over the course of time. For people who have grown to enjoy reading like myself, this is common practice. Instead of carving out an entire day to read a book I like, I let routine do the heavy lifting. For instance, I read a book recently called *Like Leaves Fall in Autumn*, a short 120-page book about a gruesome war in England. I told myself I would read a chapter a day, each chapter being ten pages long, and it takes me about two minutes per page. That's twenty minutes a day reading and five minutes writing my short summary of the chapter. Over the course of twelve days, I finished the book. This way, I am not intensely focusing for an entire day, exhausting myself mentally over a short book. Rather, I am spending a few minutes looking over it and that's it.

> "Give me six hours to chop down a tree, and I will spend the first four sharpening the axe."
>
> —ABRAHAM LINCOLN

d. Lastly, if you are struggling to find the motivation to open the book or start an assignment, tell yourself, "I'm going to just read one line" or "I'm just going to write one sentence." Seems simple, and it is! Once you get started, your brain will naturally want to continue making it harder to stop than it would be to start.

APPENDIX B

Cool, Untranslatable Words

WORDS THAT ARE UNTRANSLATABLE AND ONLY EXIST IN ONE LANGUAGE.

IN FOREIGN LANGUAGES

Abbiocco (Italian)—That sleepy drowsy feeling you have after eating a massive meal.

Cafuné (Brazilian Portuguese)—To fondle or caress someone else's hair.

Dapjeongneo (Korean)—When someone has already decided what answer they want to hear when they ask a question.

Dépaysement (French)—The feeling of being away from home, especially one's home country, and being in a foreign place.

Desenrascanço (Portuguese)—The ability to improvise a quick situation.

Fargin (Yiddish)—To wholeheartedly appreciate the success and accomplishments of others.

Gökotta (Swedish)—Getting up early and venturing outside with the express purpose of hearing the first bird songs of the day.

Goya (Urdu)—The awe or suspension of belief one feels after hearing a great story.

Hyppytyynytyydytys (Finnish)—Literally "bouncy cushion satisfaction," meaning the satisfaction one derives from a soft, bouncy cushion or pillow. I had a stroke pronouncing this one.

Iktsuarpok (Inuit)—A feeling of anticipation that causes one to check outside if someone is coming and becoming frustrated when waiting on someone to show up.

Ilunga (Bantu)—An individual who will forgive on the first offense, tolerate it if a mistake is made twice, and does not absolve after the third time.

Kyōiku mama (Japanese)—Quite literally "education mother." A pejorative term that refers to a stereotype within Japanese culture of a mother who is so adamant about her child's education it comes at the expense of the child's mental, physical, social, and emotional well-being.

Kyykkyviini (Finnish)—Literally "squat wine," meaning the cheap wine at the bottom of the shelf in a Finnish liquor store that one has to squat to look at and grab, as opposed to the expensive wine on the top of the shelf.

Litost (Czech)—A feeling felt as a state of torment, misery, humiliation. It is a torturous state brought on by the reminder of one's own misery.

Mamihlapinatapei (Yaghan)—A mutual look two people give each other that indicates they deeply desire to initiate something together but both are reluctant to do so.

Natsukashii (Japanese)—Of good memories from the past; the transitioning to a state of mind that appreciates the past, even an idyllic past that might not have existed. Not to be confused with nostalgia that has an implication of yearning for the past, and to bring it to the present.

Na'eeman (Arabic)—A sort of blessing you give someone who has just shaved or showered essentially congratulating them on looking fresh.

Onsra (Serbian)—That bittersweet feeling one has knowing a romantic love will not last long.

Oodal (Tamil)—The fake disgruntled anger two lovers show each other after an argument has ended.

Pålegg (Norwegian)—Absolutely everything you could put and fit on a slice of bread.

Pochemuchka (Russian)—Someone who asks far too many questions.

Prozvonit (Czech)—Literally "to flash," to call someone on the phone and hang up before the call is picked up to inform the receiver of something without being billed for the call.

Retrouvailles (French)—The love and joy that fills one's heart due to reuniting with someone after an extended time.

Schnapsidee (German)—A brilliant plan, so ingenious you can only come up with it while drunk.

Shīfu (Mandarin)—Used as a compliment to someone who is great at their craft or profession, but specifically in reference to barbers, taxi drivers, and repairmen.

Strikhedonia (Greek)—The pleasure one receives from throwing caution to the wind, saying, "To hell with it!"

Tartle (Scottish)—Hesitation in recognizing someone or remembering their name.

Tingo (Pascuense/Easter Islander)—The gradual process of building a collection of stolen objects with no plan of returning them, from your neighbor of course.

Torschlusspanik (German)—Literal translation is "Gate close panic," coming from a medieval phrase of the panic towns people felt at sunset to get home and lock up in time for the night or when an invading army was coming. Now, the term is more metaphorical to mean time is running out for career opportunities, marriage, and having children.

Tsundoku (Japanese)—This is the act of buying a book, not reading it, and leaving it in an ever-growing pile of unread books; this is all too relatable for the bookworms out there.

Yakamoz (Turkish) or Mångata (Swedish)—The reflection of moonlight on water.

Ya'aburnee (Arabic)—The hope and declaration that one's loved one will die after them as living without them in their life would be unbearable.

Yuanfen (Chinese)—A belief that fate, destiny, or God works to bring two lovers together.

IN ENGLISH
Cheesy—The sense that someone or something is shabby, cheap, and occasionally goofy or cringe-worthy in a humorous or simple way.

Serendipity—Good fortune, luck, but peculiarly the aptitude for making valuable discoveries by accident.

Cool—A word with many metaphorical, and sometimes opposite meanings. A lack of friendliness, compassion, enthusiasm, or approachability, but also to indicate that something is fashionable, hip, or even that past tensions and violence between people has settled down. All together it indicates peace, stylishness, and cold indifference.

Trade-off—This is a classic case of two words made one. In decision-making it refers to making one choice while forsaking another, often implying that there are always losses or opportunity costs to every gain.

Pimp—Another word with a double meaning. As a noun it refers to a criminal who makes their living by exerting influence over and extorting money from prostitutes. As a verb it can mean to selfishly and dishonorably use something or someone for their own gain, or it can mean to customize and adorn property like a car or room in a lavish and ostentatious way.

Silly—This word's many related and interpretive meanings make it difficult to translate the full range of its meaning. It can mean having a lack of common sense or weak intellect, while on the other hand, it can mean to be playfully lighthearted and amusing or to be absurd or ridiculous and dismissible.

Gobbledygook—This one comes straight from Texan American English meaning wordy and generally unintelligible language. Two good summaries are "the overinvolved, pompous talk of officialdom," and "incomprehensible or pompous jargon of specialists." For an example, read any of Michel Foucault's works.

Facepalm—This is self-explanatory as it is exactly what it says. To facepalm is to be embarrassed to the point of smacking one's palm against their face as a sign of dismay. Similar to shaking your head at someone in disapproval.

Spam—Unsolicited messages, emails, texts, mail, or advertisements often sent commercially to a ridiculous amount of people, often repetitively in a large number of places.

Language Acquisition Goal Setting Worksheet

———

For the uninitiated, goal setting is often a difficult skill to learn then turn that knowledge into practical use. Luckily, I am here to help. The best way to realize one's aims and the steps necessary to make a bullseye is by asking a series of questions. Why questions? Questions tease out *what* it is we think and *why* we think that. Questions allow *you* to realize, create, and investigate the specifics of your journey.

Asking good questions and allowing the patient to answer and work through them as much on their own as possible is a basis of psychotherapy. The job of a psychotherapist is to help the patient bring the unconscious and misunderstood to the forefront of consciousness so work can be done to learn anew. To increase your chances of learning a language these principles wholly apply. The following will be a series of questions to help facilitate your language learning, some of which I have asked throughout the book.

MOTIVATION

Vital to acquiring a language to fluency is understanding your motivations. Why do you want to learn a language? Do you want to speak with others who know that language? Do you have a friend, spouse, or family member who speaks it? Are you learning for pleasure, school, or business?

Take no longer than five minutes to answer these questions as broad or as specific as you choose.

SELECTING A LANGUAGE

What languages interest you? Is there a particular language you want to learn, and if so, why that language? What cultures interest you, and what languages do those cultures use? How difficult is the language to acquire fluency? How difficult is this language? How similar, if at all, is it to languages you know or have studied before?

FANTASY AND IMAGINATION

Imagine a future version of yourself where you know your target language. What does that future look like? Is it a better future than a future not knowing that language? What good things could happen if you dedicate yourself to acquiring that language?

What are the consequences of not learning it? If you do not learn this language, will you or others be disappointed in you?

DIFFICULTY

Acquiring a new language is difficult, yet the level of difficulty varies based on your goals. What are your fluency goals in learning this language (do you want to know a few phrases, be conversational, be partially fluent, be fully fluent, be able to read, speak, and hear or just a few of those)?

CARPE DIEM PER DIEM (YOUR DAILY COMMITMENT TO SEIZE THE DAY)

In order to become fluent in any language in an effective way, a learner has to engage with that language daily whether that be five minutes or two hours. You need to seize the day every day without exception, but this needs to be tailored to your lifestyle, habits, willingness to commit and adapt, as well as your goals. Your goals must be congruent with who you are, so do not overestimate yourself and be honest with the workload you can handle, or even if you are not doing enough.

Ask yourself: What is the bare minimum amount of time I am willing to practice language? That is your baseline and your goal, to practice that amount and attempt to exceed it daily. Then ask: What is the maximum amount of time you can—that you are mentally capable of without dipping into your mental energy for the next day—practice every day?

Bibliography by Chapter

INTRODUCTION

American Academy of Arts & Sciences. Commission on Language
Learning: The State of Languages in the US: A Statistical Portrait (2016). https://www.amacad.org/publication/state-lan-
guages-us-statistical-portrait.

Zeigler, Karen, and Steven A. Camarota. "67.3 Million in the United
States Spoke a Foreign Language at Home in 2018." Center
for Immigration Studies. October 29, 2019. https://cis.org/
Report/673-Million-United-States-Spoke-Foreign-Language-
Home-2018.

PART I

TO SPEAK IS TO SEE

Clarke, Alex, and Loraine K. Tyler. "Understanding What We See:
How We Derive Meaning from Vision." *Trends in Cognitive
Science* 19, no. 11 (2015): 677-687. https://www.sciencedirect.
com/science/article/pii/S1364661315001989.

Harper, Douglas. "Obvious." *Online Etymology Dictionary.* Accessed October 16, 2020. https://www.etymonline.com/search?q=obvious&ref=searchbar_searchhint.

The Psychology Today Editorial Team. "Synesthesia." *Psychology Today.* Sussex Publishers, LLC. Accessed October 16, 2020. https://www.psychologytoday.com/us/basics/synesthesia.

Wayne State University. "Top Ten Proverbs About Language Learning." Wayne State University College of Liberal Arts and Sciences. February 4, 2015. https://clas.wayne.edu/languages/news/top-ten-best-proverbs-about-language-learning-33572.

ANGLOPHONOSPHERE

Nicholls-Lee, Deborah. "English Is No Longer a Foreign Language in NL, but It Has a Unique Character Here." *DutchNews.* January 17, 2018. https://www.dutchnews.nl/features/2018/01/english-is-no-longer-a-foreign-language-in-the-netherlands-but-it-has-a-unique-character-here/.

Harper, Douglas. "Online Etymology Dictionary: Origin, History and Meaning of English Words." Online Etymology. Accessed September 20, 2020. https://www.etymonline.com/.

Mitch, M., B. Szonye, R. Mue. "Why Is It That Frisian Is Considered the Closest Related Language to English?" Stack Exchange. Retrieved September 20, 2020. https://english.stackexchange.com/questions/113646/why-is-it-that-frisian-is-considered-the-closest-related-language-to-english.

S., Rukmini. "In India, Who Speaks in English, and Where?" *mint.* May 14, 2019. https://www.livemint.com/news/india/in-india-who-speaks-in-english-and-where-1557814101428.html.

Encylopedia Britannica. s.v. "Frisian (_n._)." Accessed September 26, 2020. https://www.britannica.com/topic/Frisian.

Central Intelligence Agency. "The World Factbook: India." CIA. June 15, 2021. https://www.cia.gov/the-world-factbook/countries/india/.

Vega, et al. "Engelsk—English Spreading Worldwide—NDLA." ndla.no. Nowegian Digital Learning Arena. December 11, 2018. https://ndla.no/en/subjects/subject:39/topic:1:188628/resource:1:9166.

SPEAKING 'MERICAN

Hinsbergh, Gavin van. "Modern Chinese: Mandarin and Chinese Dialects." *China Highlights.* May 10, 2019.

Edberhard, David M., Gary F. Simons, and Charles D. Fennig. "How Many Languages Are There in the World." *Ethnlogue:Languages of the World.* Twenty-fourth edition. Dalas, Texas:SIL International. 2021. https://www.ethnologue.com/guides/how-many-languages.

Ibekwe, David, and Fraser Moore. "Why Universal Languages like Esperanto Won't Catch On." *Business Insider* (blog). October 18, 2017. https://www.businessinsider.com/why-universal-languages-like-esperanto-will-never-be-accepted-philip-gooden-2017-10?op=1.

Keane, John. "Why Read Tocqueville's Democracy in America?" *Democracy field notes* (blog). *The Conversation*. April 17, 2015. https://theconversation.com/why-read-tocquevilles-democracy-in-america-40802

Lampariello, Luca. "Why Learning a Foreign Language in School Doesn't Work (and How to Make it Work)" *Smart Language Learning* (blog). 2019. https://www.lucalampariello.com/learning-a-foreign-language-in-school-doesnt-work/.

Mark, Joshua J. "Kingdom of West Francia." *Ancient History Encyclopedia*. Last modified November 16, 2018. https://www.ancient.eu/Kingdom_of_West_Francia/.

McCarthy, Niall. "Chart: The Countries with the Most Spoken Languages." Statista. October 9, 2019. https://www.statista.com/chart/3862/the-countries-with-the-most-spoken-languages/.

Central Intelligence Agency. "The World Factbook: India." CIA. June 15, 2021. https://www.cia.gov/the-world-factbook/countries/india/.

"Tocqueville, Alexis de. *De la democratie en Amerique/Democracy in America*. Translated by Henry Reeve. London: Saunders and Otley, 1835.

UGLY AMERICAN

Kresia, Meredith. "From Ketchup to Mammoth: Over 50 Foreign Words Used in English." *FluentU* (blog). 2021. https://www.fluentu.com/blog/foreign-words-used-in-english/.

Merriam-Webster Dictionary Online, s.v. "Ugly American (n)."
Accessed June 26, 2021. https://www.merriam-webster.com/
dictionary/Ugly%20American.

HOPE YET

Barrère, Sébastien. *Petite histoire de Lourdes*. Pau, France: Cairn,
2014.

Bombe, Kushal. "Online Language Learning Market worth
$5.13 Billion by 2024." Intrado GlobalNewswire. Last mod-
ified August 13, 2019. Accessed June 28, 2021. https://www.
globenewswire.com/news-release/2019/08/13/1901161/0/en/
Online-Language-Learning-Market-worth-5-13-Billion-by-
2024-Exclusive-Report-by-Meticulous-Research.html.

Johnson, Joseph. "Internet User Penetration in the United States
from 2015 to 2025." Statista. July 2020. https://www.statista.
com/statistics/590800/internet-usage-reach-usa/.

Lasserre, Henri. *Our Lady of Lourdes*. New York: P.J. Kennedy &
Sons. 1906. https://archive.org/details/ourladyoflourdesoolas-
siala/page/n1/mode/2up.

Lewis, Benny. "Forget a Language: Why It Happens and How to
Avoid It." Fluent in 3 Months (blog). Mediavine Travel, November 5, 2020. https://www.fluentin3months.com/never-forget/.

Meltzer, David. "Consistent, Persistent Pursuit." Entrepreneur.
January 17, 2018. https://www.entrepreneur.com/articl/307529.

PART II

FOUNDATION OF LINGUISTICS

Clayton, Ewan. "Where Did Writing Begin?" *A History of Writing (blog)*. *British Library*, 2019. https://www.bl.uk/history-of-writing/articles/where-did-writing-begin#.

Goodreads. "Quote by Socrates." Goodreads. Accessed June 28, 2021. https://www.goodreads.com/quotes/63219-the-children-now-love-luxury-they-have-bad-manners-contempt.

Gowlett, JAJ. "The Discovery of Fire by Humans: A Long and Convoluted Process." *Philosophical Transactions Royal Society of Britain* 371, no. 1696 (2016). http://dx.doi.org/10.1098/rstb.2015.0164.

Harper, Douglas. "Tongue." *Online Etymology Dictionary*. Accessed June 28, 2021. https://www.etymonline.com/word/tongue?ref=etymonline_crossreference.

Harper, Douglas. "*dnghu-." *Online Etymology Dictionary*. Accessed June 28, 2021. https://www.etymonline.com/word/*dnghu-.

Harper, Douglas. "Language." *Online Etymology Dictionary*. Accessed June 28, 2021. https://www.etymonline.com/search?q=language&ref=searchbar_searchhint.

Scott, J. "How Culture Influences Languages." *Translation Blog (blog)*. *Trusted Translations*. November 4, 2010. https://translation-blog.trustedtranslations.com/how-culture-influences-language-2010-11-04.html.

New World Encyclopedia. s.v. "Tabula Rasa(n)." Paragon House Publishers, 2021. https://www.newworldencyclopedia.org/entry/Tabula_rasa.

Shaw, Jonathan. "Evolution by Fire." *Harvard Magazine.* November 2009.

The Royal Institution. "Linguistics, Style and Writing in the 21st Century—with Steven Pinker." October 28, 2015. Video, 2:37. https://www.youtube.com/watch?v=OV5J6BfToSw.

Kittelstad, Kit. "Examples of Semantics: Meanings & Types." Your Dictionary. Accessed June 28, 2021. https://examples.yourdictionary.com/examples-of-semantics.html.

HOW TO COUNT IN TEN LANGUAGES AT ONCE

Anonymous. "List of Greek and Latin Roots in English." Oakton Community College. Accessed June 28, 2021. https://www.oakton.edu/user/3/gherrera/Greek%20and%20Latin%20Roots%20in%20English/greek_and_latin_roots.pdf.

Basu, Sāmapriẏa. "What Are Some Amazing Similarities Between European Indo-European Languages and Indian Indo-European Languages?" *Quora.* February 14, 2018. https://www.quora.com/What-are-some-amazing-similarities-between-European-Indo-European-languages-and-Indian-Indo-European-languages?share=1.

Dictionary.com Editors. "Why Does a Cow Become Beef?" Dictionary.com. Accessed June 28, 2021. https://www.dictionary.com/e/animal-names-change-become-food/.

Hornsby, Michael. "Celtic Languages." *Languages in Danger* (blog). Accessed June 28, 2021. http://languagesindanger.eu/book-of-knowledge/list-of-languages/celtic/#:~:text=The%20Celtic%20languages%20are%20a,%2DCeltic%20and%20Q%2DCeltic.

Miller-Wilson, Kate. "29 English Words with Origins in Greek Mythology." *YourDictionary* (blog). Accessed June 28, 2021. https://reference.yourdictionary.com/resources/roots-english-words-greek-mythology.html.

Natali, Lekka. "21 English Words That Are Actually Greek (And the Stories Behind Them)." *Babbel Magazine* (blog). May 2, 2017. https://www.babbel.com/en/magazine/21-english-words-that-are-actually-greek-and-the-stories-behind-them.

Mancko. "Counting in West Frisian." Of Languages and Numbers. Accessed June 28, 2021. https://www.languagesandnumbers.com/how-to-count-in-west-frisian/en/fry/.

Peadarson, Eòghann. "What similarities are there between Gaelic and Hindi/Sanskrit languages?" *Quora.* February 8, 2019. https://www.quora.com/What-similarities-are-there-between-Gaelic-and-Hindi-Sanskrit-languages.

Powell, Erica A. "Telling Tales in Proto-Indo-European." *Archaeology Magazine.* Accessed June 28, 2021. https://www.archaeology.org/exclusives/articles/1302-proto-indo-european-schleichers-fable#:~:text=Called%20Proto%2DIndo%2DEuropean%2C,and%20left%20no%20written%20texts.

Creative Nerds Inc. "The Celtic-Vedic Connection." *SanskritMagazine.* Last modified 2018. Accessed June 28, 2021. https://www.

sanskritimagazine.com/indian-religions/hinduism/the-celt-ic-vedic-connection/.

Selvakumar, C.R., Adriano Cunha Trigueiro. "What Modern-day Language Is Closest to Proto-Indo-European (PIE)?" *Quora*. September 1, 2019. https://www.quora.com/What-modern-day-language-is-closest-to-Proto-Indo-European-PIE#:~:text=We%20can%20not%20say%20what,with%20Proto%2DIndo%2DEuropean.

Violatti, Cristian. "Indo-European Languages." *World History Encyclopedia* (blog). May 5, 2014. https://www.ancient.eu/Indo-European_Languages/.

Online ed., s.v. "Indo-European Vocabulary." Wikimedia. Last modified June 24, 2021. https://en.wikipedia.org/wiki/Indo-European_vocabulary.

Online ed., s.v. "List of Germanic and Latinate Equivalents in English." Wikimedia. November 23, 2020. https://en.wikipedia.org/wiki/List_of_Germanic_and_Latinate_equivalents_in_English.

SLANG GANG

Crain, Stephen. "Language and the Brain." *Linguistic Society of America* (blog). Accessed June 28, 2021. https://www.linguisticsociety.org/resource/language-and-brain.

Dissidenheart. "Steven Pinker: The Linguistics of Cursing and Swearing." February 6, 2009. Video, 9:55. https://www.youtube.com/watch?v=E3yRVAw6nWU.

Larkin, Bob. "100 Slang Terms From the 20th Century No One Uses Anymore." *BestLife* (blog). October 6, 2020. https://bestlifeonline.com/20th-century-slang-terms/?nab=1&utm_referrer=https%3A%2F%2Fwww.google.com.

Paskevics, Emily. "13 Quebecois Swear Words that Confuse the French." *Culture Trip* (blog). June 18, 2017. https://theculture-trip.com/north-america/canada/quebec/articles/13-quebecois-swear-words-that-confuse-the-french/.

PART III

EMBRACING THE INNER CHILD

B., Hutauruk. "Children First Language Acquisition at Age 1–3 years Old in Balata." *IOSR Journal Of Humanities And Social Science.* 2015.

Bainbridge, Carol. "How Do Children Learn Language?" *Verywell Family* (blog). March 23, 2021. https://www.verywellfamily.com/how-do-children-learn-language-1449116#citation-2.

Bainbridge, Carol. "What Do Phonemes Have to Do With Language?" *Verywell Family* (blog). January 4, 2021. https://www.verywellfamily.com/what-is-a-phoneme-1449166.

Brown, Laurence. "Brits and Americans Cannot Pronounce 'van Gogh' Correctly." *Lost in the Pond* (blog). September 19, 2013. http://www.lostinthepond.com/2013/09/brits-and-americans-cannot-pronounce.html.

Chevalier-Karfis, Camille. "In, On, An: The 3 French Nasal Sounds Explained With Audio Examples." *French Today* (blog). June 7, 2021. https://www.frenchtoday.com/blog/french-pronunciation/nasal-vowels/.

Harbeck, James. "The Subtle Sounds That English Speakers Have Trouble Catching." *The Week* (blog). August 11, 2015. https://theweek.com/articles/569137/subtle-sounds-that-english-speakers-have-trouble-catching.

Peterson, Jordan B. "2017 Personality 17: Biology and Traits: Agreeableness." March 29, 2017. Video, 49:25. https://www.youtube.com/watch?v=G1eHJ9DdoEA&list=PL22J3VaeABQApSdW8X-71Ihe34eKN6XhCi.

Peterson Clips, Jordan. "Jordan Peterson: Have Your Child Socialized at 4 Years Old." December 29, 2019. Video, 9:05. https://www.youtube.com/watch?v=r2BCHXWlLPs.

Kuhl, Patricia K.. "Early Language Learning and Literacy: Neuroscience Implications for Education." Wiley Online Library. 2011. https://onlinelibrary.wiley.com/doi/abs/10.1111/j.1751-228X.2011.01121.x.

Munnis, Dante. "How the "R" in English Differs from Other Languages." *Omniglot* (blog). Accessed June 29, 2021. https://omniglot.com/language/articles/rsounds.htm.

Sociology: Understanding and Changing the Social World. "The Importance of Socialization." University of Minnesota. 2010. https://open.lib.umn.edu/sociology/chapter/4-1-the-importance-of-socialization/.

G., Toyoda, EC Brown, N Matsuzaki, K Kojima, M Nishida, E Asano. "Electrocorticographic Correlates of Overt Articulation of 44 English Phonemes: Intracranial Recording in Children with Focal Epilepsy." *Clin Neurophysiol.* 2014.

What I've Learned. "How to Learn a Language: INPUT (Why most Methods Don't Work)." *What I've Learned.* September 1, 2018. Video, 13:57. https://www.youtube.com/watch?v=J_EQDtpYSN-M&list=PLiGTVBGDphIdNA9GpFnHs6IgAqQYH6d9k&index=5.

Wlassof, Viatcheslav. "Why Do Children Learn Foreign Languages So Easily?" *Brain Blogger* (blog). February 14, 2018. https://brainblogger.com/2018/02/14/why-children-learn-foreign-languages-easily/.

ZIPF, NADA, NOTHING

Conard, Kristin. "How to Say 'Cheers' in 50 Languages." *Matador Network* (blog). December 5, 2010. https://matadornetwork.com/nights/how-to-say-cheers-in-50-languages/.

Czekala, Bartosz. "The Rule of 2—How Many Words You Should Know (For Every Language Level)." *University of Memory* (blog). Last modified May 21, 2021. https://universeofmemory.com/how-many-words-you-should-know/.

DuBois Learning Center. "The First 100 Most Commonly Used English Words." Internet Web Archive. Last modified June 16, 2013. https://web.archive.org/web/20130616200847/http://www.duboislc.org/EducationWatch/First100Words.html.

Forsey, Caroline. "What Is the 80/20 Rule? How the Pareto Principle Will Supercharge Your Productivity." *HubSpot* (blog). Last modified June 10, 2021. https://blog.hubspot.com/marketing/pareto-principle#:~:text=The%2080%2F20%20rule%20says,t%20suggesting%20you%20work%20oless.

Gibbons, Jakob. "The Numbers Game: How Many Words Do I Need to Know to Be Fluent in a Foreign Language?" *FluentU* (blog). Accessed June 29, 2021. https://www.fluentu.com/blog/how-many-words-do-i-need-to-know/#:~:text=Fluent%3A%20 10%2C000%2B%20words.,the%20unfamiliar%20ones%20 from%20context.

Living Hour. "The Lord's Prayer in Middle English." LivingHour.Org. Accessed June 29, 2021. https://livinghour.org/lords-prayer/in-middle-english/.

"Matt 6:5-15" Wycliffe's Bible (Revised Edition). Translated by John Wycliffe and John Purvey. 1384.

Nordquist, Richard. "The Principle of Least Effort: Definition and Examples of Zipf's Law." *ThoughtCo* (blog). July 3, 2019. https://www.thoughtco.com/principle-of-least-effort-zipfs-law-1691104.

Oxford Dictionaries. "The OEC: Facts about the Language." Internet Web Archive. Last modified December 26, 2011. https://web.archive.org/web/20111226085859/http://oxforddictionaries.com/words/the-oec-facts-about-the-language.

Pageau, Jonathan. "The Mark of Cain." June 7, 2021. Video, 47:19. https://www.youtube.com/watch?v=gh9BC-wONBs&t=2152s.

Seltzer, Leon F. "You Only Get More of What You Resist—Why?" *Psychology Today* (blog). June 15, 2016. https://www.psychologytoday.com/ca/blog/evolution-the-self/201606/you-only-get-more-what-you-resist-why#:~:text=Quite%20the%20opposite.,always%20get%20what%20you%20resist.%E2%80%9D.

Stack Exchange. "Is It True That the 100 Most Common English Words Are All Germanic in Origin?" English Language & Usage. Last modified November 30, 2012. https://english.stackexchange.com/questions/8982/is-it-true-that-the-100-most-common-english-words-are-all-germanic-in-origin.

The Lord's Prayer. "The Lord's Prayer (Old English—Anglo-Saxon)." *Accessed June 29, 2021.* https://www.lords-prayer-words.com/lord_old_english_medieval.html.

Tullo, Catriano, James R. Hurford. *Modelling Zipfian Distributions in Language.* Edinburgh: University of Edinburgh, 2003. Accessed June 29, 2021. http://www.lel.ed.ac.uk/~jim/zipfjrh.pdf.

Vsauce. "The Zipf Mystery." September 15, 2015. Video, 21:04. https://youtu.be/fCn8zs912OE.

Wolfram. "Zipf's Law." Wolfram Language. Accessed June 29, 2021. https://www.wolfram.com/language/11/text-and-language-processing/zipfs-law.html#:~:text=Zipf's%20law%20states%20that%20in,after%20sorting%20by%20decreasing%20frequency.

DOOR-WEDGING

Einstein, Albert. "Old Man's Advice to Youth: 'Never Lose a Holy Curiosity.'" *LIFE Magazine.* 2 May 1955) p. 64.

Shrestha, Praveen. "Ebbinghaus Forgetting Curve." *Psychestudy* (blog). November 17, 2017. https://www.psychestudy.com/cognitive/memory/ebbinghaus-forgetting-curve.

Tamm, Sander. "Spaced Repetition: A Guide to the Technique." *e-student* (blog). April 30, 2021. https://e-student.org/spaced-repetition/.

INPUTTING OUTPUT

Joy of Languages Author: Katie. "32 Fun Ways to Learn a Language (That Actually Work)." *Joy of Languages* (blog). May 21, 2017. http://joyoflanguages.com/32-fun-ways-to-learn-a-language-that-actually-work/.

"Ask a Teacher: Study or Learn?" *Ask a Teacher* (blog). *VOA News,* October 19, 2018. .https://learningenglish.voanews.com/a/ask-a-teacher-study-or-learn-/4620573.html#:~:text=To%20study%20means%20to%20read,being%20taught%20or%20experiencing%20something.

Peterson, Jordan B. "Rule 12: Pet a Cat When You Encounter One on the Street." in *12 Rules for Life: An Antidote to Chaos.* January 23, 2018.

Szynalski, P. Tomasz. "Input—What It Is and Why You Need It." *Antimoon* (blog). Accessed June 29, 2021. http://www.antimoon.com/how/input-intro.htm.

Brown, Douglas, H. Carlos, Alfredo Yorio, and Ruth H. Crymes. "Teaching and Learning English as a Second Language: Trends in Research and Practice : on TESOL '77 : Selected Papers from the Eleventh Annual Convention of Teachers of English to Speakers of Other Languages, Miami, Florida, April 26-May 1, 1977." Washington: Teachers of English to Speakers of Other Languages. http://www.worldcat.org/oclc/4037133.

What I've Learned. "How to Learn a Language: INPUT (Why Most Methods Don't Work)." September 1, 2018. Video, 13:57. https://www.youtube.com/watch?v=J_EQDtpYSNM&list=PLiGTVB-GDphIdNA9GpFnHs6IgAqQYH6d9k&index=5.

"Why Comprehensive Input Matters When Learning a Foreign Language." *Day Translations* (blog). July 5, 2019. https://www.daytranslations.com/blog/comprehensive-input-learning-language/.

A HEALTHY BODY IS A HEALTHY MIND

Huberman, Andrew. "How to Focus to Change Your Brain | Huberman Lab Podcast #6." February 8, 2021. Video, 1:29:42. https://www.youtube.com/watch?v=LG53Vxumoas.

Desilver, Drew. "Chart of the Week: Coffee and Tea around the World." *Pew Research Center* (blog). December 20, 2013. https://www.pewresearch.org/fact-tank/2013/12/20/chart-of-the-week-coffee-and-tea-around-the-world/.

Haas, Laurelin. "Coffee, Coffee, Everywhere: Albanian Coffee Culture." *Uprooted Abroad* (blog). October 17, 2017. https://

uprootedabroad.wordpress.com/2017/10/07/coffee-coffee-everywhere-albanian-coffee-culture/.

Health Research Fund "25 Shocking Caffeine Addiction Statistics." Psychological Articles and Infographics. Accessed June 28, 2021. https://healthresearchfunding.org/shocking-caffeine-addiction-statistics/.

Liu, F., S. Sulpizio, S. Kornpetpanee, & R. Job. "It Takes Biking to Learn: Physical Activity Improves Learning a Second Language." *PloS one*, 12, no 5. (2017) https://doi.org/10.1371/journal.pone.0177624.

Lyons, Dylan. "4 Ways to Learn a Language While Exercising (And Why It Helps!)" Babbel.com. January 13, 2021. https://www.babbel.com/en/magazine/3-ways-to-learn-a-language-while-exercising.

Peterson, Jordan B. *Maps of Meaning: The Architecture of Belief.* United Kingdom: Routledge, 1999.

Reynolds, Gretchen. "How Exercise Could Help You Learn a New Language." *The New York Times.* August 16, 2017. https://www.nytimes.com/2017/08/16/well/move/how-exercise-could-help-you-learn-a-new-language.html.

Spritzler, Franziska. "9 Side Effects of Too Much Caffeine." *Healthline* (blog). August 14, 2017. https://www.healthline.com/nutrition/caffeine-side-effects#TOC_TITLE_HDR_2

Tomen, David. "Caffeine." *Nootropics Expert* (blog). Accessed June 28, 2021. https://nootropicsexpert.com/caffeine/.

Tomen, David. "Glossary of Nootropics." *Nootropics Expert* (glossary). Accessed June 28, 2021. https://nootropicsexpert.com/nootropics-glossary/#nootropic.

Wartenberg, Lisa. "How Much Caffeine Does Tea Have Compared With Coffee?" *Healthline* (blog). October 7, 2019. https://www.healthline.com/nutrition/caffeine-in-tea-vs-coffee#caffeine-concerns.

Online, s.v. "Hobson's Choice." Wikimedia. Last modified June 23, 2021. https://en.wikipedia.org/wiki/Hobson%27s_choice.

Winter, Bernward, Caterina Breitenstein, Frank C. Mooren, Klaus Voelker, Manfred Fobker, Anja Lechtermann, Karsten Krueger, et al. "High Impact Running Improves Learning." *Neurobiology of Learning and Memory* 87, no. 4 (2007): 597-609.

DIGGING YOUR TEETH IN AN EXTRA MILE: GOALS AND ROUTINES

Fridman, Lex. "Andrew Huberman: Sleep, Dreams, Creativity, Fasting, and Neuroplasticity | Lex Fridman Podcast #164." February 28, 2021. Video, 2:53:23. https://www.youtube.com/watch?v=ClxRHJPz8aQ.

Merriam-Webster Dictionary. Online ed. s.v. "Second nature(n)." Accessed June 28, 2021. https://www.merriam-webster.com/thesaurus/second%20nature.

Pratama, Iosi. "21 Examples of Personal Development Goals for a Better You." *Medium* (blog). April 19, 2017. https://medium.com/@iosipratama/21-examples-of-personal-development-goals-for-a-better-you-7dddcbc2f1b1.

Scuderi, Royale. "Why It's So Important to Know the Difference Between Self-Help and Personal Growth." *Lifehack*, (blog). Accessed June 28, 2021. https://www.lifehack.org/articles/lifehack/why-its-so-important-to-know-the-difference-between-self-help-and-personal-growth.html.

Starfire, Amber Lee. "Why Limitations Boost Creativity." *Writing Through Life* (blog). Accessed June 28, 2021. https://writingthroughlife.com/why-limitations-boost-creativity/.

APPENDIX

COOL, UNTRANSLATABLE WORDS

Bains, Grace. "29 Beautiful Words That Cannot Be Translated to English but Capture Human Emotions Perfectly." *Scoop Whoop* (blog). September 20, 2017. https://www.scoopwhoop.com/beautiful-words-cannot-be-translated-to-english/.

Constanze. "Untranslatable German Words: Torschlusspanik!" *German Language Blog* (blog). Transparent Language. August 3, 2014. https://blogs.transparent.com/german/torschlusspanik/.

Star International Translation Services. "Hyppytyynytyydytys." Accessed June 6, 2021. https://www.star-ts.com/translation/finnish-word-no-vowels/.

Hitchcock, Allie. "50 Beautiful Words from Around the World That Are Impossible to Translate." *International* (blog). *The National Student*. May 31, 2016. https://www.thenationalstudent.com/International/2016-05-31/50_beautiful_words_from_around_the_world_that_are_impossible_to_translate.html.

Adey, Oliver. "Psychology: 10 Beautiful Words from All over the World about Love That Touch You Deeply." *Get to Text* (blog). June 3, 2021. https://gettotext.com/psychology-10-beautiful-words-from-all-over-the-world-about-love-that-touch-you-deeply/.

Made in the USA
Monee, IL
11 September 2021